"The Indians told them that we were **CHILDREN OF THE SUN** *and had the power to cure or kill. . . The following day, eight men died. They were certain that we killed them by willing it.*

—The Account of Cabeza de Vaca, 1542

* * *

The Castilians had lost everything—their boat, their clothes, three more countrymen. They dug into the sand to hide their nakedness and to stop from shivering. The bodies of the dead men lay side by side on the open sand. Cabeza de Vaca was vexed. How many more must he lose before they would be delivered from this maddening world? He could not bury his countrymen. Not yet. Not until their deaths had settled in, and he was sure that this was not some harrowing nightmare.

Then the Indians returned. One Castilian whispered, "I have been to New Spain, Marshal. I know this kind. They will sacrifice us to their gods. They will eat us."

* * *

Thus began on November 1 ~~~~~~~~~~~ east Texas, an incredible story of surv ~~~~~ . It is a story of passion, love, savager ~~~~~ our lone survivors of the Narváez/Cab~ ~xpedition, the first Europeans to cross America, and the extraordinary miracle that brought them through. And it is the story of the now-extinct native Indians of Texas, their daily needs, habits, and rituals, a lifestyle considered subhuman by today's standards. It is the unbelievable story of the odyssey of Cabeza de Vaca.

* * *

". . .of all the expeditions that ever went to those lands [America], no other encountered such great dangers or had such a miserable and disastrous outcome."

—Cabeza de Vaca in a letter to King Charles I of Spain, 1542

I. Mac Perry and his wife/partner Linda Faye live in St. Petersburg, Florida not far from where Cabeza de Vaca first set foot in America.

Mac is the author of eight books including *Black Conquistador: The Story of the First Black Man in America* and *Indian Mounds You Can Visit,* which describes 165 pre-historic mounds along the west coast of Florida.

Children of the Sun is the second in a Historic Adventure Series of novels that tell the story of Florida's prehistoric people and the Europeans who drove them into extinction.

CHILDREN OF THE SUN

THE STORY OF THE CABEZA DE VACA EXPEDITION ACROSS AMERICA

A Novel By
I. MAC PERRY

Copyright © 1999 by I. Mac Perry
Library of Congress Catalogue Card Number 99-61992
ISBN 0-9663628-5-3

Publisher's Cataloging-in-Publication

Perry, I. Mac
    Children of the sun : the story of the Cabeza de Vaca
expedition across America : a novel / by I. Mac
Perry.— 1st ed.
    236 p. cm — (Historic adventure series; no.2)
    LCCN : 99-61992
    ISBN : 0-9663628-5-3

    1. Nunez Cabeza de Vaca, Alvar, 16th cent.—
Fiction. 2. America—Discovery and
exploration—Spanish—Fiction. 3.Explorers—America—
Fiction.
    I. Title.
    PS3566.E6995C55 1999   813'.54
                        QBI99-715

Cover art adapted from an engraving by Theodore de Bry, after the 16th
century paintings of Jacques le Moyne de Morgues, housed at the Rare Book
Division, The New York Public Library, Astor, Lenox and Tilden
Foundations.

Published by Boca Bay Books, St. Petersburg, Florida
Printed in the United States

I gratefully appreciate all the authors, linguists, researchers, and historians, especially: Ruth Matilda Anderson, Gordan C. Baldwin, Fanny Bandelier, Cyclone Covey, Martin Favata, José Fernández, Dan Flores, Albert Gatschet, Ives Goddard, Julian Granberry, Cleve Hallenbeck, Frederick Hodge, Paul Hoffman, Charles Hudson, Jerald Milanich, W.W. Newcomb, Jr., Alfonso Ortis, Douglas Preston, Carl Sauer, Buckingham Smith, Gene S. Stuart, John Swanton, John Upton Terrell, Carmen Chaves Tesser, and Gerald Theisen, whose dedication to unraveling the details of the Narváez/Cabeza de Vaca expedition have made this work possible.

I further acknowledge deep debt to my wife Faye for her encouragement, editorial assistance, and endless hours at the computer.

Children of the Sun is a work of faction—fiction based upon fact. The events, though written with literary license, actually happened. Cabeza de Vaca and the Spanish characters were all real people. The Indian clans of Florida, Texas, and Mexico were likewise real people and lived in the manner described here. But the actual Indian characters are fictitious. While these proud, indigenous clans, who lived in America for 12,000 years, are gone today, many of their spoken words have been preserved by linguists and are included in this work.

—I. Mac Perry

Prickly pear cactus and fruit that kept Cabeza de Vaca and the Indians alive in south Texas in the fall of 1534.

INTRODUCTION

GONE FOREVER
THE PRE-HISTORIC INDIANS OF TEXAS

In his 1542 *La Relatión* *(The Account)*, Cabeza de Vaca named twenty-three clans of Indians in Texas he and his companions encountered. Not one of these clans exists in the state today. Ethnologists believe they belonged to four culture groups.

The most primitive group were the Coahuilticans, who lived in south Texas a couple of hundred miles on each side of the Rio Grande below the junction of the Pecos, and the closely related Karankawas (the word means "Dog lovers"), who inhabited the coastal islands and mainland marshes from Galveston Bay to Corpus Christi. The clans of this culture group lived in what some anthropologists have called a "cultural sink." Their lifestyle was not unlike that of the Stone Age Indians of 6500-3000 BC, who roamed the land with portable huts, had no social structure, domesticated no animals, had no gardens, and lived as hunter/gatherers foraging off the meager products of the land. Their days were filled with witchcraft and the never ending task of warding off starvation. Most of the 250 members of the Narváez/Cabeza de Vaca expedition lived and died with these Indians in the winter of 1528.

A more advanced culture group lived between the Red River valley and Galveston Bay. These were the Caddos of northeast Texas and their dull reflection the Atakapas (the word means Man-eaters) who lived along the lower Trinity River.

16th Century Texas

In sharp contrast to the offal-eaters of south Texas, the Mississippian Caddos had vast gardens, temple mounds, a complex social system, and a high population density. The Atakapas to their south lived a lifestyle somewhere between that of the Caddos and the coastal Karankawas. They did not have gardens, and like many Texas Indians, practiced ritualistic cannibalism. For two years, Cabeza de Vaca lived alone among these Indians. It was here, as a trader, that he became the first European to see buffalo.

The Tonkawa culture (the word means "They stay together") was made up of clans who lived in central Texas up on the tableland and spilling down onto the coastal plain and the cactus prairies around San Antonio. They lived in buffalo covered teepees and hunted on the plains. Their primary food was buffalo, but they also ate rabbit, skunk, rattlesnake, tortoise, and rats. The Tonkawa religion, which kept them in constant fear of the spirits around them, would not permit them to eat wolves or coyotes. These bands lived and hunted in small, matrilineal, family clans with such names as "Blinking with the eyelids," "Mouth open," and "Long genitals." Like other Texas Indians, they decorated their bodies with tattoos and body paint and had within their ranks emasculated men who dressed as women, carried heavy loads, and provided sexual services for the hunters. Cabeza de Vaca and his three companions were living with the Tonkawas when they were first dubbed "Children of the Sun."

The fourth culture group lived along the upper Rio Grande valley west of the Pecos. They were the Jumanos, sedentary gardeners who lived in multiroom adobe houses and wore buffalo hide ponchos. The men worked the fields, while the women ground corn and made pots and baskets. They were a peripheral group of the Pueblo civilization of the American Southwest and farmed corn, beans, squash, sunflower, cotton, and tobacco in the narrow valley. Some of the Jumanos were nomadic and hunted buffalo up on the plains to the northeast, bringing hides and dried meat into the valley for trade. Because they practiced no artificial irrigation and because the valley is flanked by cactus-covered terraces and barren mountains, the productivity of the Jumano gardens was severely limited. Many farm villages disappeared in the droughts of the

1400s. When the Children of the Sun passed through their land in 1535, the few survivor villages were in the midst of a two-year drought.

In summary: the south Texas Indians were offal-eating gatherers who lived like Stone Age people, the northeast Indians were an advanced Mississippian culture who had temple mounds and chiefs, the central Indians were teepee-living buffalo hunters of the Great Plains, and the southwest Indians were adobe-living Puebloan gardeners. The clans of these four cultures are conveniently grouped together because they shared a similar mother language and lifestyle, but in fact each lived as an independent, autonomous clan made up of several smaller family groups.

Today, all four of these Texas cultures are extinct, their way of life gone forever. A remnant of the Tonkawas and Caddos eke out their twilight years on a reservation in Oklahoma, but the Coahuilticans, Karankawas, Atakapas, and Jumanos are irrevocably extinguished. It is primarily through the writing of Cabeza de Vaca that we know of their lifestyle in 16th-century Texas.

PROLOGUE

In the 35 years that followed Columbus' landing on the north shore of Haiti, the Spanish crown sent numerous expeditions and convoys to the New World. The conquistadors "pacified" the Indians and established towns on all the principal islands of the Caribbean and along the coasts of South and Central America. In 1519, Cortés entered Mexico and stole the great wealth of the Aztecs. Curious about the mainland north of the Caribbean and possible fortunes there, Ponce de Leon was sent in 1521 to establish a colony in Charlotte Harbor on Florida's southwest coast. The colony was chased off by Calusa Indians, and Ponce de Leon was shot with an arrow from which he later died. In 1527, it was time to try again.

Ruthless, one-eyed Panfilo de Narváez, who owned a large plantation in Cuba, was selected to receive Ponce de Leon's grant as governor of La Florida—all the land from Florida, across the southern US, to Mexico. The only catch: he had to pacify the Indians, establish forts and settlements, and take the gold back to Spain.

The story of the 600-man Narváez expedition from Spain to Florida is told in the first book of this Historic Adventure Series—*Black Conquistador: The Story of the First Black Man in America*. *Black Conquistador* is an intriguing tale of the first major clash of cultures in America. It is enjoyed by readers interested in 16th century Spain and the Caribbean, the ill-fated Narváez expedition, and the now-extinct Indians of Florida. A summary of that story follows below.

The rest of the expedition, an amazing eight-year wandering from Florida to Mexico, is told in this book. *Children of the Sun* will appeal to readers interested in 16th century Mexico, the now-extinct Indians of Texas, and the inconceivable Cabeza de Vaca expedition.

The two-book sequel is based on the *Account of Cabeza de Vaca* published in Spain in 1542. For a full understanding and enjoyment of the novel version of the entire expedition, it is recommended that both books be read, and in chronological order. For readers who have not read *Black Conquistador*, here are bio-sketches of the principle characters found in both books.

Cabeza de Vaca, the Provost Marshal and second in command of the 1527 Narváez expedition, is from Jerez de la Frontera in Andalusia in southwest Spain. He is short, has a bulging midriff and blonde hair. Very regal appearing. He wants but one thing out of the expedition: he wants it run by the book. He loathes the exploits of the early conquistadors under the rule of Fernando and Isabel—the brutal killing of the Indians, the forced introduction of African slaves. He wants to see a settlement established. He wants to see Indians treated humanely, converted to Christianity, living at peace alongside Europeans. And King Charles, grandson of the sovereigns, has entrusted Cabeza de Vaca to see that it happens peacefully. But not everyone on the expedition agrees with Cabeza de Vaca.

Pánfilo de Narváez is tall, muscular, has fiery red hair and beard, and wears a black silk patch over his one dead eye. He carries a quince rod in his hand, a kidney dagger on his left hip, and he's not afraid to use either one. Narváez helped pacify Jamaica and Cuba with brutality and sees no reason why Florida should not be pacified the same way. Especially if that's what it will take to achieve his real objective—get filthy rich by stealing all the Indians' gold, just like Cortés did in Mexico eight years earlier. Cortés beat Narváez to the punch then, even dashed out his eye during a power struggle. Now, it is Narváez' turn to get rich. And no sermonizing Provost Marshal is going to stop him.

Alonso del Castillo is captain of the *Caballeros*. He is fair-skinned and tall as a plank but has powerful, penetrating eyes. A graduate of the university in Salamanca, Castillo is the perfect military officer: gung ho, obedient to military law, subservient to the Crown instead of Christianity, a virtue that gets him into trouble when fosterage from a higher bidding emerges. He disagrees with Cabeza de Vaca on every issue and believes that no one could have executed the New World conquest any better than the sovereigns Fernando and Isabél.

Andrés Dorantes is captain of the crossbowmen. He went to all the military schools, but this is his first actual post. He's not looking for gold; he wants to do something for Spain, serve his country bravely. Short and stocky, muscular and baby-faced, Dorantes is honest, a real gentleman. But Narváez thinks he's a worry wart, a wool-gatherer, a rookie with little to offer to the conquest. Dorantes will just have to show Narváez a thing or two. But he has baggage—a slave who really is a wool-gatherer. His name is Estevanico and now he's Captain Dorantes' page. But Estevanico is more than a slave/page, he is Dorantes' best friend. The two grew up together, and Dorantes would do anything to keep his friend out of trouble. Even give up his life.

Estevanico is a tall black Moor with plenty of muscle. He is from Azamor in Morocco. He is not a Christian like the others. He's supposed to be a Moslem, but he can't remember even one of the Five Pillars of Islam. Slavery is the only life Estevanico has ever known. He was in Granada the night it fell and on the pier in Palos the night Columbus recruited men for his voyage across the ocean sea. The Columbus told Estevanico he was too young to go to sea but said if he wanted to be a conquistador he had to be prepared to give the ultimate sacrifice. Estevanico was seven then, Andres was two. As teens, Estevanico taught the little Spanish tike everything he needed to know to survive in the world: how to detune a guitar when the *guitarrista* went to pee, how to stampede cattle with a cane pole. Now, Estevanico is sailing on a great expedition. His goal is to become the Black Conquistador, have people cheering him, girls with big *tetas* flocking around him, calling out his name, like they did to Cortés after he conquered Mexico City. But first, he has to figure out what the ultimate sacrifice is Columbus spoke of. During the expedition across Texas, he finds out.

Here now is a summary of the events of the expedition so far as told in *Black Conquistador: The Story of the First Black Man in America.*

On June 26, 1527, six rickety ships carrying 600 inexperienced men slip out of the Spanish port of San Lúcar. But not before an old Gypsy woman warns them that the expedition is, "Doomed. Turn back now or be prepared to suffer more than anyone has ever suffered."

Six weeks on the rolling sea and finally the ships arrive at Santo Domingo, hub of the Indies. Narváez shops for horses and more recruits, but when his back is turned, 140 soldiers desert, disappear into the mountains. Quickly, Narváez musters the remaining Castilians and sets sail for Cuba only to run head on into a violent hurricane. A storm of this magnitude is new to the Spaniards. It costs them two ships and sixty lives. They are forced to spend winter in Cuba.

In the spring of 1528, they depart again and make their way to Tampa Bay, first stop in their search for a deep bay around which to build a fort. Here the conflict begins: Cabeza de Vaca wants a settlement; Narváez wants gold. Narváez and a contingent of foot soldiers circle the bay but something goes wrong. Now, an Indian chief's mother is dead, brutally killed by Narváez' dogs. The Indians are not happy, and the conflict with Cabeza de Vaca escalates.

In an audacious rage, Narváez divides the expedition. He takes three hundred foot soldiers on an overland march to search for gold in a land to the north called Apalachee. He sends the rest to sea, little guessing he will never see the ships again.

In a week, the foot soldiers run out of food. They find too few Indian villages from which to pilfer. The men are now starving, exhausted from marching through dense forests wearing heavy gear, and a stomach virus has begun to spread through their ranks. Dissension builds, but Narváez presses on. They cross the Withlacoochee. Suddenly, flint-tipped arrows fly out of the underbrush. Men fall. Wounded. Dead. The rivers and freshwater swamps and close underbrush make retaliation impossible. Still, the army forages ahead. They cross more rivers, the Santa Fe, the Suwannee, the Aucilla, and the attacks continue. Complications intensify when the Black Conquistador Estevanico falls in love with Ka•konee, a beautiful Apalachian Indian maiden. Finally, the army is forced against the Gulf coast south of Apalachee (today's Tallahassee). Defeated, they have but one choice—eat their horses and build crude sailing vessels in which to escape. The Indians of central and north Florida—the Tocobagas, the Ocales, the Apalachees—like the Calusas of south Florida who killed Ponce de Leon, once again drive the intruding Spaniards from their land.

But for the Spaniards, the story does not end here. Their escape from Florida is only a brief reprieve. Children of the Sun *picks up the story as the five crude boats are poled down the inlet in search of the open sea.*

"Cabeza de Vaca's place in history is secure. His feats, his remarkable journey, will never be forgotten. Yet there is something that historians generally seem to have overlooked in writing about him. It is the creed by which he lived."

—From John Upton Terrell's
Journey Into Darkness

SOUTHEAST
UNITED
STATES

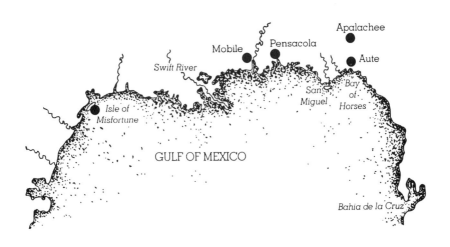

"So great was the power of need that it brought us to venture out into such a troublesome sea. . .and without any one among us having the least knowledge of the art of navigation."

—The Account of Cabeza de Vaca, A.D.1542

1

September 22, 1528
Apalachee Bay, North Florida

Cabeza de Vaca stood at the helm of boat five. If you could call it a boat. He studied the construction. A few rough-hewn pine boards caulked with palmetto fiber, pitched with pine resin. Ropes and rigging made from the tails and manes of the horses they had just eaten. Sails sewn from the men's shirts, the men now sitting in the boat like stone monuments, yellow flies buzzing around their bare shoulders. Everything held together with spikes and cleats made by melting down their armor, lances, swords, and guns. Who needed crossbows and guns when there were no quarrels, no lead, no powder. The Castilians had expended the ammunition on the Indians in their two hundred and fifty mile march through Florida.

No, these were not boats. These were barges. Crude barges with sails that were hardly more than flags. It had taken the men six weeks to build them back at the Bay of Horses, while the Indians continued to heckle and taunt. The boats, five of them, each about thirty feet long, each holding fifty men hunkered down in the water, the gunwales barely a hand above the surface. And the men, so sick they could hardly pole or paddle. Mother of God, what illness had gotten into them—typhoid, malaria? How many had died from the illness—forty, fifty? Far more than the Indians had killed. And how many days had they been paddling along this smelly inlet without food or water searching for the open sea—six, seven?

Cabeza de Vaca massaged his left shoulder where an arrow had grazed him. Twice now he'd been wounded in combat. The last time in the bloody battle of Ravenna many years ago. That time, twenty thousand had died, and the Spanish forces were driven out of northern Italy. This time they were being driven out of Florida. Only a few had died, but the hopes for the remaining two hundred and fifty were not good. The men were sapless. The sun blistered their backs. Their horse hide water bags leaked. They made camp every night and searched for fresh water, oysters, and fish to eat with the few grains of corn each man had been rationed, corn they had stolen from the Apalachee Indians back at the Bay of Horses.

Then he heard it, an open, hollow sound. A large sound, unmuted. It was the sound of the universe. The sound you hear when there are no trees, no buildings, no land around to deaden the overtones in the air. It was the sound of waves rolling against a shoreline, wind cuffing the waves. The men heard it, too. Each looked up, each turned his head one at a time.

"*Jesucristo!*" one yelped. "It's the sea."

The men dug their paddles into the mirrored water. Their boats lunged forward. Some, the healthy ones, cried out.

Cabeza de Vaca just stared. It was the open sea, all right. Now what? They had given Captain Dorantes' slave turned page—what was that *Moro Negro's* name? Estevanico? Back at the Bay of Horses, they had given to him of all people the right to choose whether to follow the shore to the east or to the west. He had made the wrong choice, Cabeza de Vaca knew it in his heart. But it sounded like the men were willing to accept that choice. It's not that they wanted an *idiota* to make the decision. They just didn't want Narváez to make it. Narváez had already made too many wrong decisions.

The boats slipped out into the gulf and swung to the west. Then—

"*Madre de Dios,* look!" someone yelled.

Cabeza de Vaca looked. Barely a crossbow shot in front of them were five dugouts. The dugouts were full of Indians. The Indians were paddling straight for them.

What could one do? There was no fight left in the Castilians. They had no weapons. Any swift movement inside the boats would surely bring water over the sides, and they would sink. The boats were too separated to assist each other. The Indians could paddle near each boat, one at a time, unleash a sling of arrows, and kill the men like grazing cattle.

The men sat still. Their boats slowed and came to a stop. The dugouts got closer, then they stopped. The Indians stared. The Castilians stared. Then the dugouts turned and raced for an island near the mouth of the inlet.

"Let's follow them," someone shouted.

"Are you *loco*," another said. "They'll kill us just for pleasure."

Then the discussion began.

"They look friendly."

"They are not friendly. They are warriors."

"They are mere fishermen."

"I saw war paint."

"That was a tattoo."

"We need food and water. We're half starved."

"It's better than being dead."

"What makes you think they have food?"

"Look! Houses."

There *were* houses. And there was smoke hanging in the tops of the trees above the houses. There would be food and the men were famished. One by one the paddles slipped into the water, and the boats eased toward the island.

When the boats reached waist deep water, they crunched on the bottom. The Castilians looked around. They saw no one. They eased over the sides of the boats and pulled them closer to shore, anchored them with large chunks of rock, which they tied to ropes.

The houses were set back in a pine thicket. There were six or seven of them, hardly more than huts, three sides and a roof covered with dry palm fronds, the front open. It looked like a summer camp for fishermen. Huge drying racks made of green branches stretched across long pits of smoldering coals. The racks were full of smoked fish. Apparently, the Indians caught and smoked the fish here then paddled them to a village on the mainland. The Castilians wasted no time. They dove into the fish and began filling their empty stomachs. They found fresh water, too, and dried coontie bread in baskets.

Narváez climbed out of boat one. Cabeza de Vaca watched him from a distance. He looked weak, but he made it to shore. Narváez ate a fish and drank some water brought to him by an *ayudante de campo*. Then he laid on a bank of pine needles, his head and shoulders against the tree trunk. Perspiration seeped out of his entire body. He shivered. Cabeza de Vaca gulped down a fish then walked over to him.

"Governor, a word with you?"

"Why not, *Señor* Provost Marshal. You have always spoken whenever you wanted to."

"I understand your goal is to discover riches. And I am aware that this expedition must have cost —"

"I know, Marshal. 'The maxim of every good conquest is to make a settlement.' You have already told me that."

"We cannot continue this way. The men will not survive without food and water. I beseech you in the name of God our Lord. Turn the expedition east. If we sail east, we will be back at Bahia de la Cruz in two days. Three at the most."

"Marshal—"

"Our ships will be waiting for us. They will have supplies—"

"Marshal, our ships are in Cuba. We left Bahia de la Cruz five months ago. There would be no reason for them to wait for us at Bahia de la Cruz."

"We can wait there. Someone will come for us. I am only thinking of the men, Governor."

"The men want gold, Marshal. They are just too sick to say so, right now. The gold is to the west. Pánuco is to the west. In Pánuco there will be medicine, food. The men can rest." Narváez coughed. He spit blood. He wiped the sweat out of his eyes. "Then we will move inland, to Amichel in northern Mexico. There we will find more gold than that found in Mexico by that *bastardo* Cortéz."

Cabeza de Vaca slammed his fish bones into the pine needles next to Narváez. *"No me importa un comino,* Governor. I don't give a damn about the gold. We have no rations. We have no horses. The men are so delirious, they leave their decision making to that *picaron,* Estevanico."

"Why, Marshal, where is your respect? If it wasn't for Miguel Quick-fingers talking in signs to the Indians, we wouldn't have made it this far."

"Governor, all I'm saying is that you were wrong in separating the army from our ships. You were wrong about there being riches in Florida. You were wrong about the Indians feeding us along the way. You were wrong in believing Bahia Honda exists on this peninsula. And I say you are wrong to head west."

"And you, Señor Marshal, lost sixty men and two ships because of a mere storm. Do you know what two ships cost?"

"Mere storm?" That *tormenta* destroyed the entire town of Trinidad. Flattened every building. It nearly took the mountain where we were hiding."

"I wish it had. Then I wouldn't have this pain in my *ano* to match the one in my stomach."

"Governor, I swear to you upon the gallantry and nobility of the *caballeros.* You will regret having made this decision this day."

Cabeza de Vaca stormed away. He left the governor sweating on the ground.

When the men had their fill and were rested, they wanted to move on. They took what little fish and roe that remained and added it to the corn they had brought with them. There was no way to carry fresh water, so they left the camp, jogged the boats into deeper water, and dragged the Indians' dugouts with them. They lashed the dugouts tight along the port rail of each boat and climbed aboard. That helped. The boats now sat two hands above the water. They paddled west.

Cabeza de Vaca looked back. The Indians raced out of the woods and began swimming to the mainland. Cabeza de Vaca knew there would be no welcoming party for them ahead.

For a week, the crude boats followed the shoreline. The men searched endlessly for ponds that might be holding rainwater.

All they saw were sand and salt marshes and great meadows of black needle rush. They came to another island. But this island was not inhabited. There was no food, no water. They navigated the pass between the island and the mainland. They called the pass San Miguel because of the day in which they passed, a day they reckoned to be September 29th. Soon winter would be upon them. They must make Pánuco before winter.

Cabeza de Vaca sat in the bow of boat five, now. The inspector Alonso de Solis was at the helm. How much longer could the men last? They no longer talked. Most were raging with the fever. Some lay like rags in the wet floor of the boat. How many would still be alive if they had to spend winter in this desolate place.

Days turned into weeks. The food ran out, except for a few grains of corn doled out by the *sargentos*. Precious hours were spent each day exploring inlets and bays, some extending far inland, looking for fresh water. Rarely did they find it.

Finally, a cloud rose in the east. It swung to the south then moved toward them. An island appeared. The barges arced for the island. The Castilians dug holes, lined the holes with green palm fronds, then waited. The rains came. The holes filled. The men drank till their stomachs bulged. Many vomited, then drank again.

Cabeza de Vaca felt sorry for them. Most were young, inexperienced. They had followed a dream, followed the promises of the most vicious conquistador who had ever sailed the Main, a butcher of humans, who had promised them great wealth in the land of La Florida. A man who once sat like a marble statue upon his stallion while his soldiers chopped and mauled an entire Cuban village of three thousand. Natives whose only crime was being in Narváez' way. Now, they were following him again, an insane man delirious with fever. They would not make it to Pánuco. Cabeza de Vaca knew it in his heart. The boats were still heading west. Pánuco was south. Who knew how far west they must paddle before turning south? Then how far south they must paddle to get to Pánuco? Surely death would come first.

Cabeza de Vaca knew it in his heart.

2

Village of Pensacola

Estevanico sat in boat three. "I'm thirsty," he said. He spoke to no one in particular.

Captain Dorantes stood at the helm. He glanced down. "You have said that a thousand times, *amigote.*" Dorantes' throat was as dry as dust. His skin was flaking. His nose and forehead were cratered with broken blisters caused by the sun and dry air. He dared not touch them for fear the salt on his finger would sting the raw flesh.

The sun had dropped to the horizon in front of him, now. The five crowded boats turned a point of land. Dorantes looked at his men. They were forlorn, exhausted. He knew not one of them would think twice about toppling into the sea to relieve his agony. Their rations were dangerously low, and they had not found fresh water for days. It was time to look for a campsite and hopefully a pool of water.

"I can't even spit," Estevanico said.

Dorantes saw his friend stare at the water splashing onto his hand where he worked his paddle. He watched Estevanico carefully these days. Besides the physical suffering they all felt, Estevanico was depressed. Ka•konee, the Indian girl who had been killed back at Apalachee was the only woman Estevanico had ever shown any real affection for since Dorantes had known him. Estevanico had been with dozens of women, actually, hundreds, always searching for love, but he never found it. Not until Ka•konee.

"Don't even think about it," Dorantes told him. "We have lost five men so far from drinking that salt water. It just doesn't work."

"How long has it been since we left Bahía de Caballos, Andrés?" The Castilians called their departed shipyard at Apalachee the Bay of Horses, because of the stench of horse heads and rotting carcasses left there.

"Seven, eight weeks. Counting the week we were penned down from the storm back at that last island."

Estevanico's head dropped and bobbed. The big gold ring, a gift from Dorantes when they were younger, rocked in his left ear. He spoke again. "Andres, do you remember that golden rattle you found when we landed back at Bahia de la Cruz?"

"*Si.*"

"And that old shaman who said whoever took the rattle would die the death of a thousand arrows?"

"*Si.*"

"And you gave the rattle to me to carry?"

"*Si...* Estevanico, you don't think—"

"I gave the rattle to Ka•konee, then she got shot with an arrow."

"Surely you can't believe—"

"It was my fault she died. Can't you see?"

"That was Indian hokus pokus, old friend. It means nothing." But he knew Estevanico did not hear him.

What had Dorantes gotten his old companion into? So many years they had been together. In fact, Dorantes could not remember a time when Estevanico was not with him. He was just a child, barely walking, when his family moved from Béjar where he was born to Gibraleón. That's when his father went to Palos to pick up the new slave boy. He was sure his father had purchased an older slave boy so that Dorantes would have someone close enough in age to be a playmate, yet old enough to keep him out of trouble. But having Estevanico watch over you was like having a gorilla scratch your *huevos*.

In their younger years, Estevanico was almost twice the height of Dorantes, was almost that still. No one bothered Dorantes

26

as long as the big fellow was around. They could go anywhere, do anything. But keep him out of trouble? That was something Estevanico was not gifted at.

He was *desordenado*—a wild man, always taking Dorantes farther from home than he was supposed to be, teaching him how to steal apples in the marketplace when they were hungry, how to sneak out of a window at night when everyone was asleep, and later teaching him the finer points of *coito* in the brothels of Córdoba.

When Dorantes decided to go to military school, he insisted Estevanico go with him. Estevanico roamed the streets of Toledo until classes were over, then he was Dorantes' servant in the *residencia*. When Dorantes was to go off to war for his country, Estevanico was to be his page. Together, they would see the world, bring honor back to Spain. But somehow things had not worked out the way he'd planned. Here he was with his page, but there was no honor for Spain in La Florida. He noticed Estevanico had set his paddle aside and was starting to figure.

"Andrés, what is a lot?"

"A what?"

"When I was a kid, the old caliph at Granada told me a great adventure would someday fall to my lot, that it would linger only a moment. I figure eight weeks is more than a linger, don't you, Andrés?"

"You've been in the sun too long, Estevanico."

"I'd hate to think this little trip to Pánuco is my adventure."

"If you don't turn to on that oar we'll never get to Pánuco."

He knew Estevanico would become remorseful if he figured too long. He had to keep him busy, hopeful.

But Estevanico was apparently too tired, too dried out to do much figuring. He wasn't going to paddle, either. He was going to sit and do nothing, and there was nothing Dorantes could do to stop him. Then he spoke again.

"Andrés, why do the people I love always end up at my feet with an arrow sticking out of them? My mother at Azamor. The old Caliph at Granada. Ka•konee at Apalachee."

"Not everyone. I don't have an arrow sticking out of me, do I?"

Suddenly, an arrow zinged past Dorantes'' head. He jerked aside. "Castillo!" he shouted.

Captain Castillo was asleep on the floor. He sat up. The men stopped paddling. They stared. Thirty dugouts squatted dead in the water directly in front of them At the bow of each stood a tall Indian with long, shaggy hair and dressed in a fur robe that hung down to his knees. The seated Indians yelled, *"Esteehatkee! Esteehatkee!"* Then the dugouts turned and the Indians waved for the Spaniards to follow.

Cabeza de Vaca's voice boomed across the bay from boat five. "God our Lord has shown His favor in this our time of great need. Those *pobre hombres* are sure to have food and water."

Dorantes was alert. He saw no weapons. The Indians looked friendly enough,. yet someone did shoot at him. Perhaps to get his attention. Still, he was cautious. He leaned on the rudder and followed them.

The five boats glided into shallow water. The Castilians helped the sick disembark. The musky amber scent of the civet-marten fur from the Indian's robes rankled Dorantes' nose. The village was made up of several mat houses sitting on a slope beyond the shore. At the center of the village sat a large, round house and four partially enclosed sheds with benches. Each shed faced one of the four cardinal directions. Dorantes and the Castilians followed the Indians into the village.

An enormous Indian came out of the round house. His wild unbridled hair hung over his robe and nearly touched the ground. A small Indian wearing a hide loincloth walked beside him.

Dorantes moved beside Narváez. He motioned Estevanico to join them. Narváez was visibly in pain and perspiring heavily. The small Indian spoke and gestured with signs. Estevanico interpreted.

"He says, 'We receive you at our *tulwa*. We are the Pensacolas—the Hair People. I am the *yateka*, chief speaker for the *mikulgi*, the wise ones. Why has the Breath Holder *Hisagita immisee* brought you to our *tulwa?*'"

Narváez answered and Estevanico made signs back to the Indians. 'We seek water and food. Our men are sick.'

28

Dorantes surveyed the village. He saw no weapons. But he didn't trust the Indians. All Indians had weapons. Why were they hiding them?

The big Indian looked at the Spaniards. He stared at the daggers on their hips, then whispered to the smaller Indian who signed. 'Your men are *heethleko*, out of balance with nature. They have bear sickness. We will give them *choska*, a drink from the bark of big oak.' He turned to the villagers and slapped his elbow twice with the palm of his left hand. The villagers brought clay jars filled with water. The Castilians drank, then the villagers led them to the drying racks scattered throughout the *tulwa*. They gave the Spaniards smoked fish. The small Indian beckoned Narváez to follow. He and his chief turned and walked toward the square ground nearby.

Dorantes whispered, "Governor, I will bring a contingent of twenty of our healthiest men."

Narváez nodded. Dorantes turned and snapped his finger.

At the square ground, the small Indian signed, 'Your men can stay here at the *tupas*.' He gestured to the four open sheds. 'You will come into the *chokofa*.' The small one and the chief entered the round council house. A huge ugly Indian stood beside the entrance.

Dorantes looked around again. He still saw no signs of hostility. Narváez gestured for Cabeza de Vaca, Castillo, Dorantes, and Estevanico to join him, the twenty soldiers could wait outside. Then he touched the handle of his dagger. It was apparent that Narváez did not trust these Indians, either.

Inside, the big mat house was smoky and dark. Four torches burned near the center. Dorantes squinted his eyes. He saw a dozen or more, strong-looking men along the wall of the round house.

"Why is it I don't like this, Andrés?" Estevanico whispered. Dorantes motioned for him to hold still.

The small Indian pointed at the men and signed, 'These are the *tustunukulgi*, our leading . . . men.'

29

Estevanico said quietly that the Indian had struggled to sign 'men' and not 'warriors.' But any fool could see these were warriors.

'They have fish for you,' the small Indian signed. He nodded for the strong men to bring two baskets of fish. They did.

Dorantes sat with the officers and Estevanico. He ate the fish and drank more water. The food revived his energy somewhat, but he never took his eyes off the open door or the huge Indian who stood just outside.

The sun was gone now, and except for the glow of the coals under the drying racks, darkness enshrouded the village.

Dorantes had been in and out of the council house several times without any hindrance. He was starting to feel safer among these wild looking people. Apparently, the Castilians had free run of the village too, but it was late now, and most of the men had returned to the beach to their makeshift campsite. Cabeza de Vaca and the chief had entertained each other for hours, the marshal giving brass and glass beads, the chief bringing more fish and pots of water, which Dorantes sent to the boats by Estevanico. Narváez, still too sick to sustain long periods of activity, had fallen asleep on a fur robe that had been supplied him.

Estevanico reentered the council house. He signaled to Dorantes that he had noticed a small group of Indians following him in the darkness.

"All is well on the beach, Andrés," he said loudly. "Most of the men are asleep."

Dorantes was seated beside the Cabeza de Vaca. He had long since stopped correcting Estevanico for not calling him Captain when he was with the officers. So far from Spain and under these trying circumstances, where every man found it necessary to do his utmost just to survive, it seemed inappropriate. "Soon, we too will rest, Estevanico," he said.

Suddenly, without warning, six Indians raced through the open door and began throwing rocks at the officers. Narváez bounced up. One of the rocks smashed him full in the face, split his forehead. Blood spurted out on the straw floor. The Indians screamed. *"Esteehatkee heethleko!"* Dorantes figured that meant they were still not in balance with nature.

Rocks streaked everywhere. The marshal and Castillo rolled on the floor. They tried to dodge the stones that were bouncing off them like hailstones on the streets of Madrid. Dorantes raced to Narváez' aid.

The big chief scrambled to his feet. He rose to a full stance. Estevanico fell in behind him, grabbed his arms, and pulled his elbows back. But somehow, Estevanico got tangled in the fur robe fastened at the chief's neck. The Indians, seeing their chief held captive, dropped their rocks and ran to wrestle him away from Estevanico. In a moment, Estevanico was standing with the scented robe in his hands, the chief and the six Indians racing out of the house.

Estevanico threw the robe over Narváez's shoulders. He helped him to his feet and half dragged him out of the house. Dorantes, Castillo, and Cabeza de Vaca followed.

Outside, shadowy bodies raced off into the underbrush. Dorantes heard cries coming from the beach. The Indians were attacking the Castilians in their sleep.

Estevanico heaved Narváez on his shoulders, and they all raced for the shore. When they arrived, the Indians were retreating from their first attack. They had apparently run out of rocks. They would be back, Dorantes was sure of that.

Men lay everywhere, groaning, crying, screaming with split skulls, broken cheek bones, sagging twisted chins. The attack had come so swiftly, so unexpectedly, they had not been able to establish a defense.

"Put the governor in his boat!" Dorantes ordered. "Put all wounded and sick men in the boats. Send them out in the bay. All able-bodied men are to stay here with me on the beach. We can't sail until sunrise. We'll have to hold them off till then."

Fifty men remained. Two hundred got into the boats

No sooner had the boats been shoved off the shore than the second attack came. Dorantes didn't have time to form the Castilians into ranks. Rocks flew in every direction. One bashed Cabeza de Vaca in the face, knocked him unconscious. In the darkness of the night, amid the screams and confusion, the Indians again ran out of rocks. They disappeared into the marsh elders that lined the bay. There was not one Spaniard who hadn't received a wound or a bruise or a broken bone or a split skull.

The third time the Pensacolas came, Dorantes was ready. He had the men in ranks. Those with daggers had them drawn, the rest had stacked piles of rocks for some hurling of their own. But this time, the Indians came with bows. They kept a stone's throw distance away and fired into the confused ranks. Castilians began to fall, wounded under the avalanche of arrows. Three fell and never rose. Again, the Indians ran out of ammunition and retreated. It seemed to Dorantes there was nothing he could do to thwart the Indians. One by one the Spaniards would fall as the Indians attacked all night long.

He screamed to two of the captains. "Penalose! Téllez! Muster fifteen men. Circle around behind them. When the Indians attack next time, ambush them, trick them into thinking we have them surrounded and outnumbered.

It worked. When the Indians made their fourth attack, Penalose executed the plan. The Indians retreated and did not return.

Dorantes couldn't sleep that night. He paced the beach and talked to the *guardia*, made sure they did not fall asleep on watch.

In the morning, the boats and the sick men returned to shore. But with them, there came a northerly storm that blew so violently and coldly that the Castilians were afraid to sail.

Cabeza de Vaca had regained consciousness and took charge. Narváez lay in a protected ravine with Enríquez the purser and the other feverish men. The marshal ordered that the thirty dugouts along the shore be burned to keep the Castilians warm. Dorantes took a contingent of soldiers to see what the Indians were up to.

"The Indians have fled the village," he told Cabeza de Vaca when he returned. "But they left dried fish and these water jars." His companions brought the fish and water. "Estevanico caught one and beat Hell out of him. He learned that the chief believes that we evoked Thunder Man and Thunder Snake to roar and streak the sky. He says the Indians will not return until we are gone."

By late afternoon, the storm had subsided. The men buried their dead, refilled the water jars, and loaded onto the boats all of the feverish, the wounded, the water jars, a small amount of fish, and what little corn remained. Cabeza de Vaca swung his boat into the lead. Dorantes pushed out behind him. How long would they last this time before the water and food ran out?

Who would be the next to die for a few jars of water?

3

Village of Mobile

Cabeza de Vaca crouched in the bow of boat five. The inspector Alonso de Solís, still feverish, attended the helm. The other four boats trailed behind. The marshal's blonde hair had grown shaggy and long. It whipped around his swollen face. His head throbbed. Pain shot down the back of his neck. Where had things gone wrong? It wasn't supposed to be like this. War against the Indians was supposed to be declared only with approval of the cleric. But the cleric was too busy defending his own life. How could one be forthright and considerate when the Indians were pinging rocks off your face?

He remembered the tales of slaughter and abuse on the Canary Islands told by the Guanche slaves that had served in his home in Jerez when he was a child. Had it been like this then? Had the Indians attacked first? He never fully agreed with his grandfather Pedro de Vera, who told him it was righteous and holy to kill heathens, and that a man who showed compassion to the unholy was no more than unholy himself. But what if you're attacked in your sleep? What if men lay around you with arrows in them? What if you are desperate and need water and food in order to survive? Does a starving man have the right to steal and plunder from those who refuse to give him food?

The five boats had drifted westward three or four days, now—who could remember any more—when in the distance, Cabeza de Vaca spied another bay. Its shores swept far inland. He had learned that such bays were frequently inhabited by Indians who fished the calmer waters. Perhaps these would be friendly Indians. But he thought not. News sped along the shore much faster than their boats drifted at sea. It was unfortunate that the Castilians did not have the necessary lines, nets, and skills to catch fish for themselves.

An image rose in his mind—dead Castilians lying on the shore. It was a distinct possibility, but one had no choice, really. One had to have food and water. One would perish if he stayed at sea.

Dorotheo Theodora— the clever Greek who had made the oakum and pitch for the boats—interrupted Cabeza de Vaca's thoughts. "I cannot take any more, *señor*. The hunger, the thirst. Not knowing who will be the next to die."

Cabeza de Vaca looked at him. "We must recommend ourselves to God our Lord and pray that He will deliver us from evil. It is all we have."

Then Theodora tugged on the marshal's arm. "*Señor*." He pointed. At the mouth of the bay sat a lone dugout filled with Indians. Beyond the dugout sprawled a frighteningly large village. Cabeza de Vaca eased his boat closer. Captain Dorantes' boat three slipped up beside them. The Indians signed and spoke. Estevanico interpreted.

'We are the Mobiles. We have heard of your misfortune with our enemy the Pensacolas. We will give you fresh water if you have something to put it in.'

Excellent. They had a mutual enemy. Surely this was grounds for friendship. Cabeza de Vaca signaled for the Indians to come alongside. He gave them the empty pots and a handful of hawkbells. Suddenly, Theodora splashed into the water. "I will go with them," he shouted.

A Negro porter leaped behind him. "Me, too," he yelped. The Negro was part Taino and had joined the expedition in Santo Domingo. Despite Cabeza de Vaca's pleas, the two would not return to the boat.

"Seize two of the Indians," he finally ordered, surprised at his own aggression. "We will keep them hostage until these men return in good stead." Showing hostility was the last thing he had wanted to do, but one had to protect the men.

The Indians did not like this action, but they could do nothing about it at the moment. They departed with the pots and the two crewmen.

"*Adiós, hombres,*" Theodora yelled.

Cabeza de Vaca didn't like the inflection in his voice. If it came to it, could he depart without those two?"

No one slept that night. Several times the two Indians tried to jump overboard and had to be restrained. At dawn, the bay was full of dugouts. Six of them carried long-haired headmen dressed in robes similar to the Pensacolas' but of finer quality. The robes had patterns of fawn-colored furs and were held snug with panther-skin sashes. The Indians showed no evidence of anger. They carried no bows. Still . . .

They signed, 'Give us our two companions, and we will return your men and give you all the water and food you need.'

Cabeza de Vaca's eyes darted from boat to boat. He did not see the two men. What had they done with them? Then slowly, the dugouts began circling behind them, blocking their exit from the bay. He did not like this. Narváez' boat one was nearby, but the governor was too ill to make a decision. It would be up to Cabeza de Vaca to decide. The Castilians were in no condition to fight, that was for sure. The cold, the wounds, the thirst and hunger, the sickness, all held them in a state of lethargy. The two men had jumped ship freely on their own accord, choosing to desert the Crown. They must suffer their own consequences. But then he remembered having watched the Indians who were brought to Spain wither away in the cruelest of fates, separated forever from their own kind. Could he bear to subject two of his countrymen to this destiny? The Castilians stared at him. They waited for a command. They were beyond even suggesting what might be right or wrong. Then, in a flash, the decision came to him. "Row the boats!" he shouted. "Turn to. Race for the open sea!"

The men snatched up their paddles. They struck out at the water. Cabeza de Vaca could sense the jolt of energy racing through their bodies. The Indians shouted. They fanned more boats around them.

"Row! Row for your life!" the marshal shouted.

Then the Indians crouched down inside their boats. They bounced up with slings—long strands of hemp cordage tied to small hide pouches. They dropped heavy stones in the pouches. They whirled them over their heads and let fly the fastest traveling rocks Cabeza de Vaca had ever seen.

Fighting back was out of the question. It was all the men could do to row. It would be a running fight. The dugouts of the Indians were faster and easily blocked the passage, but the five boats were much larger and pushed the dugouts aside.

Stones sizzled past them. Many struck the Castilians in the head, in the neck, the body. Some of the men were knocked overboard and had to be snatched back in. One stone ripped through the side of Peñalosa's boat four, and the hole had to be stuffed with a pair of trunk hose, leaving one man naked. Another snapped loose the mast of the *fraile's* boat two.

When the Indians came alongside the boats, they swung poles with large rocks tied to the ends of them. Cabeza de Vaca heard men scream, but he kept shouting. "Keep to the paddle. A wind has arisen. The Lord is on our side." He could see Narváez' lead boat with the strongest men heading through the pass.

"See, the governor is free. Paddle hard." The wind continued to blow from the north. The boats picked up speed. Several dugouts capsized in the choppy bay. Finally, the Indians retreated.

For two more days, the flotilla of five crude, leaky barges drifted west. Cabeza de Vaca's boat five took the lead, but his men no longer paddled. They were spent. They let the wind blow them wherever it wanted. They knew the end was near. They were ready to make their final confession. The last escapade had all but done them in. They had received no food or water at the village of Mobile and had expended their last flicker of stored energy. All hope of ever getting out alive had left them. They lay on the floor of the boat, unable to move, the sick raging with fever, the others totally exhausted.

At sundown, the boats drifted around a promontory and came to a ravine near the mouth of a swift river. Cabeza de Vaca knew the men could not go on without food and water. Should they give up and die here at the ravine or simply drift on forever? May God have mercy upon them.

He dropped his hand into the water. He licked his fingers. "The water's fresh!" he shouted. The river must be feeding fresh water to the ravine. The men cupped their hands. They hung their heads over the sides and drank their fill. All they had eaten that day were a few grains of corn that had been softened when they had fresh water. Now, they needed firewood to parch the last of their corn. But they saw no trees in the marsh. They'd have to sail to the mouth of the river for wood.

They pushed on, but the closer they got to the river, the farther they were carried away from shore. The current was swift, much stronger than Cabeza de Vaca had anticipated. He leaned against the rudder. The few who could tried to paddle against the current. But it was no use, night was upon them.

It was as dark as sable fur. The boats separated. Cabeza de Vaca called into the night but heard no return. He tried again. Nothing. Half a league off shore he tried to take a sounding and found no bottom, even at thirty fathoms.

As if the current were not enough, the wind freshened out of the north and pushed them still farther, beyond the silhouette of land. The salt stung Cabeza de Vaca's face. The sea spilled over the boat rail. Was this how it was going to end? Was drowning a more merciful way to die than starvation? May the good Saint Sebastian be with the Castilians

Then abruptly, Cabeza de Vaca stood tall. He threw back his shoulders. No. The Castilians would *not* die here in this unknown land. He would not allow it. He would stand fast and encourage them till the final breath of life was sucked out of him.

For two more days and nights Cabeza de Vaca's boat drifted endlessly, never once seeing another boat. Eventually, he found the coast. He held the rudder firm. The wind continued to blow from the east, but the men were useless. They lay in a heap in the floor, waiting to die. They had not eaten or drunk for two days. Cabeza de Vaca thanked God hourly for giving him the strength to stand at the helm and speak encouragement to the men. But his lips were cracked and bleeding, his nose peeled raw, his throat so parched he could barely talk, and his head still ached from the rock.

Near sundown, he caught sight of two of the other boats, and beyond them, the smoke of many fires rising from the mainland. He closed his mouth. He tried to moisten his throat but couldn't. He yelled in a cracked voice.

"Saludos! Amigos!"

Narváez' boat one came alongside them. The governor reclined in the bow, his one good eye sunken and dark. He was dehydrated and did not look well. His voice was weak and scratchy, barely audible.

"What do you think we should do, Provost Marshal?" Cabeza de Vaca was surprised he could talk at all. "I think we should join the boat up ahead and thereupon, follow God's directing."

"Nonsense." Narváez' voice grew clearer. "Can't you see that boat is drifting out to sea? I'm heading for those fires. If you wish to follow you'll put your men to the oar. With this contrary wind, it is only by the strength of your arms that you'll ever get to land."

"My men are too weary to paddle."

"Captain Pantoja here says if we don't get to shore tonight, the wind will hold us away for six more days. By then we'll all be dead." The frail Captain Pantoja stood at the helm. He did not move or even blink. "If your men want to live, they'll row." Narváez nodded. Then his men paddled away.

Cabeza de Vaca left the helm and took up a paddle. He would follow Narváez. Seeing his determination, a few of the Castilians attempted to help him, but their strength just was not there. Finally, he yelled out, "Governor, throw us a rope. We cannot row against this wind. You have the largest boat, the strongest men. We can hook up and go together."

"It is no small effort on our part alone to reach the shore tonight, Marshal," Narváez yelled back.

"Then tell us what we should do."

"This is no time for orders, Marshal. From here on, it's every man for himself. Damn the expedition. That's the way it is, and that's the way it's going to be."

Narváez' boat slowly disappeared into the glow of the setting sun. Cabeza de Vaca could not believe what he had just heard, his commanding officer abandoning his post. Had Narváez gone berserk? The men on Cabeza de Vaca's boat and all the other boats, wherever they may be, were now *his* responsibility. He wished he had them all together. He'd ask the opinions of every man. Together, they would somehow reach a decision on what to do.

He looked up and saw the second boat drawing nearer. It was boat four of the captains Peñalosa and Téllez. Their rudder had broken off in the outpouring current of the river, but they had a small quantity of corn and water, which they shared. Slowly the two boats drifted westward. Four more days they drifted, the men on the edge of death.

Then a storm raged. It chilled the air. The men shivered, their emaciated bodies unable to give off heat. Cabeza de Vaca held the rudder firm, but Peñalosa's boat drifted out to sea. There was nothing he could do to catch them. That dark night the marshal believed he would never see the men of boat four again. He crossed himself and held tight to the rudder. May God our Lord have mercy upon them. He must save the men in his own boat, now.

On into the darkness the weather-torn boat drifted. The men were in a heap. No one moved. Several had slipped into unconsciousness. Death was sure to come with the next wave surge. Not a sound was heard from them. They had run out of prayers, run out of groans, run out of hope. Resolutely, they awaited death.

But Cabeza de Vaca would not give up. He clung to the rudder as if it were the breast that fed them. He was the only man on his feet, but he would give up his life in a moment if he could somehow get the Castilians on their feet. Had it been his fault they

41

were in this condition? He was, after all, second in command. Perhaps he should have been more insistent about staying with the ships at Bahía de la Cruz, even to the point of arresting Narváez for direct disobedience to the Crown. Perhaps he should have sided with the *caballeros* and ridden back for the ships instead of eating the horses. Perhaps he should have been more insistent to force the men to sail east instead of west out of the Bay of Horses. Perhaps there had been a dozen things he could have done to save them from this wretched moment. But no, he had done none of them.

Inspector De Solís, thoroughly exhausted, had gone to sleep in the bow, holding his stomach. Cabeza de Vaca had told him he'd take his shift at the helm. Around midnight, thinking De Solís might have died, he went to shake him. He found he was well enough to pilot the boat for awhile.

Cabeza de Vaca fell into the inspector's spot, but he was unable to rest. The responsibility of the men lay heavily on his shoulders. He felt the cold waves crushing over the side of their boat. Fall had come and his men were still alive. He felt the dangerous rocking and swaying. He wondered if Peñalosa and Téllez in boat four had survived. He wondered about the two men left at the village of Mobile. He wondered if Narváez had made it to the village, and how many men in the other boats, wherever they were, were already dead.

Sometime before dawn, Cabeza de Vaca heard a sound, a low roar that he had not heard before. He lifted his head; the sound was still there. Wearily, he rose and joined the inspector at the stern.

"What do you make of it, Alonso?"

"Sounds like a surf to me." De Solís spoke weakly.

For a moment longer, they both listened. Yes. It was a surf. Somewhere up ahead.

"Can we hold the boat off till sunrise?" De Solís asked.

"We'll try." Cabeza de Vaca took an oar. He fought against the sea, but the wind was too strong behind them. Steadily, it nudged them toward the rumbling surf.

The boat began to shake and rocked violently. Water spilled over the sides in great washes. One wave picked up the boat and threw it a horse's length out of the water. When it crashed down, the men scrambled out of their unconsciousness. The next wave toppled the boat end to end, and all of the men splashed into the cold, shallow water.

They battled the surf in a state of shock. But eventually fought their way to the beach. They crawled ashore. Cabeza de Vaca was with them. He fell face first in the sand. He kissed the sand. He rolled over and stared into the deep starless sky. He raised his weary arms to the heavens and uttered a *Pater Noster*.

"Our Father, who art in Heaven . . ."

TEXAS

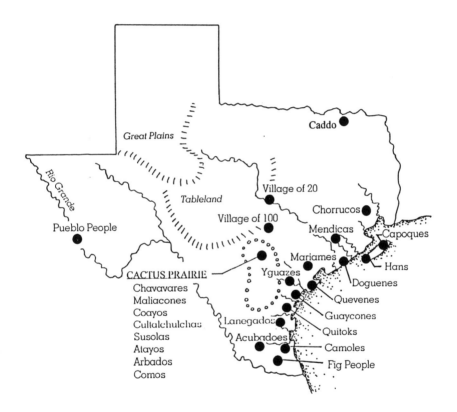

Caddo

Great Plains

Rio Grande

Pueblo People

Tableland

Village of 20

Chorrucos

Village of 100

Mendicas

Capoques

Mariames

Hans

CACTUS PRAIRIE

Yguazes

Doguenes

Chavavares
Maliacones
Coayos
Cultalchulchas
Susolas
Atayos
Arbados
Comos

Quevenes

Lanegados

Guaycones

Acubadoes

Quitoks

Camoles

Fig People

"The Indians wanted to make medicine men of us. We laughed, taking it for a jest, and said that we did not understand how to cure. Thereupon, they withheld our food."

—The Account of Cabeza de Vaca

4

November 15, 1528
Village of Capoque

A bizarre chorus of wails lifted out of the marsh. A frightened egret bolted to the sky. Seagulls squawked and flew for the mainland. It was dawn. The seabirds had never gotten used to that unnatural sound in their feeding ground each morning.

Below the birds, in a smoky scrub on the bay side of the island, forty oval *cahas* sat in a thicket. The huts were little more than long willow poles pushed into the ground in a circle, their tops bent over and lashed together, their sides covered with reed mats and deer hides. In front of one, a skinny boy, his mother, and her two sisters knelt in the dirt among sedges and rattlesnake weed. They whined and bawled and moaned, but there were no tears. Two village women came down the trail that led to the backwater sloughs. The women would spend the day digging roots from the mire. But first, they must stop and join the ensemble of wails

The boy Tadpole wanted to be fishing with the men or chasing deer on the mainland—even though no deer had been seen since spring. They needed meat. He was so hungry he could eat a *xo*. He had eaten nothing but lotus roots for two moons. It was time he did something on his on, time he stopped depending on others. Besides, would he not soon have his breast pierced and his body painted to show the village girls he was available? He was almost a man, almost twelve winters. Soon, he would no longer be a *clox*.

He rolled over onto his back. He raised his feet into the air and bellowed long and loud enough to chase the night herons out of the marsh elders.

"Tadpole! Do not overdo it," the mother snapped. "You will anger the witches."

"Why do we have to wail every sunup, every sunhigh, and every sundown in the first place?" Tadpole said.

"We must mourn your sister's death, you know that. It is the shaman's command—mourn the dead for three moons. It has only been two moons.

"But Little Bird herself lived only one moon. And the shaman has been dead since last coldtime. He does not even know what we do."

"Stop saying the name of the dead out loud, you will anger the witches. They will fill you full of sticks and bugs."

The two sisters stopped wailing. One spoke. "Itch Vine, we must go now. We will be back at sunhigh." They stood. They were frail as palm twine and naked as a grub, except for a small patch of moss hanging in their front and rear to keep the men from knowing when they were issuing blood, to keep the men from beating them and accusing them of tainting their yopon during drink time. The four women left and followed the trail to the sloughs.

"We did not mourn when the old shaman died," Tadpole said. "And he was your father, like Little Bird was your daughter.?"

"We do not mourn old men. They lived their life. And if you say your sister's name one more time I will club you with this hammerstone."

She would not, of course. The Karankawas never beat their children. They loved their children. Besides, Tadpole was her only *clox* now that Little Bird was gone. Tadpole rose and started to follow the women. He was tired of mourning. He must do something about their hunger.

"Stop!" his mother barked.

"Do not worry, Itch Vine. I will be back at sunhigh. I will not forget Little—

"Ahhht!" Itch Vine raised a skinny finger. Then, "I will feed you first. You had nothing at all yesterday. I will not have you dropping by the trail like your father."

"There is nothing here but sumpweeds and knotweeds. Why can I not go to the root fields and dig with the others?"

"We are not allowed to dig or gather until the mourn is over, you know that. The villagers will continue to feed us. Come into the *caha* by the fire where their is heat."

Reluctantly, Tadpole followed his mother through the opening. Three pairs of deer skins lay on the floor around the wall of the *caha*, two pairs for Itch Vine's sisters and their *saylas*, one pair for Tadpole and his mother. He wondered if Itch Vine missed his father, her *sayla*. He wondered how she felt when her sisters and their *saylas* panted and grunted in the night, sometimes accidentally kicking the mats off the walls of the *caha* then laughing behind muffled mouths, pretending the wind had blown them away.

He watched his mother sit by the fire, the smoke drifting upward through the mats. Her face was gaunt and bony; her ribs pushed against her skin.

"Not today, Itch Vine." he said. "You are too weak. Save your strength. I will go find us some oysters."

"The oysters will not be ready until spring. Come." She patted her skinny thigh. "*Haka.*"

Tadpole stretched out on his back. He laid his head on his mother's thigh. She leaned forward, directed her flaccid breast into his mouth, and began to hum a song, one he had heard a thousand times.

Tadpole sucked gently on the long nipple as he had done for twelve coldtimes. But he knew he would get no milk. Itch Vine was dry. She had dried up right after Little Bird died. He did not want to tell her, for soon he would get his first tattoo, then she would no longer invite him to suck.

After several moments, he stopped. He rose. "Maybe I will bring you an *am* today, Itch Vine."

"Stay away from the bay; the mourn is not complete. You will anger the witches."

49

"I know." He headed out the door. "We would not want to anger the witches."

"Do not forget the ceremony tonight," she yelled. "The coldtime has returned. It marks the time your grandfather's body washed up on the shore. I told him he was too old to swim across the bay. You stay away from that bay, Tadpole."

Tadpole left his mother watching from the opening. But as soon as she went back inside, he circled around and came in behind the *caha*.

He thought about his grandfather, the old shaman, and the magic he had. Whenever one of the village women got sick, the old shaman laid a warm stone on her belly then dropped his head between her legs until the woman shivered and jolted up squealing that she felt wonderful. The new shaman was older than the old shaman, but he did not have the old shaman's magic. He blew smoke on the sick women, made cuts, and sang chants, but he did not drop his head between their legs. Sometimes the women got better; sometimes they died. Tadpole wanted the old shaman's magic. When the old man named him *Tadpole*, he said that would be his village name. Tadpole hated the name. But many seasons later the old shaman whispered his spirit name to him—*Kele*, the wrestler. Tadpole knew the name had magical powers, but he was never allowed to speak it out loud. He knew that someday, he would be the greatest wrestler among the Karankawas all along the coast.

Shortly after that, the old shaman was taken to the mainland to collect some of his magical herbs. Growing tired of waiting for a fisherman to pick him up, he decided to swim back to the island. He never made it. His dead body was pulled from the bay, bundled with his whooping crane flute and shell necklace, and put to the fire. Shamans were never buried like common villagers. Later, his bones were pounded and mixed with water. Tonight at the ceremony, Tadpole, his grandson, would drink the crushed bones, for the shaman had only daughters, and daughters did not drink the bones of the dead.

Tadpole came to the back of the *caha* where the *saylas'* bows were kept. The *saylas* would not need them today; they were on the mainland searching for firewood. They were not allowed to hunt until the family mourn was over.

He grabbed a bow and one arrow and ran off through the salt flats to the bay. There were many dugouts pulled on the shore, for this was the season to pull roots, not shoot *ams*. Still, Tadpole wanted an *am* for his mother; she looked so weak.

He threw the bow in the floor and pushed off. He climbed upon the triangular platform on the rear of the dugout. When he came to a cove, he stopped. He laid aside his pole, slapped the water, and waited. No *am* came. From cove to cove he poled and slapped until finally he shot an *am*. It was bony and scaly and not very large, but it was meat.

Tadpole returned the dugout and raced back to the village. But something had happened while he was gone. He could hear the commotion long before he arrived. Something was wrong; the villagers were gathered in the clearing. He slipped to the back of the *caha*. He returned the bow and arrow. No one was at the *caha*, so he laid the dead *am* on the stump where the villagers set their scraps. Itch Vine would never know who had shot it. A gift from a villager, she would think.

A hundred *saylas* had gathered with the women. The women were handing them their bows and reed arrows. Tadpole saw his mother. He raced to the clearing.

"Itch Vine!"

"There you are. Where were you?"

He ignored the question. "What has happened?"

"While the villagers were at the root fields, a strange man came and stole a *xo*, a cooking pot, and some dried *ams*. They say he headed toward the sea. Three villagers are following him. The *saylas* are going there now."

"What did he look like? Was he a Han from the other end of the island. Was he a Chorruco from the forest?"

Itch Vine squinted, her eyes full of fear. "His skin was as white as the morning sky, and his face was covered with hair."

Cabeza de Vaca heard someone yell. He looked up. He and the men of boat five were huddled in a ravine behind a high dune that partially blocked the harsh sea winds. They had a small fire, but there was not much firewood. They had found a little fresh water but not nearly enough. Their boat lay upside down in the surf, but they were alive, at least for now.

"It's Lope de Oviedo, returning," he hollered to the inspector.

Oviedo, being the only one strong enough to move about, had been sent to reconnoiter the inland. He was returning with what looked like dried fish, a cooking pot, and a small dog. He approached Cabeza de Vaca.

"This is an island," he said. "About a half league away, on the bay side, there is an Indian village. That's where *they* came from." He turned and pointed.

Cabeza de Vaca looked up. He saw a hundred Indians standing a crossbow shot behind Oviedo. Their bodies were tall, their heads narrow. Reed canes three palms long pierced their breasts, a shorter one protruded from their lower lips. Each Indian held a stone or a bow. Each looked angry. The Castilians could not stand another fight. Food and shelter were all they needed.

Cabeza de Vaca had to go talk to them. He had to make them understand they meant no harm. "Alonso, do you feel up to a confusing conversation with barbarians?"

The inspector replied, "I have nothing to lose, Marshal. All they can do is club me to death, and right now that would be a welcomed pleasure."

Cabeza de Vaca and Alonso de Solís gathered up beads and hawk bells from one of their supply sacks. They approached the Indians. When they held out the gifts, no one came forward. Finally, a skinny boy about twelve cautiously came and stood in front of them. They offered him a bell. He refused the bell. He pointed to the dog held by Oviedo.

"*Xo*," he said and gestured that he wanted the animal returned.

Oviedo brought the dog and handed it to the boy. "The little *perro* never barked, anyway," he said. "I think he is *loco*."

Cabeza de Vaca signed as best he knew how and asked the boy's name.

"Kele," the boy whispered so the others would not hear. Then he signed, 'The wrestler.'

'You are very brave,' Cabeza de Vaca signed.

The boy took the dog and returned to the villagers. One by one other Indians came forward. Their faces and skin were streaked with grease and mud. Their bodies smelled repulsive. Each took a bell or glass bead and each gave an arrow. They signed and said, 'We are the Capoques of the Karankawa People. Who are you?'

Cabeza de Vaca did not answer; they would not understand. Instead, he told Alonzo, "An arrow gift is a gesture of friendship."

By vague hand signals, Cabeza de Vaca was able to convince the Indians to bring them food and water. The Indians were so happy to have the hawk bells that they did. And for the next few mornings, they continued to bring fish, roots that tasted like bitter nuts, and brackish water. Each day, Cabeza de Vaca gave them more bells and beads.

Each night, after the Indians went back to their village, cold winds sliced down the beach. It carried tiny pellets of grit and salt. It stung the arms and faces of the men, so the men buried themselves in the sand for protection.

Cabeza de Vaca lay in a heap of sand. He studied the stars. Winter was closing in. He had to get the Castilians off the island and into the land of the Christians before they all died from exposure.

On the morning of the fourth day, he told the men, "We must repair the boat and depart forthwith."

The boat was almost completely covered with sand at the edge of the breakers. The Castilians removed their clothes, bundled them as tight as they could, and splashed into the cold water. They spent the day shivering, righting and repairing the boat. Then they boarded. Preferring to remain naked until they were safely beyond the turbulent surf, they stuffed their clothes bundles safely under the thwarts. They had hardly put to the paddles when the raging sea crashed into the side of the boat and tore loose the oar sockets. Several men fell overboard. When the others leaned over the rail to help them, another wave got under the boat and flipped it completely over again. Cabeza de Vaca was one of the few who could swim. He sucked down a deep breath to overcome the shock of the cold water. Surprisingly, he found the sand bottom in the trough beneath the waves. The men yelled and spit water and struggled to remain on their feet. But each new wave lifted them and tumbled them into the rollicking surf.

"Alonso is under the boat!" someone yelled. "He is trapped with two others."

Cabeza de Vaca knew the inspector could not swim. But also knew that at any moment a wave could lift the boat and send it crashing down on top of him. Still, he struggled to get to the boat. His heart pounded. The water was freezing. His breath was shallow. His open sores and wounds sent stinging pain screaming through his body. Before the next swell, he took sight, dove, and swam underwater toward the boat. His timing was off. The boat shifted, and he emerged just a few feet away from the bobbing hull. Before he could readjust, a wave slammed the stern into the side of his head. His ears rang with a high-pitched chime above the roar of the surf. Somewhere in the background, he heard the cries of the Castilians. For a moment, all went black. He felt himself slipping into the sea. But the unfair odds of the cold, the hunger and weakness, and the relentless sea, brought him to anger. His thoughts cleared.

He took another deep breath, slipped under the surface, and found a surprising calm. Through the foggy sea water, he saw the hulking shadow of the boat. Frantically, he swam underwater and emerged gasping for air in the belly of the hull. He grabbed a thwart and hung on. He looked fore and aft. He saw no Alonso. He let go and swam to the bow. He slammed his fist into the hide hull. He shouted, "Alonso! Alonso!" But Alonso was not there. He held his breath again and swam out. He saw that the Castilians had made it to shore, but he would not give up. He made several more dives searching for the three men. Finally, he had to stop and swim in.

Most of the Castilians lay coughing and shivering on the sand. A few had formed a huddle farther down the beach.

"Marshal, down here," someone yelled.

When he arrived at the huddle, the men parted, and he saw the drowned bodies of the three men in a heap on the beach.

* * *

The crude camp behind the dune was quiet that afternoon. They had lost everything—their boat, their clothes, three more countrymen. The Castilians dug into the sand to hide their nakedness and to stop from shivering. The bodies of the dead men lay side by side on the open sand. Cabeza de Vaca was vexed. How many more must he lose before they would be delivered from this maddening world? He could not bury his countrymen. Not yet. Not until their deaths had settled in, and he was sure that this was not some harrowing nightmare.

At sunset, the Indians returned. They knew nothing of the attempted departure. When they saw the Castilians naked and trembling, they jolted. Then they saw the three dead bodies. Immediately, they began to wail and bawl and roll in the sand. This they did for half an hour—but there were no tears.

Meanwhile, Cabeza de Vaca spoke with a few of the men who were still able to stand.

"I am going to ask them to take us to their village."

Two older men became incensed. One said, "We have been to New Spain, Marshal. We know this kind. They will sacrifice us to their gods. They will eat us. We have been to Tetzcoco and Tlacopan. We've seen the great temple steps at Tenochtitlan stained with sacrificial blood where they rolled the bodies down to the butchers below. We must stay away from their village. You see how savage they are."

"I see only Indians somewhat frightened and defensive at having their land invaded by foreigners, but with enough compassion to feed us and mourn our dead."

"They are fattening us up for the feast, I tell you."

"There is hardly anyone fat here. Besides, even if they do kill us it's better than suffering a slow and agonizing death of cold and starvation. Look around you. We have no clothes, no food, no tools, no weapons. Everything was lost with the boat."

The two men continued to complain. They walked away and tried to get support from the others. But Cabeza de Vaca was still in charge, and his mind was made up.

When the Indians stopped wailing, he asked them by signs if the Castilians could go to their village and sleep in one of their houses. The Indians seemed surprisingly happy. Cabeza de Vaca did not know why. Perhaps the two older men were right. Still, he had to chance it. He had no choice.

The Indians ran ahead and built fires at intervals along the trail to keep the men warm while crossing over to the bay side. Then they led the Spaniards—carrying the lame and the three dead men—through the dunes and salt barrens to the scrub where they came to the village.

The scrub gave some protection against the cold wind but provided harborage for thousands of mosquitoes that immediately attacked the soft, pale skin of the Spaniards. The Indians gave them some of their lotion to rub onto their skin. When asked what it was, they pointed—mud and oil from *el largato,* the big lizard. The alligator oil was rancid and turned their stomachs. Many of the young Castilians threw up. The Indians laughed.

There were no temples at the village, no mounds, no plaza. Only huts covered with reed mats that looked like they would hold a family of six or eight. There was one lodge large enough to hold the forty or so men left under Cabeza de Vaca's command.

The Indians led them into the lodge. Several small fires burned near the center. The men had to crouch or lie to keep the smoke out of their eyes. Many of them were so exhausted they fell asleep right away. Cabeza de Vaca sat and watched through the open doorway. Outside, the Indians were building a large fire. They looked to be preparing for some sort of ceremony.

The sun was well below the horizon now, and the only light outside was the fire around which several naked Indians danced in frenzied gyrations. Two of them pounded a hollow log, while others shook turtle rattles. They were preparing for something, that was for sure. The later the night grew, the louder the drum sounded.

The soldier who had been to New Spain came and sat beside Cabeza de Vaca. "They are savages, I tell you. I swear we will not see the light of a new day."

Many who had slept earlier woke. They sat up. The incessant beat of the drum would not allow them to sleep.

"I'm going outside to see what's going on," the soldier told Cabeza de Vaca.

Cabeza de Vaca tried to calm the men with reassuring words, but he wasn't so sure himself, anymore. In his mind, his thoughts reeled. Where were they? Where was Narváez? What were the Indians up too? Had any of the boats made it to land? If it would only please God our Lord to deliver the men from this night.

Suddenly, the soldier dashed back into the hut. Even in the orange glow of the fire, he was as white as milk, his eyes as big as sea snails.

"Did you talk to them?" Cabeza de Vaca asked.

The soldier was breathless. He stared into the dark space at the ceiling of the lodge."

"Well?"

"I do not understand signs all that well, Marshal. But I swear to you they said . . ."

"Said what?"

"They said, soon, they would drink the crushed bones of the dead."

.

5

Village of Han

"I know you're going to think I'm crazy saying this, right?" Estevanico sat on a log eating a smoked fish. He watched the Han villagers laboriously dig roots out of the mire and pitch them onto the bank.

"Everything you say is crazy, *amigote*," Dorantes said. He didn't bother to look at Estevanico. He snatched up several roots, washed them, and placed them in a reed basket. Their boat three had crashed on the south end of some island his men were calling Isle of Misfortune. The friendly Han Indians had taken the half-dead Castilians to their village and for several days had fed them. The men recovered some of their strength and were now helping with chores.

"I'm going to push one of those reeds through my *pecho* like those *nativos*."

"What?"

"You think it would hurt?"

"Not near as bad as the one I'll push through the top of your head if you do that."

Estevanico knew Andrés would never do what he said. Who'd keep him out of trouble if Estevanico wasn't around? "But I like the way it looks."

"Speaking of the *nativos*, have you noticed how the farther west we go, the more primitive the Indians are? Look at these Hans. They have no chief. They use only stone tools. They settle quarrels with their fists, rob each other routinely, and change wives two or three times in the middle of the night."

"Sounds like pretty good living." Estevanico said. He stood up. He needed to get a closer look at those reeds. Maybe he'd stick one through his lip, too, like some of the *nativos* had done.

"Don't even think about it, Estevanico. Besides we're leaving this morning. While the men continue to repair our boat, you and I and Captain Castillo will take a guide to the north end of this island. The *nativos* say another boat has landed there."

Estevanico lagged behind. He tripped along in the footprints of the three men. He needed a little time to himself to do some figuring. He was already tall like those Hans, only he was much darker. The *nativos* liked dark people. What he needed now was a couple of reeds stuck here, a couple stuck there, flatten his head a little, probably do that with a log, get him a couple of tatoos on his *culo*, then they'd make him chief for sure. They needed a good chief, somebody to invent the wheel for them, show them how to use forks, how to have a little rabbit farm. Besides, Estevanico was well-timbered. The Hans were more in the frog-dicky category; had serious limitations on their ability to pleasure the princesses. Estevanico would call the princesses Sweet Cake and Honey Hunker, things like that. Make them feel real good so they'd bring him some crabs, and chunks of venison, lay down beside him, present themselves to their chief.

Estevanico was thinking less and less of Ka•konee with each passing day. Having had many near-death experiences in the past several weeks, he had decided that life was little more than a bunch of grapes whose pleasures were to be plucked as often as possible before his plucker wilted.

The morning turned to afternoon. Finally, they came to an overturned boat on the shore. A man in a skin robe peered into the wreckage.

"Marshal! Provost Marshal!" Dorantes yelled. Estevanico ran and caught up.

Dorantes and Castillo hugged Cabeza de Vaca and shared stories of their grueling voyage from the village of Mobile to

Misfortune. Cabeza de Vaca told them how they thought they were going to be eaten that first night in the village and about the things that had happened since their arrival.

"Let me get this straight," Estevanico jeered. "When these nativos came and saw your naked bodies, they cried for half an hour?"

Cabeza de Vaca did not laugh. In fact, he rarely responded to anything Estevanico said. Instead, he invited the officers to the Capoque village. They talked further about Narváez relinquishing his command and what they might do about their present condition. Then two Castilians and a guide from the village of Han arrived.

"They finished repairing the boat, Captain," one of them told Dorantes. "It looked good, but when they pushed it into the water, it sank. Waves tore it to pieces. Tavera drowned"

"The same thing happened to us" Cabeza de Vaca said. He uttered a quiet prayer and made the sign of the cross. "That settles it, We will stay here on the island for the duration of winter. We'd never survive traveling in this cold weather. We will select four of our strongest to journey by foot to Pánuco. If by Divine favor they should reach the Christians, they can inform them of our ill being and sorrows and send a ship for us."

"I have just the men, *señor*," Dorantes said. "They worked several days on our boat without falling to the fever: Méndez the Portuguese carpenter, Álvaro Fernández, Astudillo from Cafra, and Figueroa, a native of Toledo. I'll get a *nativo* from Han to be their guide. Meanwhile, it would perhaps be best if we stayed with the Han while your men remained here with the Capoques. Together, we would be too great a burden for one village. We have a few clothes and some supplies. We will share them with your men."

Winter came. The weather was cold, bitter, tempestuous. The men who were sick got sicker. Most of them died. Those who were not sick became feverish. Then they began to die. The Castilians lay around night and day unable to work. To make matters worse, the lotus had begun to sprout, and the roots were too bitter to eat. The season had run itself out, and the winter tides no longer brought *ams* into the bay. Estevanico traded his gold earring for the last two smoked *ams* in the village. He gave them to two starving men. Starvation was now the daily disposition of both the Indians and the Spaniards.

At the Village of Han, Estevanico stalked back and forth in the lodge the Indians had provided for them. The lodge was nearly empty now. It was February.

"If I have to bury one more man I think I'm going to throw up."

"Stop pacing, *amigote*," Dorantes told him. "Conserve your strength."

"I don't even think I could throw up. There's nothing down there to throw. How can you throw up something that isn't?"

"Why don't you go live on the beach awhile. At least you won't have to slap mosquitoes or listen to moans."

Moans weren't the half of it. Bellyaching, crying, praying all day, all night. If he didn't get out of this place soon, he thought he'd explode. If he didn't get something substantial to eat, there wouldn't be anything to explode.

"Who is at the beach?"

"Sierra, Diego, López, Corral, Palacios, and Gonzalo Ruiz."

"Allah go on. That's one *loco* bunch. Any of them got the fever, do you think?"

"Didn't have when they left."

"I'm not sure my dogs can make it that far."

"Careful what you say. You know how the *nativos* love their little dogs."

"*Xos*, Andrés. Dogs bark. *Xos* just run around peeing on everybody that's lying down. If I could catch one of those varmints when he was hiking his leg on me, he'd be *xo* chops in Estevanico's belly. You know how long it's been since I had meat?"

"Don't think about it. Go to the beach. Pretend you're making a pilgrimage to Mecca."

"Never went there."

Estevanico left the village. He shambled off toward the gulf. A jaunt that should have taken twenty minutes took two hours. His wizened body had never suffered such disregard and inattention. He stopped frequently to give it rest. Finally, he spied a sloppily constructed mat house on the backside of the dunes. He entered. Inside, it was shadowy and still.

"What are you doing here?" It was Gonzalo Ruiz. The skin around his eyes was dark and sullen.

"Just thought I'd spend a little time out here."

Gonzalo looked nervous, a little crazed. His eyes darted from Estevanico to the fire pit. The smell of smoked meat drifted in the air. Where'd they find meat?

"What's that?" Estevanico sniffed.

Gonzalo hesitated. He looked at the other man. There were only two of them in the hut.

"Food for survival," Gonzalo finally said. "There is enough for you. Would you like some?"

"Where are the other men?"

Gonzalo looked to a pile of brush in the corner.

"Dead?"

Gonzalo nodded.

"Why haven't you buried them?"

Gonsalo did not answer. He was nervous. He began to fidget. "It is tasty, not bad at all." He held out a piece of meat for Estevanico. Estevanico's stomach groaned. His mouth began to salivate.

He looked back and forth between the meat and the pile of brush. This was crackbrain, savage. "You're not. . ."

For a long time Estevanico stared at the meat in Gonsalo's hand. He was near starvation, would probably die soon himself if he didn't eat something. But this? The flesh of another man? He wrestled with images flashing in his mind. He'd heard about Indian cannibals from soldiers who had sailed the Spanish Main. Once he figured himself eating the flesh of a man, pictured himself holding a charred arm, nibbling on the fingers like it was a chicken neck or a pig tail, skin popping between his teeth, gristle sticking to his gums. But that was just figuring. That wasn't real. This was real. He stared at the meat. There were no fingers, no bone, no skin, just a roasted piece of flayed meat. It could have been a side of pork or beef. He remembered what Dorantes had told him once: a hungry man will eat anything.

He had to do it. He had to keep from starving. It'd be easy. Just reach out, grab it, say something like: So how's the weather been doing out here? Take a bite, look around.

He reached and took the meat. He said, "So how's been doing out here in the weather." Bite, now, while Gonsalo is answering, What'd you say. Just munch down, chew, swallow, say something like: It's a little cold back at the village.

He wasn't munching.

He wasn't chewing.

He began to sweat.

In this cold, sweat?

Gonsalo asked, "What'd you say?" The other man stared at him. No one moved.

Suddenly, a shadow dropped onto the sand floor; a body blocked the door opening. It was the kid from Capoque, the one they called Tadpole or Kele or something. He was holding a smoked *am*.

Estevanico threw the cooked flesh into the fire. He grabbed the kid, snatched him outside away from the hut. The kid gave him the *am*, and Estevanico ate it quickly, thankfully. He couldn't believe what he'd almost done. Thanks be to Allah, to Lord our God, to Gomez Arias the bull fighter and dead-eyed Dagger Dick wherever he may be.

'He wants you to come,' the kid signed. 'The Hair-faced ones are nearly all dead. The village people are sick in the belly.'

Cabeza de Vaca had sent for them. Estevanico must tell Andrés and Captain Castillo. They'd go see what was the matter.

Tadpole listened to the *saylas* arguing about the Hair-faced People: They do no work, they eat each other like the *ams* eat their own dead, and now they have brought their stomach sickness to the Capoques.

The Hair-face People must die.

Tadpole knew the *saylas* were right. He had watched half of the villagers groan, hold their bellies, and die. Every cold season it was expected that some would die—usually the old ones. When the *ams* left the bay in the cold season and did not return until the oysters came, it was the time for the old ones to die. But never had they lost this many, and never from the bellyache sickness. Now, Itch Vine had become sick, too. She moaned all night and visited the pit by the edge of the village much too often. She was weak and moved with great pain. How many suns before she too would die?

The Hair-face People had brought an evil witch to their village. Only by killing them would the witch leave. The new shaman had no power over this witch, over any witch for that matter.

Kele the Wrestler would be the first to make the kill. He had the magic of his grandfather's bones inside him now, and his body was scabbed in long streaks where he had been bled during the ceremony. He would lead the villagers with his new power.

When the Great Sun Spirit went to sleep behind the trees on the mainland, Tadpole dipped his finger in oil. The oil had been darkened with charcoal. He streaked his face from his forehead to his nose and made several marks on his arms. Then he slipped silently to the rear of his *caha*. There, next to the bows, was the *saylas'* stone club. They used it to club deer after chasing them all day, but they would not be needing it this night. He grabbed it up.

He had watched the three Hair-face leaders sit on a tree log every night since he had delivered the message. Which one would he kill? The tall, skinny one who looked like a pole? No, his eyes were so strong he was probably a spirit himself. Kele could not kill a spirit. The one with hair the color of the morning sky who had come to them first? No, he lived with the Capoques and had become one of them. It would be the short, muscular one, the one who hollered at the black man all the time.

Tadpole sidled around the village until he saw the log and the bulky images of the three men. They were sitting and talking in their nightly spot by the fire. Silently on his knees, he crawled through the scrub, getting closer to the images. Even in the dark, he could tell who they were: Sky-hair on the left, Spirit-man in the center, Muscle-man on the right. He would pounce on Muscle-man, wrestle him to the ground, leap up and club him to death.

He could hear the fire popping, now. Sky-hair leaned to the right, blew a snort of stink-air on the tree log, then sat back up. Spirit-man said something, Muscle-man laughed.

Do it now, while they are distracted.

He leaped into the air, gave a shrill cry, and pounced on the broad shoulders of Muscle-man. The two rolled forward barely missing the fire. Muscle-man did not fight back; he seemed dazed by the surprise attack.

Kele the Wrestler found his footing, leaped up and felt the power of the old shaman swell inside him. He raised the stone club. Muscle-man's head was just beneath him, lying in the sand, reflecting the fire. This would be easy. Soon the witch would be gone. Soon Itch Vine would be well again.

The club started it's downswing, but something caught Kele's arm. He could not move it. A hand gripped his wrist and squeezed so tight he had to drop the stone club. Maybe this wasn't the right night to kill Muscle-man.

Without looking back, Kele freed himself and raced off into the scrub. He veered right, left, sent sand flying in a flurry. But racing feet followed him, very close now, chasing him. Then the chaser tackled him. They tumbled to the sand. The big body leaped on top of him. In the pale light he saw his club being raised in the air over his head. In the next moment he would be dead.

But the club never came down.

The man sitting on top of him stopped. It was the black man, the one he'd given the *am* to. When the black man recognized him, he lowered the club. He climbed off. Kele jumped up. He turned and fled. The black man did not chase after him.

Back at the *caha*, Kale told his family what had happened.

"Maybe they have secret powers of protection and cannot be killed," one of the *saylas* said.

Kele thought about that a moment. "If that is so then they can use their power to chase away the witch." He looked at his mother lying in the corner, holding her stomach, her eyes a blank stare. She had not spoken in days. She awaited death. "Spirit-man. The one with the piercing eyes. It is *his* magic that keeps them alive."

Kele the wrestler had used his secret powers to figure it out. Now, he would tell the people. They would make Spirit-man their new shaman.

Alonso del Castillo paced back and forth on the beach. A chilly breeze ruffled his thinning hair. So, now it had come down to this. Instead of being an engineer or a conquistador, he was to be a shaman, a shepherd healer. And if he refused, the *nativos* would not feed them. Then it would be just a matter of days before they all died.

He thought of his days at the University of Salamanca, the great learning center of Europe built by King Alonso IX of León in 1218. The school was a hundred years older than Madrid University. His physician father had wanted him to attend one of the newer universities sprouting up in Seville, Valencia, Barcelona, even the newest, the University of Alcalá de Henares. But Castillo had wanted the oldest, the biggest, nothing but the best, Salamanca, where he would study Latin and mathematics.

The University of Salamanca had amassed over six thousand students from all over Europe. Its library contained hundreds of incunabula including works printed by the Englishman William Caxton and the German Johann Gutenberg, works such as the 42-line Bible Gutenberg and his ex-partner Johan Fust printed before Fust sued him and won the print shop. Castillo had spent many fascinating hours at the university reading that Bible, even memorizing large sections. He didn't actually comprehend the spiritual aspect of it—he even questioned it sometimes—but he loved the great adventures of the prophets and the journeys and healing ministry of the Lord Jesus.

At first Castillo had wanted to be an engineer and work on Salamanca's new Romanesque cathedral that was replacing the old one built four hundred years earlier and now suffering under the pressures of time and population growth. But he had received a calling—books. He loved to read. In the afternoons, after classes, he crossed the old Roman bridge near the university and sat on the bank of the Tormes where barbel and tench swam in the shallow waters. In the shade of olives and cork oaks, he read such popular novels of chivalry as *Amadás de Gaula* and *La Celestina* and the writings of the theologian Juan de Valdes and the philosopher Juan Luis Vives, whose advanced thinking included the education of women. Castillo liked that idea, a modern society where everyone was educated. He especially liked the pastoral poetry of Juan Boscán Almogaver and Garcilaso de la Vega, which dealt with the manners of fictional shepherds. After five years at the University, he received his *licenciado*, but he was quickly conscripted into the new war against France, where with his strict adherence to military rule, he soon won his captain's bars. With the war settling down, he'd decided to join the expedition to La Florida in hopes of finding some of the great adventures he'd read about in his novels and in Gutenberg's Bible. But it never occurred to him that someday he might actually become a fictional shepherd, a poetic healer in a hostile land. He kind of liked the idea.

He left the beach and returned to the village.

"I'll do it," he told Cabeza de Vaca. "What's to lose."

"I don't like it," the Provost Marshal said. "It mocks the Holy Spirit. Only the Holy Spirit can heal. How can we expect such humble souls as ourselves—"

"Military training teaches us to survive, Marshal." Castillo could care less about the Holy Spirit.

"Not if it endangers the lives of others."

"And healing does that? If I try and fail, what have we lost? But if someone just happens to get well, then look what we've gained."

"What have we gained, Captain?"

What sense was it to argue with a man who considered Fernando el Católico a criminal? The Provost Marshal was living in More's Utopia. This was not fiction; this was real. This was the bowels of the earth, and Castillo would do anything to be out of it.

Before other words could be spoken, a band of *saylas* appeared. They were ready.

Castillo went with them. Cabeza de Vaca, Captain Dorantes, and Estevanico followed at a distance.

They came to a *caha*. The *saylas* gestured for Castillo to enter, but they would not look into his strong eyes. Castillo hesitated. What if the Marshal had been correct; what if this wasn't right in the eyes of the Lord? Castillo had lost everything but his salvation. Could he now lose that? What would a fictional shepherd do in this situation? Be Christ-like. But what would Christ do? Christ would enter and touch the sick.

Castillo entered. He was in the *caha* of the kid Kele. And here was Kele's sick mother lying by the fire. She was flanked by two *nativo* women—one pregnant, one nursing—and her two sisters, their *saylas*, and the kid. He knew the mother had been incoherent the past few days and was unable to recognize her own son. Castillo grew nervous. He was way out of his league on this one.

He knelt beside the woman. He saw the cut above her eye where the shaman had made a gash. He sucked her blood, and spit it into a gourd bowl. He had seen the two *nativo* women drink the blood and spittle because they believed it would make their babies stronger. What was he going to do? He felt her forehead. Very hot. He felt her pulse. Very weak. He lifted her hand, let go. It fell limp. Very sick. He was no doctor. Even if he was, he had no medicine.

Beside the woman sat a bowl of nuts, a small stone mortar, and pots of other things left by the shaman. Suddenly, a passage flashed in Castillo's mind, something from the book of Mark he'd remembered from Gutenberg's Bible: *Lay hands on the sick and they shall recover.*

He broke a few nuts. He crushed them in the mortar and dabbed his finger in the oil. He anointed the woman's head with the oil. He left his hand on her forehead and recited an *Ave Maria*. The woman opened her eyes. She looked up into Castillo's eyes. He jerked his hand away, stared into the woman's eyes. "Almighty God, you have said that whatever we ask in your name you will do. I ask, in your name, that you take the sickness from this woman."

That was all he could do. He was no saint. He made the sign of the cross over the woman and stood. Then another passage came to him. This one from somewhere in Isaiah. He couldn't recall ever having so many verses come to him all at once, but surprisingly, they were there. This one had the ring of victory in it. He looked up into the space in the top of the lodge. He felt strength in his eyes.

He spoke aloud. "Thou hast been a strength to the poor, a strength to the needy in his distress, a refuge from the storm, a shadow from the heat. Amen."

Suddenly, the woman sat up. She said, "Tadpole, bring me an *am* and some water. I feel as though I have not eaten since the new moon. Why is everyone looking at me? We have chores to do; let's get busy."

The women and the saylas were astonished.

Dorantes, Cabeza de Vaca, and Estevanico were astonished.

Castillo and the kid were astounded. This woman should be dead, but here she was sitting up, talking. Castillo looked at his hands. He looked at the woman, at his companions. They were all staring at *him*.

What had he done?

6

Spring, 1529
Villages of the Coast

A runner arrived at the Isle of Misfortune. The oysters were ready for harvesting. The Capoques and Hans folded up their mat houses, stacked them and their wares on the dugouts, and crossed the bay to the mainland. For weeks, the two clans and the Castilians, in dozens of small bands, harvested oysters and drank dirty water around the river inlets and shallow bay waters. By early April, the oysters were depleted. The Indians wanted to pole their dugouts farther upriver and hunt peccaries and antelope on the big prairie. But they knew the Chorrucos and other Atakapa people would kill them if they moved into their hunting grounds. So, the Capoques and Hans remained shut in against the Gulf where they had been for as long as anyone could remember. Their world was a world of marshy, coastal meadows, grasses, and far too little rain. There were oysters, mussels, turtles, fish, and duck. But there was never enough. Some of the Indians would spend the summer picking blackberries and scavenging the mainland coast for whatever they could find. The rest would migrate back to their little island to await the season of the fish and lotus roots.

The Castilians returned to the island with the first dugouts. Dorantes rounded up all the men he could find. He looked at them, just a handful now, peaked and undernourished. The stomach sickness and vigorous paces the Karankawas had put them through had taken its tithe. He had to get these few survivors off the island. He had heard there were others farther on who, like themselves, had shipwrecked along the shore. He must try to find them.

"Where is the Provost Marshal?" he asked the men.

No one had seen him. Dorantes asked around the village. One Capoque said Sky-hair was at a small camp over on the mainland, but that no one would want to see him the way he was. Dorantes told the Castilians to prepare to leave the country. Then he bribed the Indian to take them over. He gave him the robe of marten-sable that Estevanico had taken from the Pensacola headman.

Two of the Castilians, Lupe de Oviedo and the notary Heironymo Alaniz, were too sick to leave Misfortune. Their bowels would not permit travel. They would wait for the ship sent by Figueroa and his three companions. Surely, Figueroa would be at Pánuco by now.

Dorantes and the others found Cabeza de Vaca on the mainland. He looked like leftover death—quivering, eyes shadowy, skin perspiring. He'd lost at least twenty percent of his body weight.

"*Señor!*" Dorantes squatted beside him. "Why didn't you send for someone?"

"You and the Castilians must leave right away." Cabeza de Vaca's voice was low, hoarse. "If you stay you will die."

"We won't leave without you. We'll make a *camilla* and carry you."

"No, I would never make it. I'll wait for Figueroa, too. A ship will be arriving soon, now that the weather has broken. This sickness knows no mercy. Is there a *fraile* among you?"

"*Sí, señor.* Asturiano is here."

"I wish to have confession and a prayer."

Dorantes did not like this. Confession in the coastal scrub meant death. He had seen too many confess and die that winter. From the hundred who had landed on Misfortune, they were reduced to. . . how many? He counted. . . sixteen, counting the two still on the island. But he knew the Marshal was right. If they did not leave right away, they too would die, one by one.

Reluctantly, Dorantes stood. He beckoned *Fray* Asturiano. "*Dios guarde a usted*—may God be with you, my friend."

The Castilians headed south. They mired through flat, mosquito-infested marshlands and struggled across swift rivers. They came upon a band of friendly Karankawas who called themselves Doguenes. The Indians acted as guides and taught them how to catch crabs and how to boil kelp. These provided modest nourishment, but the kelp bloated their stomachs.

Alonso del Castillo followed Dorantes and the guides. He decided not to interfere. The young Captain Dorantes was doing as good a job leading the men as Castillo could. Besides, Castillo still felt humbled and confused as to how a woman whose grave was already dug could return to good health so quickly, all because of the touch of a hand and the uttering of a prayer. He had read in Gutenberg's Bible how such things had happened long ago, when the Lord Jesus came down off the mountain in Galilee and met a leper, put forth his hand, touched the leper, and immediately the leper was cleansed. And when Jarius of Capernaum took the Lord Jesus to his dead daughter, and the Lord Jesus touched her hand and said *Talithacumi*, and the girl rose from the dead.

Castillo had said that word over and over after he'd read that passage. But he shuddered at the thought of the dead rising.

In any case, such healings had occurred a long time ago, when the role of the church was to heal people. Things had changed since then, thanks to Fernando and Isabél who, fifty years earlier, had petitioned for and been granted papal approval for a Spanish Inquisition. Now, the role of the church was to cleanse itself of Marranos, Islamics, and Protestants, not heal the lame or raise the dead. Give the heretics thirty days to admit heresy, put them to the tribunal, torture them until they confessed, burn them at the stake. Things were much simpler these days, more controllable. But, Castillo noticed that there was one glaring difference between these two roles of the church, one saved people, the other killed people.

The Castilians trudged on. After several days, they came to another wide bay. They built rafts. During the crossing, a northerly wind arose and pushed one of the rafts out into the Gulf. Four men drowned. When the bodies came ashore, *Fray* Asturiano knelt beside them and administered the sacrament of *extreme unction*:

"Ruego a nuestro Padre celestial por la salvación de tu alma. En el nombre del Padre, del Hijo, y del Espíritu Santo."

When the fray left, Castillo came and stood over the drowned men. He was still thinking about Jarius' daughter, wondering why things had changed in the church. Wondering if maybe the church had never really lost its original role. It wouldn't hurt to try. He knelt. He touched the hands of the dead men and said, *"Talithacumi."* Then he recited a *Pater Noster.*

The men did not rise.

Castillo hadn't really expected them to. Things had changed. He helped bury the dead men, then he and the others laboriously continued their journey.

After several more days, they spied one of the five boats sunk and stranded in an inlet. It was boat two of the purser Enríquez and the *fray commisario* Juan Suárez. But there were no signs of any survivors.

Castillo remembered that Hernándo de Esquivel from Badajoz had been on that boat. He always liked that pudgy little Andalusian. Esquivel was one of the first to go ashore with Enríquez when their ships landed at Bahia de la Cruz. He'd spent half the day making signs to the Indians, trying to convince them that the expedition was on a peaceful mission. But his signs didn't work. As soon as he left to return to the ship, the Indians loaded their goods into their dugouts and abandoned the village. The men had teased Esquivel, saying with his fat little belly, the Indians must have thought he was going to eat them. In truth, Esquivel was so picky about what he ate, Castillo wondered how he had made it this far. Now, perhaps, his suffering was over.

After more creeks and more hardship and more deaths, seven survivors found themselves looking out across another wide bay. There were Indians nearby, picking blackberries. They fled and the Castilians helped themselves to the berries. While they were eating, a dugout slipped across the bay. There were two people in it, one was Indian, the other—

"Figueroa!" Castillo shouted.

74

"*Sí*, it is I, *Capitán*." The dugout hull scraped onto oyster shells scattered along the shore.

"You never made it to Pánuco?"

"Who knows where Pánuco is, *Capitán*."

"Where are the others?"

"Méndez, he was killed by the *nativos*. Fernández and Astudillo, they died in the cold and hunger last winter. I have been a slave to the Lanegados in the south." He gestured to the Indian who had brought him.

Castillo, Dorantes, and the others sat in the shade of the groundsel trees that grew along the shore. They shared stories with Figueroa.

"After I was alone," Figueroa said, "a *nativo* came and told me that another Christian was living with the Quevenes. He spoke by signs, because, as you know, all of these clans speak different tongues. I went to their village and found Hernándo de Esquivel from the purser's boat."

"Esquivel from Badajoz? He is still alive?"

"He was when I last saw him. Esquivel told me a tale of their crew and those of the governor's boat."

"Governor Narváez is still alive, too?"

"Perhaps I should tell you the story as Esquivel told it to me. It happened last winter:"

The Previous Winter
Somewhere off the Texas coast

Esquivel laid his hand on his round, little belly. It felt smaller than when he was a kid growing up on the Guadiana in southwest Spain. He had not come from a wealthy family, but there was always something to eat. Never in his life had he felt the hunger he felt during the last few weeks, since leaving the Bay of Horses. He was losing his shape. They couldn't call him *Bala de cañón* anymore.

He was sitting on the front thwart of boat two piloted by the *comisario* Enriquez and the *frailes*. *Fray* Juan Suárez was at the

75

helm. The wind was much stronger now, and the men did not have to paddle. The wind had pushed them to the southwest, but they were still in sight of land.

"*Virgen!*" Esquivel groaned. "My stomach feels like a deflated *globo*."

Enriquez sat beside him as he had the day the two of them went ashore to meet the Indian fishermen at Bahia de la Cruz. "You know, Esquivel, we have not seen another boat since we passed the mouth of that river and were blown out to sea."

"Do you think they are still alive, *señor?*"

"*A la verdad*, I do not know. Between the fever and the hunger, I am surprised any of us is alive.

"Perhaps Pánuco is not far, eh, *señor.*"

"Perhaps we have already passed Pánuco, Esquivel. The *frailes* mutter among themselves that we passed it during the night many days ago. It is but a small slave station. We would not have seen their lamps in the darkness."

The wind was bitter, now. It swung to the west and pushed the crowded boat toward an inlet. Fray Suarez leaned on the rudder, but there was nothing he could do to hold the boat off shore. Cold water poured over the gunwales. The boat dropped deeper into the water.

The *comisario* shouted, "To the paddles, *compañeros de armas.*"

Enriquez grabbed a paddle. He dug into the turbulent water. But the others were weak. Their attempts to paddle had no effect on the boat.

The rocks, *señor*," Enriquez said. "We are going to smash into the rocks."

"Brace yourselves, *compañeros.*" The men were too sick to brace themselves. Too sick to even shout. They sat still and big-eyed as the boat locked into the trough of a wave. The bow dipped down. The stern rose. The boat swung sideways. The starboard bow slammed into the rocks. A large hole ripped through the bow. Water poured in. The stern continued to rise. The boat flipped. It slung Esquivel and the men into the shallows beyond the rocks.

76

"Ayyeeee! Esquivel shouted. The November water felt like ice on the high Nevada to him. His heart pounded. His mouth sucked air. His knees sprang to bounce free of the water. Everyone clambered and crawled until they were out of the sea and panting on the shore.

"Aye caramba!," Esquivel said. "What next?" He watched as the wind buffeted the boat into the shallows. The bottom was destroyed, and they had no way to repair it. The rest of the trip would have to be made on foot.

That night, the men tried to build a fire to dry their clothes, but all the firewood was wet. One by one they fell asleep, shivering in the salt marsh. At dawn they were still shivering. They found a few crabs and kelp to lessen their hunger, but Esquivel refused to eat weeds. Weeds were for rabbits. He was no *conejo*.

"Compañeros," the *comisario* said. We must leave this place. We will continue south. In the name of the blessed virgin we will find a village and *nativos* who have food." The *comisario* had the dual role of commissioner and lieutenant to the governor. He was a trustworthy and efficient man. The Castilians believed him. They would rather follow him than Narváez himself. They no longer trusted Narváez.

When the sun topped the distant trees, it began to dry Esquivel's clothes. But still, he shivered. The Castilians followed the salt marsh, wading through creeks and collecting firewood when they could find it. By mid-afternoon they saw another boat far out to sea. They built a fire to attract the men. When the boat got close, Esquivel saw that it was Narváez and his friend Captain Juan Pantoja, Lord of Ixthahuaca, who had commanded a company of crossbowmen for the governor during his expedition to Mexico.

"Companeros, are we glad to see you!" the *comisario* shouted. The Castilians pulled the boat into the shallow water. Most of the men on board jumped off. Narváez and a few remained.

"The governor does not look well," Esquivel said.

"He will not leave the boat," one of his men said. "He sleeps on it every night when we make camp. He has a stone he uses for an anchor."

Then the governor's boat began to slip back to sea.

"*Amigos*, where are you going?" the *comisario* yelled.

"The governor says there is not room enough for everyone," a voice came back.

"But you can't abandon us here. By *Santiago*, I command you to return the boat."

"The governor says he does not want to linger. We will follow you by sea. Signal us if you find food."

With that, nearly a hundred Castilians were left standing on the shore.

"I do not trust them," Esquivel said. "Did you see the governor's eyes. He looked like *el diablo*.

"They will not leave us, Esquivel. Come, we must organize the men and continue on."

The party of men shuffled slowly to the south. Eventually, they came to a large bay, which they could not cross. Narváez' boat drifted toward them.

"See, Esquivel? They come for us."

"They come because they need us to search for their food."

The afternoon was spent ferrying the men across the mouth of the bay. The *comisario* and Esquivel waited for the last boatload. Once on board and the boat was pushed off, Narváez spoke to them. His throat was hoarse, but it was still deep and commanding.

"Alonso Enríquez, by the powers vested in me as governor of La Florida, I strip you of your command. Your role as lieutenant to the governor is revoked, and I give this post to Captain Pantoja."

Everyone on board was stunned. Everyone looked at Pantoja then at the *comisario*. The *comisario* sat still.

"Why would he do this?" Esquivel whispered.

"It does not matter," the *comisario* replied. "As long as Pantoja remains on the boat, I will keep the shore team organized."

Narváez said no more. He looked at no one.

As the sun began to set, the boat slipped up to on shore . The Castilians had a fire going and had already made camp. When everyone was offloaded except Narváez, a pilot, and a sick page, the boat pulled away. It would anchor offshore.

"There is no food or water on board," Esquivel said, watching them depart.

"There is no food or water anywhere, *Soldado*."

The voice behind Esquivel was harsh, cold. He turned. It was Captain Pantoja.

That night, Esquivel left the fire and walked to the beach. He squatted in the spartina grasses growing along the shore. The moon was full. It was a clear night, but the north wind picked up. He gazed out at Narváez' boat bobbing in the water. Then he saw a strange thing. Someone on the boat—he could not tell who—leaned and pulled up the anchor and sat it inside the boat. Then the boat drifted out of the bay and into the sea.

Next morning when the men rose, they saw that the boat was gone.

"The storm must have torn the anchor loose and pushed them out to sea," someone said.

"Without food or water they can't last but a few days," another said.

"Without a crew to hold the boat in this wind, they won't last through one day," said a third.

"Poor Narváez," said a fourth.

Esquivel did not speak. To tell them Narváez deserted them would only lower their morale. They had enough to worry about now; Pantoja was in charge.

Esquivel and the Castilians broke camp and resumed their march. They moved slower. Many were stricken with fever and had to be helped. Pantoja sifted through the ranks, barking at the men, "Move along faster, we are not making time. You walk like *Mariquitas*. If that man can't walk on his own, leave him."

On and on they went. More and more Pantoja yelled at them. Finally, they came to another bay and with great difficulty made rafts to float across. It took them an entire day.

On the south side, they approached a wooded point on a beach. A small band of Indians lived under the trees. When the Indians saw the large quantity of men, they rolled up their mat houses, loaded them into their dugouts, and paddled to the far end of the inlet.

Pantoja liked this spot. There was fresh water in a small creek, crawfish, crabs, and shellfish in the water, and a dense canopy of trees that would give the men protection against the coming winter. He barked the command. They would spend winter here rather than chance the bitterness of traveling and camping in the open marshland.

As days turned into weeks, the nights got colder. Food became very scarce. There was never enough to feed all the men every day. To make matters worse, Captain Pantoja continued to batter and debase them. The weak ones grew weaker: the fever, the churning stomachs unable to hold down mere victuals, the cold cutting to their bones. One by one they began to die. One by one, they were buried in shallow graves at the edge of the camp.

One night, Esquivel sat on a log with Sotomayor, the camp master.

"Tell me about your brother, *señor*," he said.

"Vasco Porcallo? He is a daring man. You know, at one point, when Governor Velásquez revoked Cortés' commission, he gave it to my brother. If Cortés hadn't taken matters in his own hands, my brother would have been the conqueror of Mexico."

As they spoke, Captain Pantoja began one of his rages. He started at the far end of camp and worked his way toward the two men. He pushed weak men to the ground. He kicked those who already lay on the ground. He shouted at those asleep.

"I did not know that." Esquivel said. "When our ships were in Cuba, before you joined the expedition, Vasco Porcallo offered Narváez an entire warehouse of provisions. When Cabeza de Vaca sailed to get them, a *tormenta* blew in and sank his two ships. Killed sixty of our men."

"*Si*, I heard about that. Captain Pantoja was with Cabeza de Vaca on that trip, was he not?"

"*Si*, he was."

I was in Havana at the time. I wish the *tormenta* had taken Pantoja instead of the horses." He watched the approaching captain.

Pantoja came and stood in front of Sotomayor. "You are supposed to be camp master here. Why don't you have men in the shallows catching crabs? The tide is moving in. We need meat."

"The men are tired. They need rest. They worked hard all day digging roots and trying to catch fish."

"They were lying in their own vomit all day. I don't see any fish.

"The fever and hunger makes them vomit."

"I have a good mind to break camp and leave the weak ones here. They are going to die anyway."

The argument began to escalate. Sotomayor rose to his feet. Pantoja paced in front of him.

"The way you left sixty men on a ship in Trinidad when a *tormento* was rising," Sotomayor said.

"What?" shouted Pantoja. "Who are you to judge me? The *bastardos* could have gotten off the ships anytime they wanted to."

"They had no boats to go ashore. You took them."

Pantoja's face showed rage. He flew into Sotomayor. He knocked him over the log. Esquivel backed away. The two men slugged it out, first one striking the other, then the other striking the one. Pantoja reached for the dagger on his hip. The blade fleshed in the firelight as he swiped back and forth at Sotomayor's face. Sotomayor dove and rolled and when he came up, he had a fire log in his hands. With one wide swing he struck Pantoja in the head. The strike was so swift and sure, it crushed Pantoja's skull. The man was dead before he hit the ground.

The *comisario* and others heard the ruckus. They raced over. Enríques was the first to speak.

"That is one *picaron* who deserves to die. Lay him on a bed of pine straw. We will bury him in the morning."

"*Señor*, I have a better idea," one man said. The men are starving. Pantaja said they need meat. So give them meat. Give them Pantoja. Flay his flesh and smoke it over the coals. We can bury the rest in the morning."

Esquivel jolted back. "You can't be serious. Eat the flesh of one of our own?

"It has been done before, *señor*. Once the meat is cleaned and dried. It is like any other meat. *Amigo intimo*, a man will do strange things when his only alternative is to die."

81

The more the men thought about it, the more they realized it was their only choice. They dragged the slain body to the edge of camp and began slicing off the meat. Esquivel slipped deeper into the shadows. He would take no part in such an outrageous act.

Spring, 1529

Castillo and the men around him began to squirm as Figueroa told them what had become of Narváez, Pantoja, and their countrymen.

"How many made it through the winter?" Castillo asked.

"As the winter got colder, the men continued to die. Each time, the ones left alive ate the flesh of the ones who died. It was all they had to eat. The crabs were gone and the land around them was barren. The smoked flesh sustained them for awhile, but before spring came, every man had died—except for two."

"And they were?"

"Sotomayor and Esquivel. They would not leave because Sotomayor wanted to head south and Esquivel believed Pánuco was to the north. Besides, it was still too cold to travel and Sotomayer had caught the fever. He knew he would be the next to die. He told Esquivel that he must do what he had to do. Esquivel said he would never eat human flesh. He had sustained himself on kelp and roots."

"Then Sotomayor died?" Castillo asked.

"*Si.*"

"And Esquivel lived?"

"When Esquivel told me this story, he began to cry at this point. He did not have to tell me. I knew. He had flayed the flesh off the body of his good friend and eaten it. That is the only way he could have made it to spring. When the weather warmed up, the Indians returned to their woods. They found Esquivel alone. They were the Quevenes. They took Esquivel to their village. That is where I found him. I proposed that we escape together, head south to Pánuco. He still insisted that Pánuco was to the north. He would not go with me. One night, he escaped. The last I heard of him he was living with the Mariames in a river valley the *nativos* call Guanpacti—river of two waters. If you go there, you will probably still find him. But I do not recommend it. The Mariames are as savage as they come. They even kill their own babies if they are girls."

"*Jesucristo!* Why would they do such a thing?" Dorantes asked.

"When the girl babies grow up, the Yguages come and take them away. They mate with them. Their children become warriors who fight the Mariames and make slaves of them. So they kill the girl babies. They are not good people, *señor.*"

"*Aye caramba,*" Dorantes said. "Do they have food?"

"In the summer, they eat snails and prickly pears from the cactus prairie to the west. In the fall, they eat bean pods, nuts and roots, which the women bake a couple of days in their ovens. The rest of the year they eat lizards, snakes, spiders, ant eggs, worms, even deer dung to stay alive. They are like wild animals, always searching for food. When they can't find it, they steal from each other and from the Quevenes nearby. They are liars, cheats, and drunks, too, *señor.* They stupefy themselves on a brew made from the root buttons of a cactus, then they dance all night. They frighten me. I'd stay away from them, *Capitán.* I tell you, the *nativos* who live in this country are the lowest creatures on the earth."

Castillo leaned back against the trunk of his tree. Four boats and their crews could now be accounted for. Where was boat four, that of the captains Téllez and Peñalosa? Had they made it to Pánuco? Was help on its way?

The Lanegado who had brought Figueroa offered to transport the Spaniards across the bay and feed them if they'd come to his village.

Castillo suspected if they went, they'd be made slaves.

They went.

83

Estevanico, Dorantes, Castillo, and the handful of survivors *were* made slaves of the Lanegados. When they first arrived, the *nativos* took away what few clothes they had and gave them roasted rats and acorns to eat. Before they'd give them anything else, the men had to carry heavy pots of water from the Guansan—the little river, gather firewood, and drag dugouts over flooded lands. Their backs became raw, their muscles sore.

A week or so after their arrival, Figueroa and *Fray* Asturiano vanished into the night. It had been the hope of Dorantes and the others that the two men would make it to Pánuco and send a rescue ship, but after many months they lost hope of ever being rescued. Their ranks continued to diminish. It had now been over a year since they left the Isle of Misfortune.

Estevanico had taken about as much *mierda* from the Indians as he cared to take. It was bad enough being a slave once, but being a slave to a slave was taking it too far. If Dorantes didn't yell at him all the time to not resist, he'd snatch a couple of bamboos out of those little brownies' lips and shove them up their *culos.*

"Enough is enough, Andrés." Estevanico caught up to Dorantes on their way to the river to help gather nuts from the trees. "First they kill Diego and Valdivieso, club their bodies till they look like La Mancha *salsa,* then they kill De Huelva just for moving from one of those weed domes they live in to another. Andres, remember what that old gypsy told us in San Lúcar before we set sail?"

"I remember."

"She said the expedition was doomed."

"I remember, Estevanico."

"She said the child who follows the sun would never return."

"It is not the best of conditions, *amigote,* but we can't just run away. They'd kill us instantly, and there are only three of us left.

They arrived at the river and threw their skin sacks on the ground.

"But I'm tired of those little wart hogs running up to me, shouting in my face like they're something fierce, putting arrows to my chest, then laughing. Back in Córdoba, I'd've planted those turds in the ground and grew a pile of manure big enough to fertilize all the fields of Castile."

Suddenly, out of nowhere, two Indians raced up to Dorantes, grabbed him, and threw him on the ground. They shouted Indian words and put fists in his face. One of them cuffed Dorantes in the jaw, while the other pounded him with a stick.

Estevanico wanted to leap on them, snatch them up and dunk the little *mocosos* in the river.

"Stand still, Estevanico," Dorantes yelled. "I can take it. I have been beaten so many times I don't even feel it."

The Indian who had cuffed Dorantes put his foot on the back of his head and pushed his face in the dirt. Dorantes spit. "If you make one move. . . *ptew*, others will come and. . . *ptew*, kill us both."

Estevanico caught himself. Andrés was right. He knew they were outnumbered. But he'd sure like to smack him a couple of brownies.

"Meet me at the river tonight," Dorantes said through the dirt that was being rubbed in his face. The Indians laughed. "A half league upstream. Just after sunset. Bring Castillo. We will escape, together—tonight."

"If Castillo and I can't get there, don't try to go alone," Estevanico warned. He was sure glad Andrés had come to his senses. "We'll tell the *nativos* you had the squirting stinks and will be right back. They'll be glad you left the village to take care of that business. Then we'll try again later."

"Just be there," Dorantes burbled."

Dorantes made it to the river. He puffed, his heart thumped. He hissed the name of his companions at every thicket, but his companions were not there. He knew it would not be easy for all three of them to slip away at the same time, they were watched constantly. He waited as long as he dared. If the *nativos* discovered him missing, they'd come looking for him. The results would not be pleasant. He could wait no longer. He had to go on without them. He'd join up with them later, somewhere. He waded across the shallow river and swung north. Late the next day, he arrived at the Yanaguana River, the name the *nativos* gave to the southern arm of theGuanpacti. He was heading for the village of the Mariames. Hopefully, Esquivel would be there, and the two of them would return and help Castillo and Estevanico escape. Then the four could head for Pánuco.

He saw nuts on the trees along the shore. When he stopped to gather some, he heard voices downstream—the Yguazes. If they found him they'd enslave him, and he'd never get to the village of the Mariames. He slipped across the river and darted through the underbrush.

After two more days, he heard the rush of water and more voices. He made it to the Guanpacti and crouched in a thicket. He spied *nativos* along the bank—Mariames. They were on the opposite bank. They were drunk, stupefied. He watched them burn leaves on a flat bolder, hang their heads over the smoke, and suck down the vapor. They staggered and whamed into the trees and fell into the river. They gurgled and spewed saliva and socked each other in the face. Now, what had he gotten himself into? Why hadn't he listened to Estevanico and returned to the village? Sometimes he took Estevanico for granted, forgot he was even there, like he was a shadow you never pay much attention to. Only sometimes, that shadow disappeared and could not be found for half a day. But he must admit, here in this diabolical country, Estevanico seemed to be surviving better than either him or Castillo. Already, he had begun to miss his old friend.

Dorantes tried to scoot away, move upstream, but the Indians heard him. "*Arre-aca,*" they yelled. They snatched up their bows and whizzed wild arrows into the underbrush. Dorantes scrambled out and ran right into the arms of a small band of Indians who had crept up behind him. He had learned long ago to never resist them.

The Mariames were larger than the Lanegados. But they were not as tall as the Karankawas on the Isle of Misfortune. They had long pointed fingernails and, like the Karankawas, wore body paint and had reeds thrusts through their breasts and lower lips. They did not appear happy that Dorantes was there.

The Mariames marched him back to their village. The village sat in a wooded glen bordering the river, thirty or so round huts made of grass and reed mats slapped onto bamboo poles. The smoke of many rotten wood fires hung in the air, but it didn't seem to deter the thousands of mosquitoes and gnats that clouded the village. The *nativos* swatted the clouds, squirmed their shoulders, and blew out before they inhaled. This the did all day without thinking about it.

After a few days, it was evident that Esquivel was not with them. When Dorantes learned to communicate, mainly by signs that most of the clans knew, he asked what had happened to the Spaniard who had lived among them.

They told him that one of their women had a dream that the Spaniard was going to kill her son. So, they killed the Spaniard. They kill everyone who shows up in someone's dream. If you live in the dream world, how can you be a person, you must be a witch, so they kill you. Then they showed him Esquivel's sword, his rosary, and his prayer book. Dorantes hoped they never dreamed about him.

He also learned some other sad news. Sky-hair , who lived with the Capoques to the north had died.

Dorantes' heart dropped. Cabeza de Vaca was dead.

For the first time, Dorantes felt alone. He wanted to run, but he knew they'd kill him. There was no way to escape; now, he had no choice. He must wait for Castillo and Estevanico and hope they can escape.

The Mariames made a slave of Dorantes. He quickly learned how painful their sharp fingernails could be. When he did not work hard enough—which was all the time—they stiffened their fingers like knife handles and sliced his naked body. Sometimes, he thought they just cut him for practice.

Life with the Mariames was far worse than it had been with the Lanegados. Their village was filthy, smelly. The men beat their children often. In retaliation, the young boys tormented Dorantes day and night. Whenever he came out of his hut without being told, they stoned him. Whenever he stopped to rest or eat, they yanked his beard. It would be suicide to fight them. For a year and a half, he lived as a lonely, tortured, low-life slave to brutal savages, whose eating habits included picking seeds out of human dung that lay in piles all over the village. He gave up on Estevanico and Castillo ever coming to find him. He felt sad that he might even have been responsible for their death.

Winter, 1531

One day, shortly after the Yguazes made a late night raid on the Mariames, killing two of them, the Mariames gathered up the abandoned arrows and moved south. They took Dorantes with them. He thought they were going on a two-day deer hunt. He had been before, had watched how they burned a circle around a vast field to trap deer inside. But this time they didn't go to a field. They backed up to a curved ravine and made camp. Under cover of darkness, they dug trenches on the approach side of the camp and covered the trenches with sticks and grass. Then they hid in the ravine behind their temporary houses. Dorantes did not like the looks of this. Deer were not what they were after. They were after men, and they hunted like dogs, one moment fast asleep, then at the snap of a twig, leaping up yelping.

Early in the morning before sunrise, after several false alarms, the attack came. Yguaze hunters raced up to the camp with their bows drawn. They tripped in the trench. The Mariames sprang upon them. They yelped and smacked them with their clubs. Bones cracked, skulls split, blood flowed. Dorantes could not believe how brutal the Indians were to each other.

Suddenly, as the battle raged on, two men popped out of the darkness near the edge of the trench. It was Estevanico and Castillo. They had been brought by the Yguazes.

"Andrés!" Estevanico yelled. The men hugged and hid in the ravine while the battle raged on. Indians were hard to stop. Unless you speared one in the heart or entrails or crushed his skull, he would keep fighting. Finally, the battle ended.

With several dead on both sides, the Yguazes retreated back to their village The Mariames left their severely wounded to die or revive, whichever, then took the three Spaniards back to their village.

It was the happiest night of Dorantes' life. He had long since considered his old friend dead. The amused Mariames laughed and pointed at the Spaniards hugging each other. But since it did not take much to anger the Indians, the Spaniards did not laugh back. Dorantes learned that Estevanico and Castillo had escaped the Lanegados a week after he had but had been captured by the Yguazes and held as slaves, carrying heavy loads alongside the emasculated freaks who dressed like women and lived with other men.

Another year passed. The three Spaniards remained slaves to the Mariames, teetering at the threshold of starvation, insanity, and death from abuse. They had long given up hope of ever finding another Spaniard alive. Then one day in the spring of 1533, a Doguenes Indian arrived to trade. He said there was a Spaniard living among the Quevenes on the coast. Dorantes was ecstatic. Who could it possibly be? There was no one unaccounted for. A survivor of Téllez and Peñalosa's boat four? Hardly, not after all these months.

They asked the Indian if he could bring the Spaniard to them. He said he would try.

For the next few weeks, the three men kept their eyes pasted on the trail that led from the east. They saw no Spaniard.

Finally, one afternoon they looked down the trail and saw him, skinny as a bird's leg, naked as the rest of them, skin crusty and flaking, the color of charred copper.

Dorantes was the first to recognize him.

"He is alive!"

7

The tides were up and the fish had returned to the bay. It was time to go back to the island.

Cabeza de Vaca dragged another reed mat off the side of the hut. He laid it on the stack. Three months had passed since Dorantes and the others had left. In, March, when the oysters were gone, many of the Karankawas had left with them, returned to Misfortune. The others had spread out into small family camps up and down the coast to harvest the blackberries that were coming into season. Now, the blackberries were gone.

He grabbed another mat. He felt he must look a sight, naked as the day he was born, skin blistered and peeling from the sun, body bruised from the beatings, ribs exposed from the hunger, face and shoulders covered with alligator grease and mud. But he was alive. He had declared that if God our Lord would bring him through the sickness, he would take it as a sign that he was being preserved for a special reason. He did not know what that reason was, but he swore, once back on his feet, he would do everything that was necessary to stay alive until he determined that reason.

When he had been unable to move, lying there on the dirt floor, the Indians had fed him. At first, they brought blackberries. Then they brought snakes, skinned and cooked, and grasshoppers roasted as crisp as ice on a winter puddle. When the firewood ran out, he had to learn to eat things raw.

For weeks, he laid in a pool of sweat and body excrement. The Capoques came every day to catch the flies that buzzed around the excreta. The flies were added to the soup that sat in the center of the camp. For a long time, he thought the Indians kept him alive just to bait the flies. But soon, he learned it was for another reason.

When his fever finally broke, Cabeza de Vaca walked down to the marsh and bathed. Then he followed the gatherers on their daily scavenger hunt. That's when the beatings began. There were fifteen of them: a grandfather, his three tall sons who robbed each other incessantly, their wives, and their eight children, all about grown now, in their early teens. One of the teens had a child born that spring, but Cabeza de Vaca never saw it. The girl had gone off into the woods alone one morning. When she returned that afternoon, she was issuing blood, but there was no child.

Another one of the teens was a dullard. He was the oldest but acted the youngest. His body was knotted and cut in a thousand places where he had stumbled on an oyster bar or fallen headlong into a patch of needlerush. He was energetic and active but totally uncoordinated. He wandered off into the night. He never slept. No one could control him. He was the reason the Capoques kept Cabeza de Vaca alive. When Cabeza de Vaca was back on his feet, it became his job to watch over the dullard, day and night.

He untied the willow poles. He wrenched them from the circle of holes and stacked them beside the mats. The Capoque camp on the mainland had been home base from which he and the gatherers made daily excursions up and down the coast. There was a single oak on a knoll whose flanks were covered with golden broomsedge. Off to one side, there was a shallow marsh filled with water grass. In and around the marsh Cabeza de Vaca had pulled so many roots, his fingers bled to the touch. The roots staved off starvation, but these were not the lotus tubers so popular in the fall. These roots made his stomach cramp. Once, a young alligator had come into the marsh. The gatherers saw him and ran and circled him. They jabbed his eyes out with a long pole, leaped upon him, then drove the pole down his throat so he could not bite them. They beat the animal for hours with clubs and stones until he no longer moved. The dullard pulled him back to camp, and the others

92

roasted him on a grate made of green branches. They collected the rendered fat to rub on their skin. It helped some, but at sunset every night, thousands of mosquitoes rose out of the marsh and fell like a spell over the camp. Cabeza de Vaca's skin was speckled with their bites.

"We are leaving," one of the gatherers yelled and signed. During the weeks he had been alone with the Indians, Cabeza de Vaca had become proficient with signs and could speak and understand many of their words.

"*Arre-aca*," he yelled. He beckoned the dullard to join him. The dullard came and picked up all the poles and mats. Cabeza de Vaca was glad it was ending. The daily beatings, the starvation, death tapping him on the shoulder at every bend in the trail. These had been the most miserable three months of his life. Several of the Karankawas who had stayed on the mainland had died. There just wasn't enough food. The mourning had made it worse. Many who could search for food did not. They mourned and had to be fed. Now, the mourning was over. They would join the others on the island where there would be fish. He wondered if Lope de Oviedo and the notary Heironymo de Alaniz were still there? If they were even still alive?

Cabeza de Vaca walked to the center of the camp. The gruel in the pot was all but gone. He reached in, grabbed the clam shell cup, and scooped up the last of the liquid. He swallowed it down. Returning the cup, he saw a lizard drowned in the bottom of the pot. He pulled the drowned creature out, held him by a thin leg and stared at him: slimy, limp, uncooked, for they had not had a fire in weeks. He knew what he had to do. He'd done it before. Many times. He had to eat the lizard. He had made a promise to stay alive. But he had invented a way to make eating easier. He thought of his wife in Jerez de la Fontera. Her dark eyes, her thick hair. He opened his mouth, tossed the lizard inside. Her thin body lying on top of him, making love to him. He bit down. The lizard popped. Their little cottage along the Guadalete, the vineyards in the fertile plain. He swallowed. The *bodegas* along the narrow streets where the sherry was stored. He wiped the juice that seeped from his lips. He missed his wife very much. Missed holding her in his arms. He had not been with a woman since they had sailed out of San Lúcar in the summer of 1527. He stayed away from the women in Santo Domingo when they first arrived in the Indies. He avoided the ladies in Cuba where they spent the winter, waiting for the season of the *tormentas* to end. And he did not copulate with the Indians at *Bahia de la Cruz* where they set to shore in La Florida, although he had seen the men do it—against his orders. Now, two years had passed. He wondered if he still had his manhood.

Cabeza de Vaca leaned over and picked up the heavy pot. He cradled its round bottom in his arms and walked down the trail into the coastal marsh. The trail passed through a field of smooth cordgrass, to a meadow of black needlerush, to a little salt creek where the dugouts were bulked up with the mat huts, the Indians, and their meager possessions. He climbed aboard and sat behind the dullard. Slowly, the log boats eased down the creek toward the bay. The women and the teens huddled inside. The tall, skinny Capoque fathers stood on the triangular platforms at the rear of each boat, long poles in their hands. Cabeza de Vaca sat near the bow of the lead boat, the pot between his legs, holding the dullard so he wouldn't fall overboard.

"It is Pepok Pela!" a youngster shouted. The youngsters frolicked on the shore, wrestled in the weeds, shot little arrows at fiddler crabs. Two barkless dogs darted around their feet. The youngsters threw down their bows, splashed into the water, and pulled Cabeza de Vaca's dugout ashore.

The *saylas* were at the center of the village in the scrub. Cabeza de Vaca saw them moving about, loincloths hanging to their knees, reeds stuck through their breasts. The women were engaged in some form of activity beyond them. He hoisted the big pot up on his shoulder, got out of the dugout, and headed up the trail, the youngsters circling around him, shouting, "Pepok Pela! Pepok Pela!" He did not see his two countrymen.

The dullard was close behind Cabeza de Vaca. He carried the heavy load of mats and long poles. Suddenly, he stubbed his toe. The bundle flew off in all directions, and the dullard toppled onto the scattered pieces.

The others paid him no mind. They bucked over him. But one son, after stumbling on the dullard, punched Cabeza de Vaca squarely in the chest. Cabeza de Vaca spun to the ground. The pot flew from his arms and broke into a hundred pieces. The other two sons heard the crash and came back. They kicked Cabeza de Vaca in the ribs and back then headed on up the trail. Cabeza de Vaca groaned to his feet. He helped the dullard up, then gathered the mats in his arms and carried them up the trail. The dullard lumbered after him, carrying the poles.

When they got to the scrub, the *saylas* began to weep and wail and roll on the ground. This they would do for half an hour. The women continued to work. They chopped and broke wood for a big fire and tended fish on a smoke grill while a youngster dragged a skinny, dead deer by his tail all over the village. There were two *saylas* who were not wailing. They were fighting, no doubt because one had robbed the other. No one paid them any mind.

While Cabeza de Vaca stood staring at all the activity, the youngster with the deer came his way.

"Pepok Pela, look! I shoot a deer." It was the kid, Tadpole. "I shoot him myself with my bow." The kid was ecstatic. He dragged the deer back across the sand.

Through the dust, the grating wails, the fistfight, the eye-watering smoke, the shouting youngsters, Cabeza de Vaca saw what he had waited three months to see—Oviedo and Alaniz sitting under a distant scrub thicket. They scraped bits of flesh from a coyote hide, ate the raw scraps, and pounded the skin on a log. When they saw Cabeza de Vaca, they jumped up and rushed over to greet him.

"Provost Marshal, it is you." Alaniz said. "I hardly recognized you."

"*Si*, it is I, *amigo*. What happened to you?" Their bodies were bruised and swollen.

Alaniz ignored him. He hugged Cabeza de Vaca. "*Como esta usted?*"

"I am hungry, that is how I am. "*Tengo hambre.*" Cabeza de Vaca rubbed his empty stomach. "What is all this about?" He fanned out his hand.

"They prepare for a *mitote*." Alaniz said. "It is sort of like a feast of thanks, although, I don't see a whole lot here to be thankful for. They had a *mitote* this spring when the bay began to rise. Have you heard anything from the others?"

"Nothing. Why are they calling me that name?"

"Pepok Pela? It means, 'the one whose hair is the color of the morning sky.' The Indians heard how you cured yourself on the mainland. They have been waiting for you."

"For me? Why?"

"Soon, you will know, *señor*. Soon, you will—"

"Hear me, *amigo*." Cabeza de Vaca grabbed the notary by the shoulders. We must escape from this place, now. It is impossible to travel in the wintertime. The three of us must go, today. Head south to Pánuco."

"But, *señor*. The fish have returned. There is food."

"We are the only ones left." Cabeza de Vaca looked from face to face. "I beseech you in the name of God our Lord, we must escape."

"I do not know, *señor*," Oviedo said. "They will kill us if we try to escape."

"Look at you," Cabeza de Vaca's voice was sharp. "Look at me. We can't go on this way, menials to the lowest form of life on earth. I have been dragged through the mud, smacked with a pole, even stabbed. I am but a beast of burden, deprived of food, deprived of sleep, deprived of clothes. . ."

Alaniz handed him the coyote skin. "Tie this on, *señor*. It will make you feel more like a man."

Suddenly, a commotion rose along the shore.

"Now what?" Cabeza de Vaca said. He took the skin, tied it around his waist.

"It is the Chorrucos. They come from the forest on the mainland."

"The Chorrucos? Aren't they enemies of the Capoques? Have they come to fight?"

96

"They come for the *mitote, señor,* for the *muchachas.* Their young hunters are exploding with desire." Alaniz cupped his crotch. "Their *huevos* have dropped, their little *bischos* are hard like a nail."

"Don't they have their own girls?"

"They are not allowed to take girls from their own clans, *señor.* That produces cross-eyed babies with six toes."

"*Aye,* so they mix it up a little, do they."

"They mix it up a lot, *señor.* Prepare yourself for the *mitote.*"

The afternoon was spent with clan members from the wooded inland rivers reuniting with their families on the island. Just before the sun set, the Indians came to the cook fire and bathed in its smoke. They pulled the vapor into their faces and over their bodies.

Then the sun dropped behind the trees. A firelog was set to the big brush pile. The drum, a coyote skin pulled tight across a hollow log, boomed across the village. The *saylas,* their wives and daughters, the Chorrucos, and the young boy hunters began to migrate to the clearing at the center of the village. Cabeza de Vaca and his two companions watched from the edge of the clearing. For the *mitote,* the *saylas* wore woven fiber sandals. Their loincloths were decorated with seeds, animal teeth, and small shells. The alligator mud had been washed off, and their faces were painted half black with charcoal, half red with ochre. Many had their tattoos blackened over. The women wore thick masses of gray moss to their knees. Their breasts remained exposed, and their bodies were painted in stripes. Some had designs of animals or flowers. Some had tattoos. Their eyes were reddened and their eyebrows blackened in sweeping arches. The young girls wore deer skins around their waists, and a stripe painted from their foreheads, across their noses, to their chins. They wore shells around their arms or legs. The boy hunters were shamelessly naked, their bodies lean and tall, muscular and washed clean of alligator mud.

Now, turtle rattles and reed whistles with the shrillest, harshest sound imaginable joined in. Those who had come to the clearing began to dance around the fire. Their feet barely moved, their shoulders dipped ever so slightly. Then one of them let out a shrill screech, and they all leaped into the air and hopped to the beat of the drum. Some chanted. As the dance grew more intense, the boy hunters danced closer and closer to the girls. Their bodies rubbed, bumped. The wiry little *bischos* grew stiff and swung like flags into the backs and buttocks of the girls. The girls giggled until they were grabbed and pulled off into the scrub. The dowry of a bow and two arrows would be paid later. Now, it was time for some testing. Cabeza de Vaca saw Tadpole slip into the underbrush, a girl in one hand, the deer tail in the other.

The dance continued with the participants shouting out prayers, asking for victory in battle, a deer to chase, better success in their robberies. Meanwhile, several of the older women pulled fish from the smoke rack and passed it around. Some of the dancers stopped long enough to eat, but at no time did the dance ever cease.

Cabeza de Vaca and his companions were the last to be fed. They received their fish humbly with their heads held low, so the women in a fit of displeasure would not withdraw their food. A feat which they had done many times.

When everyone had eaten—the first and only time during the year that there was enough food to feed the entire village at once—the musicians ceased their whistles and rattles. The drum, however, continued for those dancers who would not stop. It was time for the tattooing.

The boy hunters came out of the woods. Tadpole led them. The girl was not with him, but he still pulled the deer. Four Chorruco *saylas* came to the fire. One wore three folds of coyote skin, a bear claw necklace, and smoked a pipe.

"It is the *coma*," Alaniz whispered. "He is their shaman. He speaks for their gods Pichini and Mel. The Capoque's shaman died this winter, so they borrow the one from the Chorrucos.

"May God our Lord help us," Cabeza de Vaca said. Then Tadpole stopped in front of him.

"Pepok Pela can have my bed," he said. The kid looked happy. "I will not need it, anymore." Then he spun around and dragged his deer out to the fire.

Cabeza de Vaca thought about Itch Vine and how she had looked the last time he saw her, so frail and debilitated. "May God our Lord help me," he said.

The Chorruco boy hunters, like their parents, were an ugly lot. They had short bodies and overly large heads, so unlike the tall, and in a primitive way, attractive Capoque girls. Their skin was much darker, and their hair dirty and coarse, bushy and matted. It stood upright on their heads and gave them the appearance of being top heavy.

For a moment, Cabeza de Vaca remembered his courting days in Jerez, each boy trying to match up with the prettiest girl who would have him, each girl trying to match up with the handsomest boy who would have her. But these girls had no choice. They had to go with whichever *Negrito* pulled them off into the scrub.

Tadpole and the Chorruco youngsters, all of whom had proven their manhood since the last *mitote* by killing a deer, stood before the *coma*. The *coma* bleated out a couple of incantations to Pichini and Mel, then blew smoke over their bodies. His assistants rubbed herbs into the chests of the boys. Then the *coma* removed his necklace and used the bear claws to cut long incisions across each of the boy's chests. To cry out or even flinch would be to show a lack of courage and was likely to result in a beating. Then the *coma* rubbed charcoal and resin into the cuts. They had received their first tattoo.

As the night wore on, the dance intensified. Cabeza de Vaca saw the *coma* pass a cup of liquid to the dancers. It clearly made them inebriated.

"It is peyote," Alaniz told him. "Cactus juice." Sometimes, they simply eat the roots. It is how they visit Pichini and Mel."

From time to time, a dancer fell out onto the ground, shaking, jerking, waving an arm. Then he'd pass out. The *coma* came by, shouted out to Pichini and Mel, and gave the dancer a scratch with a bear tooth to revive him.

Off to the side, the *saylas* had begun a wrestling tournament. But soon, the wrestling turned into a fistfight. Cabeza de Vaca noticed that in the midst of all the events, the Capoques were continually trading things with the Chorrucos: whelk shell dippers for red ochre so they could dye their faces, tiny sea beads for pieces of flint, dried fish for mesquite beans.

Then Oviedo spoke. "*Señor*, you must see this." He grabbed Cabeza de Vaca by the arm, pulled him closer to the gathering. The *coma* was off to one side of the dancers. He was ministering to the afflicted. "Do not get too close," Oviedo said. "Someone will smack you." They stopped.

Indians came forward. They clutched their heads, their stomach, their shoulder. The *coma* uttered songs, blew smoke on the ailing area, sucked on stomachs, cauterized open wounds with a fire log. Most of the ailing were Capoques, for they had lost their own shaman.

Suddenly, one man came forward and fell at the *coma's* feet. He clutched his stomach and groaned as if he were dying. The *coma* raised his hands. Everyone stopped. Except for the dancers. Nothing could stop the dancers. He knelt beside the man and waved his hands over him. Cabeza de Vaca watched carefully. While the *coma's* left hand swept back and forth, his right hand slipped between the folds of his loin cloth. When the hand came out, it was closed. Then he closed his other hand. He slammed both fists onto the man's stomach, droned out a bizarre chorus, then rotated his fists in small circles on the man's flesh. The Indians slipped closer. They were in awe.

"Watch," Oviedo whispered. "He's going to pull the vermin causing the sickness right out of the man's stomach."

The rotations got faster. The chorus got louder. The people got quieter. Suddenly, the *coma* spanked the stomach flesh with his left hand and opened his right. Out jumped the largest *cucaracha* Cabeza de Vaca had ever seen. The cockroach fluttered its wings as if it were glad to be free from the man's stomach. The people fell back. The insect landed on the *coma's* tattooed forearm and ran up his shoulder, neck, and buried himself into the *coma's* thick hair.

The circle of Indians sprang back. No one wanted the creature to go inside their body.

Meanwhile, one small dancer had fallen in the midst of the throng of people and had been kicked and stumbled upon time and again by everyone. The *coma* pointed at him. The dancers broke their circle. The *coma* circled the man three times then knelt at his feet. He removed the necklace and carefully searched for the proper bear claw. He found the one that would do the job. The fire had dwindled, but there was enough light for everyone to see. The people stooped over. The *coma* stooped over. Cabeza de Vaca and his two companions stooped over. The *coma* reached out with the bear claw, but before he could scratch the man, the man leaped up. The *coma* and the people leaped up. Cabeza de Vaca and his companions leaped up.

"It is Badthing!" the people yelled, almost in unison. The drum stopped. The dancers stopped.

During the eight months since Cabeza de Vaca's boat had crashed on the Isle of Misfortune, he had seen many strange things: dancers who could twist and contort their bodies into unimaginable shapes, men with heads flattened and pointed by crude planks. But never in his life had he seen a thing as hidious as what vibrated before him.

The creature was more beast than man. He was a ghastly ball of moss as wide as he was tall. His hair stood out at all angles and was beaded with sticks, feathers, and balls of dried deer dung. His face was marred and streaked with outrageous designs. His eyes glowered and darted, never fixing on anything. His features were barbaric, indiscernible. On his chin, he wore a thin beard. He made a mortifying screech without moving his lips and gave off an odor akin to vomit and stale urine. The moss was so thick on his body, he looked to have no arms. The moves he made were not human. He rotated first this way then that way as though not sure where he wanted to go.

Suddenly, he reached out and grabbed one of the women. He jerked her to her knees. He plummeted into the woman. When he withdrew, the woman had three gashes in her side. The crowd was hysterical. For the first time ever, Cabeza de Vaca saw fear in their eyes.

Again, the hideous creature plummeted into the woman. When he sprang back this time, there were entrails dangling from his hands. The woman was devastated. She reached for her side. She felt for her stomach. Her eyes rolled back. She fainted. Badthing fished his flint knife from the bundle of moss. He sliced off one end of the entrails and threw it into the fire. The moisture sizzled and sparks drifted off into the trees. The trees caught on fire and blazed wildly. But the people would not take their eyes off of Badthing.

Then the pesky moss ball waddled over to one of the huts. He went inside. Groans and gurgles drifted out through the mat walls. Suddenly, the hut began to shake. It came off the ground. It spun around faster and faster, then toppled over and crumbled into a heap. For one brief moment, all was quiet except for the cracking and popping of the trees. The people stepped closer to see what had happened to Badthing. With a harrowing cry, he bounded out of the rubble. The people fell back. Badthing rotated three more times then disappeared off into the scrub.

Fear drifted away from the Capoques, now. It was replaced by anger. The Chorrucos had brought Badthing with them. He had burned their woods, wrecked their hut, cut their woman. In the Indian world, there was no such thing as forgiveness. Someone was going to pay for this.

Fists started flying. Several Capoque *saylas* grabbed the *coma*. He yelped and struggled and fell to the ground. They grabbed him by his ankles and dragged him out to the clearing where the dancers had been. Cabeza de Vaca didn't like the looks of this. He started to move. Alaniz grabbed his shoulder, pulled him back, told him it would be sure death to interfere.

Several Capoque *saylas* wrestled with the *coma*. They kicked him, pulled his hair, and stripped off his clothes. The *coma* stopped resisting. The Capoques were much taller and greatly outnumbered the Chorrucos. Besides, the Capoques were mad, and that gave them extra strength.

102

They pulled the *coma* to his knees, pushed his head down. A *sayla* appeared behind him with a stone club in his hand. He raised the club and in one swift swing crushed the skull of the *coma*. The man fell face first into the dirt. But before his head hit the pool of blood, the cockroach flew out of his hair. It fluttered off into the horde of viewers. The viewers screeched and yelped and tried to get out of the way. No one saw where the witches sent the bug but one thing was known by all—the bug had gone into somebody's body and that somebody would soon get sick and die. Without a shaman or a *coma* to speak to Pichini and Mel, there was only one thing left to do—dance. The drum burst forth into a violent rhythm. The Capoques broke into a wild, frenzied dance. The men jerked and twisted their bodies into grotesque angles. The women stomped and wailed. Who had the witches hexed? Who would be the next to die? The Chorrucos, on the other hand, were mad. They had just lost their only shaman. They grabbed up their trade goods and started to leave. Then they stopped and shouted as loud as they could.

"Who will be our shaman? Who will be your shaman? Look at what you have done."

The drum softened. The dancers slowed. The *saylas* were stunned. The Chorrucos shouted again.

"Who will be your shaman?"

The *saylas* stood silently. They looked around. Then they pointed directly at Cabeza de Vaca.

"Pepok Pela will be our shaman."

Cabeza de Vaca was a spiritual man. Had been most all his life. He remembered clearly as a child the day his mother Teresa Cabeza de Vaca died, and the weeks that followed with him trying to help take care of his sister and two younger brothers. Religion had helped him get through. His father remarried but his new stepmother could never replace their mother. The four children were placed in a *curatela*, a kind of guardianship. Since nuns were a major part of the *curatela*, Cabeza de Vaca was taught to be holy and righteous, for his body was the temple of God. And he was taught that the greatest sin, the only unpardonable sin, was blasphemy against the Holy Ghost. He would never, ever commit that sin. He had gone on to study architecture and alchemy, and the new sciences of cartography and navigation, but he never strayed from an ardent study of the word of God. He felt very comfortable as a spiritual being in daily contact with God our Lord. And, although the nuns never clearly explained exactly what blasphemy against the Holy Ghost was, he was sure it included praying to Pichini and Mel.

The *saylas* rushed over to Cabeza de Vaca. They grabbed him by the arms. They pulled him out to the clearing, then brought a small log stool.

"*Haka! Haka!*" They yelled.

Cabeza de Vaca sat, but he shook his head and shouted, "No! No!"

The *saylas* shoved him and said "*Haka! Haka!*" They pointed to the sky and yelled, "*Apel!* Pichini, Mel, *Apel!*" But Cabeza de Vaca said no, he wasn't going to talk to Pichini and Mel. He had promised to do whatever was necessary to stay alive, but that did not include committing the unpardonable sin. He would never pray to any god except God our Lord. The Chorrucos gathered at the edge of the village. They started to laugh and mock the Capoques. The *saylas* pushed Cabeza de Vaca harder. But the harder they pushed him, the louder the Chorrucos laughed. They rolled in the dirt and held their stomachs. The Capoques started punching Cabeza de Vaca with their fists and slapping him with their open hands. Oviedo and Alaniz tried to come to his aid, but other *saylas* beat them and dragged them off.

The *saylas* knocked Cabeza de Vaca off his stool. They kicked him in the shoulder, the head, wherever their feet landed. The Chorrucos bellowed, now. Pain rushed through Cabeza de Vaca's side. Maybe they would kill him this time. Maybe he would not have to deal with Pichini and Mel. All he heard was a cacophony of laughter, shouts, insults, and commands. All he saw were flying feet, dirt, and smoke from the tree fire that had spent itself out. Then, he saw the pole coming. It was a push pole, the kind used to shove dugouts through shallow water. The pole was sweeping an arc across the dark sky. There was nothing he could do to stop it. The pole landed squarely on his head and everything went black.

When Cabeza de Vaca came to, he was lying on a mat in a *caha*. He ached all over. Someone was attending his wounds, rubbing a wet hand through his hair. Slowly, the face came into focus. It was Itch Vine. Her sickness was now a thing of the past. The spring had been good to her. She had flushed out and looked healthy and alert.

"*Clé,*" she said, meaning water. She dipped her hand into a bowl. When she spoke, she spoke carefully and slowly. Cabeza de Vaca was able to understand her.

"I was afraid you would die. Tadpole and his friends brought you here."

Cabeza de Vaca heard the drum pounding in the distance. The *mitote* was still going on, the dancers were still dancing. But his internal clock told him it must be nearly sunrise.

"The Choruccos have gone," Itch Vine said. "If they had not taunted the *saylas*, I do not think they would have beaten you." Cabeza de Vaca doubted that. His body was full of bruises from past beatings. "You will stay here. I will look after you until you are better."

"My two companions," Cabeza de Vaca said. "Are they well?"

Itch Vine was silent. She brushed more water through Cabeza de Vaca's hair. When she leaned forward, her leg lay against him. She was very close. She smelled of pine bark and wild rosemary. She smelled like a woman. She smelled good.

"Why will you not be our shaman? We know you have magic."

"I can't talk to your gods. I have my own."

Her damp hand came down across his face, moved to his chest. Her touch was tender. Cabeza de Vaca's defenses left him.

"Where does it hurt?" She asked.

"Everywhere."

She turned and rose to her knees. She reached across him, dipped both hands into the bowl of water and swept her hands over

105

her own body. Her skin was smooth and brown and glistened in the dim light that drifted in from the distant fire. Cabeza de Vaca felt a gentle rush through his loins. He had never looked at an Indian woman this way, never noticed the regal lines in Itch Vine's face, the confidence in her eyes, the strength in her high cheek bones.

Itch Vine leaned forward again and lay at an angle across Cabeza de Vaca's body. Her flesh felt cool, soft, delicately refreshing. His senses quickened. She began to hum softly and to knead the muscles of his thighs.

"My father was the greatest shaman this village ever had," she said. "He had magic. I can teach you his magic."

Cabeza de Vaca did not speak. Itch Vine hummed awhile longer, then she slid down across his middle to his feet. She turned and lowered her head to his stomach. Her hair was soft and fanned out across his skin. His pain began to subside.

"He had a special way of healing the women that kept them returning everyday for their bellyaches and pains."

Cabeza de Vaca still did not speak. "*Tots 'ntule*," she said, then lowered her face to his groin and took him into her mouth.

Cabeza de Vaca responded quicker than he remembered ever responding. Blood pulsed through his veins, adrenaline sped up his spine, his heart pumped fiercely. For a moment, he forgot all the sorrow of the past months: the loss of nearly three hundred of his countrymen, the lengthy separation from his family back in Jerez. The hunger. The beatings. But this was not how it was supposed to be done. This was not a natural act. He reached down and pulled Itch Vine up. She squatted over him, her feet coming to rest beside his hips. Her eyes looked into his. Then she dropped down and gently received him. For the longest moment, Cabeza de Vaca lay still, staring at the ceiling of the *caha*, the Indian woman locked around him, massaging him with her inner muscles, not touching him anywhere else. He closed his eyes. His pain was gone, now. His mind drifted back to Jerez, to his wife tending her garden. He could smell the newly turned soil, see her curly locks glowing in the morning sun, taste the salty perspiration on her shoulders.

Man was not meant to be without woman.

8

Winter, 1530
Village of Chorruco

Cabeza de Vaca kicked the dead turtlegrass that had washed onto the beach at high tide. A hundred springtails whipped up onto his feet and bare legs. He leaned and picked up a few pieces of mineral pitch he saw lying in the wrack. He dropped them into the basket slung over his shoulders. The Capoques used the pitch to line their pots to keep them from leaking.

The dullard shuffled behind him. Cabeza de Vaca kept his back to him. He knew the *lunático* would bump into him in order to stop. Either that or fall down.

Wham! He bumped into him.

"*Eh, eh, eh.*"

The dullard could speak a little, but he would rather imitate the grunts he'd heard from the animals. He said *eh, eh, eh* when he was excited about something.

"What have you found, *loco rematado?*" Cabeza de Vaca took the hard, brown object away from him. "Ah, you've found another sea bean." He recognized it as a seed he'd seen on a tree in Cuba. He looked out to sea. He wondered how long it had taken the seed to drift from Cuba. He wondered how much farther it was to Mexico, or to any place where there were civilized people. He wondered if his countrymen would ever come for him, if Dorantes or any of his men had reached Pánuco. He thought not. Surely they must all be dead. Only he, Oviedo, and Alaniz were left.

The three men had lived with the Capoques for two years now. Many times, Cabeza de Vaca had begged his companions to escape with him, but they had steadfastly refused. They said if the others had made it, there would be a ship on the shore. And since there was no ship, their companions had to be dead. If they left, they too would be dead. But today, Cabeza de Vaca had made up his mind. Today would be his last day on the island. If God our Lord had preserved him for a special task, he was sure that task was not on Misfortune.

He shoved the sea bean deep into the basket of pitch so it would not be seen. He looked back across the sea. A sheet of darkness was rising off the horizon. "That is enough for today," he told the dullard. "Let's go back to the village."

They followed the trail they'd taken when the Spaniards first crashed onto the island. In his mind's eye Cabeza de Vaca could see his shipmates, fifty of them, running naked from fire to fire to keep from freezing. He missed his countrymen. He held the dullard by his arm and guided him quickly along. He knew if he was late getting back, the *saylas* would beat him. His body still ached from the last beating, when three of them had jumped him just to have something to punch. When the *saylas* were busy fishing, collecting oysters, hunting, or tanning hides, they did not bother him. But when they stopped, they turned to him and his companions for entertainment. It seemed the *saylas* never rested.

When he got to the scrub, the blanket of darkness had nearly covered the village. Soon, the *saylas* would return from the bay. He didn't have much time. Through the short trees, he saw the first hut. He crouched. Then he saw Oviedo. He was pulverizing fish bones with two rocks. The meal would later be added to the gruel pot. He sat the dullard in the shadow of a scrub oak and told him, "*Haka*." He sidled around the huts so as not to be seen. If the *saylas* caught him talking to Oviedo that would surely be worth a couple of punches to each of them.

"Pssst, Oviedo." He whispered from the underbrush. "Do not turn around." Oviedo continued as if he had heard nothing. "Tonight, I am leaving the island. Itch Vine is going to take me to the Chorrucos. She said they are in the marsh across the bay and soon will be going back into the forest. Come with me."

"You are crazy, *señor*," Oviedo hissed. "They will kill you."

"They *are* killing me."

"That would not be if you would be their shaman."

"You be their shaman, Oviedo."

I tried to cure one of them, remember. When he died, they beat hell out of me. If the dullard hadn't stumbled into the lot of them, I'd be dead myself."

"I swear to you by the code of the *hidalgos* you will not last another winter out here. Come with me."

"I cannot leave, *señor*."

Cabeza de Vaca thought for a moment. "I am leaving, Oviedo."

"You would leave us alone out here?"

"I will come back for you. I will search for a way out of this hellhole and come to get you next summer."

"I will be ready, then, *señor*."

"I shall pray to God our Lord that your souls do not get harmed."

"*Gracias, señor*. May the good Saint Sebastian be with you in your travels."

Now, there was only one thing left to do. Cabeza de Vaca slipped deeper into the scrub and circled back to where he had left the dullard. The dullard was no longer sitting. He was standing, leaning against the tree.

"*Augh*," he said. He said *augh* when he knew something was happening but he didn't know what it was.

Cabeza de Vaca put his hands on the dullard's shoulders and gently pushed him back down. "*Haka,*" he said.

The dullard sat. Cabeza de Vaca squatted beside him, looked him in the eye. "I have to leave, *amigote*. I won't be here to help you anymore. You'll have to make it alone."

The dullard stared blankly back at him. Cabeza de Vaca knew he wouldn't understand, but he had to tell him.

"I am going away for awhile. I will be back next summer. You sit here. They will find you."

Then he rose. He dropped back into the shadows. He could feel the dullard's blank stare on his back as he ducked into the underbrush.

Darkness was all around them now. Cabeza de Vaca and Itch Vine slipped through the trees. Tallowwood thorns tore at their flesh. The scent of rancid alligator oil drifted in the breeze. Twigs snapped under Cabeza de Vaca's feet.

"Don't make noise," Itch Vine said. "They will hear you."

"Do you have the sea beans?" Cabeza de Vaca asked her. He had found and saved ten sea beans. Itch Vine had told him the Chorrucos loved to make necklaces from them. And if he took them some, they would be happy to see him.

"I have them," she said.

They arrived at the bay. Cabeza de Vaca saw the shadows of the dugouts on the shore. The two crouched low and darted out of the underbrush into the open. If they were to be caught sneaking off into the night, it would mean slow death for both of them.

Cabeza de Vaca eased one of the dugouts into the water. The boats were crude and unstable. Most of them still had bark on the trunk. They were not fit for fishing at sea; the *saylas* used them only for crossing over to the mainland.

Itch Vine walked out into the water. Cabeza de Vaca steadied the dugout while she stepped into the boat. She set the small basket of sea beans at her feet. That's when Cabeza de Vaca heard the slap of feet on the muddy shore behind him. His heart sank. He didn't know whether to push the dugout into the bay or make a run for it. Either way, he'd be dead. He could never outmaneuver the *saylas* on the water, and he surely couldn't outrun them on land. He had seen them chase a deer all day until the deer dropped from exhaustion. Then he'd seen them club the deer to death with a stone, which was exactly what they would do to him and Itch Vine for trying to escape.

He stood. He turned around to face the consequences. It was not the *saylas*.

"*Eh, eh, eh!*" It was the dullard.

Cabeza de Vaca rushed over to him. "You must stay here. This is your home. They will look after you. Do you understand?"

"*Eh, eh, eh,*" he said again and pointed to the dugout.

"*Haka, haka,*" Cabeza de Vaca told him. "You can't go with us." He pushed the dullard to the ground and rushed back to the boat. He shoved the boat into deeper water and climbed onto the triangular platform at the rear. He began poling out into the channel. Then the shouts came.

"*Arre·aca! Arre·aca!*"

Cabeza de Vaca looked back. Three *saylas* stood at the water's edge. They were madder than hungry lions. They had rocks in their hands. They pushed one of the longer dugouts into the water. Cabeza de Vaca had a lead, but it wasn't enough. It would not be long before they would overtake him. He knew exactly what they would do then. He had seen it done before whenever the Capoques captured an Akokisa or a Patiri who strayed down from the forest to steal their oysters. They would drag him back to the village and beat him. Then they would lash his wrists and ankles with strips of rawhide and stretch him in a pole frame facing into the rising sun. The next day, the women would come and amputate his fingers. The following day, the old men would come and slash his arms and thighs and bleed him. They would feed the warm blood to their women and children. Then a day or two later, the *saylas* would cut an incision around his scalp and peel away his hair and skin. Then, he would die.

The thought of such torture made Cabeza de Vaca push harder on the pole. Itch Vine leaned over the side. She paddled with her palm. But it was no use. The *saylas* were closing the gap too quickly. Cabeza de Vaca stopped paddling. He looked back. The three Capoques were lined up on their knees inside the dugout. Their dugout was slicing through the water just a few lengths behind them. But then he say a fourth figure in the boat, in the rear. Cabeza de Vaca squinted. It was the dullard. Somehow, in the excitement, the dullard had managed to get into the dugout without the *saylas* knowing it. Cabeza de Vaca saw him swaying, first to the left then to the right. The *saylas* paid him no mind. They paddled, the dullard swayed, the boat rocked. Closer and closer the

111

edge of the boat dipped to the water. When the *saylas'* boat got alongside Cabeza de Vaca's boat, they reached out to grab hold. That's when the dullard fell overboard. The dugout came over with him. All three *saylas* toppled into the water. Cabeza de Vaca's dugout glided away from them. The *saylas* yelled and splashed and shook their fists. But it was to no avail. Cabeza de Vaca and Itch Vine sped on into the darkness.

May God our Lord bless the dullard.

"*Clon,*" Itch Vine said. She rubbed her eyes and pointed. She lay in the bow of the dugout where she had been sleeping.

"Yes, it's the sun," Cabeza de Vaca answered. The sun had just topped the trees to the east. Cabeza de Vaca had poled all night across the wide bay to the north of the island. He was looking for the mouth of a river. Itch Vine had told him they would find the Chorrucos somewhere up the river. They came to what appeared to be a river, but he was not sure since many inlets were mere fingers that jutted up into the marsh a half a league or so, then stopped. They saw two Indians fishing with spears at the water's edge. Itch Vine yelled and asked them if this was the river that led to the Chorruco camp. The Indians said no and pointed that it was farther north up the shore.

"Turn in here," she told Cabeza de Vaca.

"But they just said this is not the river."

"That was a lie. These people lie about everything. This is the river. I can smell the freshness in the water."

They spent the rest of the day poling along the edge of the river where long, silver strands of moss hung from bald cypresses. Near sunset, they came to a camp.

"It is the Chorrucos," Itch Vine said.

Cabeza de Vaca saw a row of huts lined across the top of an old shell mound. The mound was made from shellfish that had been brought up to the camp from the bay.

A dozen or so Chorrucos came to greet them. They shouted.

"They know who you are," Itch Vine said. "They say the shaman has come to them."

Cabeza de Vaca shook his head. Not again, he thought. He got out of the dugout and followed them into camp. He felt like a giant in their midst; they barely came to his chest. Besides, they were ugly, and that frightened him a little. Their heads were wedge shaped and they had big platelike ears, prominent noses, wide mouths, and their heads seemed to sit on their shoulders without a neck to join the two. Their lips were swollen like Andalucian plums ready for harvest. Their teeth were stained dark yellow. And as if that were not enough, their bodies were covered with tattoos and their faces rife with decorative scars from cuts.

Their camp was nestled in the river lowgrounds, among tall tupelo trees and sweet gums whose leaves lay scattered on the ground like fallen stars. Cabeza de Vaca and Itch Vine were given a hut. The Chorrucos called it an *añ*. It would be awhile before Cabeza de Vaca learned their language, but Itch Vine seemed to have no trouble communicating.

The huts were similar to those of the Capoques, but had a hole in the roof to let the smoke out. Cabeza de Vaca went to his hut. It was filthy. It sat in a low spot. The floor was damp, a dozen spiders and water bugs crawled over the walls, and a smelly pile of human excreta lay in one corner. The opening was covered with a strange looking hide of some creature Cabeza de Vaca could not identify. Some creature much larger than a coyote or even a deer. He wondered what the animal might be and if they had its meat in the camp. If he could find a reliable source of meat, perhaps that would entice Oviedo and Alaniz to leave Misfortune.

When the sun dropped below the trees, the Chorrucos added wood to the communal fire. Some of it was rotten and created a smoke screen. But it did not repel the thousands of mosquitoes that filled the air like particles of dust. Cabeza de Vaca came to the fire and sat on a log next to a woman with long hair and a tattoo around her ankle.

Itch Vine dropped to the log on the other side of him.

Cabeza de Vaca was tired and hungry. He had not eaten all day or the night before. The fire pit was lined with oyster shells, but he saw no oysters. Many of the Chorrucos sat on deer hides, but he saw no deer meat. There were a few pieces of fish, some worms,

113

and lumps of dry deer dung, but Cabeza de Vaca did not see any red meat. He took a little fish and passed on the rest.

"These people are starving," he whispered to Itch Vine. "There is no meat. Why did we come here?"

"Look." She pointed up through the bare limbs. A bright star shone in the east. "It is 'The Dog.' The season of the deer and *cokon* has come. Soon, we will move upriver where there will be meat."

"*Cokon*?"

Cabeza de Vaca's question was interrupted by an old man with a bulging stomach and sagging face. He stood by the fire. As he spoke, Itch Vine interpreted.

"We are honored that Pepok Pela has come to stay with us. He has brought sea beans, the gift of the Great Sea. Tomorrow, he will go with us to the lake. He will talk to the gods and make the fish come."

Cabeza de Vaca felt uneasy. He was not a shaman and could not make fish come to anything. And he was not about to talk to Pichini or Mel. The woman next to him slipped closer. Her thigh touched his. What was *she* up to?

"Tonight, we celebrate by telling the tale of our beginning," the old man continued. "Go fetch the young ones."

The children were throwing gum balls near the edge of camp. They were brought to the fire. The old man waited until they were seated, then he spoke.

"Once, a long time ago, the land rose out of the sea. The sea was full of oysters, and it became crowded. Some of the oysters decided to leave the sea and live on the shore."

Cabeza de Vaca could feel the eyes of the tall woman next to him moving over his body. She was dressed like the other women, a hide tied around her waist hanging to her knees, no top, no shoes, long pig tails clasped at the end with rawhide. She leaned forward so he could not fully see her body.

"The oysters that came to live on the shore were very big, and they grew bigger until they became Chorruco people. The land was full of animals, so the people moved inland and began to hunt

114

the animals. There was one among them who was very wise. He spoke the wisdom of the one who made all things."

The woman chuckled in a low, stilted voice. She nudged Cabeza de Vaca at the end of every statement, coaxing him to laugh with her. Itch Vine leaned forward, stared at the woman.

"He said that those men who do well will go above when they die, and those men who do not do well will go under the earth into the shades when they die. But he said that those men who are eaten by other men will go nowhere. They will be dead forever."

Cabeza de Vaca grew more uncomfortable. The fatigue, the hunger, the darkness and remoteness of the camp, the ugly people, the woman next to him vying for his attention, and now, the old man speaking about men eating men. He had heard there were cannibals in these parts, but he had not met any.

"Then it began to rain," the old man continued. "It rained every day for a long time, and the land began to flood with the rain. Some of the men and some of the animals climbed up onto the mounds and they were saved. But most of them did not and they were not saved. The ones who were saved became our *pérea*, our ancestors. They continued to live in the forest and eat the animals. But they never forgot to build their huts on top of the shell mounds when they came to the river."

Then the woman made her move. She swung around and reached for Cabeza de Vaca. One hand fell upon his back, the other on his thigh. Steadfastly, the hand on his thigh began to move up, the one on his thigh moved down. When she had turned toward him, Cabeza de Vaca saw that her chest was as flat as a man's. And she didn't have the face of a woman. In fact, she wasn't a woman; she was a man. A *berdache*. A man who had cut off his *pene* and *huevos*. A man who was attracted to other men and gave them sexual favors. A man who dressed like a woman and did the work of a woman but also did the labor that no man wanted or could do. He carried heavy loads when the village moved. Carried stones when the village did battle. Carried the sick and tended to them until they died. Carried the dead into the forest. Cabeza de Vaca was too shocked to move. The callused hand of the *berdache* kept coming.

Suddenly, Itch Vine was on her feet. The *berdache* never saw her coming. In one swift motion she bounded across Cabeza de Vaca's outstretched legs, balled her fist, and slugged the *berdache* squarely in the nose. Blood flew. It splattered on Cabeza de Vaca's legs. It spurted up Itch Vine's arm. It spewed from the *berdache's* nose like milk from a dropped coconut. The *berdache* rolled backwards. His momentum carried his feet high in the air. When he rolled forward again, his face was full of surprise, and blood poured down onto his chest. He never knew what hit him. He stared at Itch Vine. Itch Vine stood solidly in front of him. She shook both fists in his face. She spouted out a string of words that even Cabeza de Vaca's sharp mind was unable to decipher. The Chorrucos laughed. They bellowed out loud, grabbed their stomachs, fell off their logs, pointed at the *berdache*.

Itch Vine had had enough. She grabbed up Cabeza de Vaca and pulled him off to the river. The echo of laughter drifted through the forest behind them. Cabeza de Vaca sat on the bank, while Itch Vine washed the blood from her arms and his legs.

"You will have to go with the fishermen tomorrow," she said. "They will not let you stay in the village."

"I know."

"Will you speak to the gods and bring fish to the lagoon?"

"No."

"They will beat you like my people did. They will take away your food."

"They have done that before."

"Why will you not bring the fish? You have more magic than the witches. You and all of your people. I have felt your magic."

"My people are all dead, Itch Vine. Tell me, what is a *cokon?*"

"It is the beast of the prairie. It is the meat of the Caddos. We are not allowed to hunt on the prairie, but sometime our hunters go anyway. Many times, they do not return."

Morning came too soon for Cabeza de Vaca. He touched his stomach out of habit. It was flat. The skin was loose. He massaged his nose. He would never get used to the smell of human feces. Today, he would have Itch Vine clean out their *añ*.

Outside, the camp bustled with activity. The women added limbs to the fire and blew on the ashes. They joked and cackled. Today, when Pepok Pela returned from the lagoon, they said, the coals would be ready for the fish. The men gathered up long spears "*Yal*," they shouted to Cabeza de Vaca. "*Yal*," meaning carry. They handed him an empty basket and pointed to a pile of leg-length poles. Cabeza de Vaca took the basket and picked up the poles. Until he proved to them that he could bring fish to the lagoon, he would be treated as a menial.

The Chorrucos walked out of camp into the low marsh. Cabeza de Vaca followed them with his load. They stepped over cypress knees, sloshed through dark mire, and followed a trail of bent flags and maidencane. The stench of marsh gas smarted Cabeza de Vaca's nose, but a light morning breeze gave him a moment of refreshment. Then the land rose They passed through a region of saw palmettos and tall pines and came to a small lake, hardly more than a pond. *Ciwon*, the Indians called it. The surface of the *ciwon* was dusty and green, and the borders were thick with pondweeds. Cabeza de Vaca could not see how any fish could live in that stagnant water.

Some of the fishermen disappeared into the flatwoods. Others circled the pond holding their spears, sharp deer bone points tied to the ends, bark floaters tied along the shaft. Cabeza de Vaca dropped the poles to the ground. He wondered why they had brought them. From time to time, one or two of them would come to him and argue that he should speak to the gods now, make the fish come. He refused. As the morning sun grew higher, the fishermen lost their patience. When Cabeza de Vaca would not help them, they slapped him with open hands and kicked him with muddy feet, then returned to their fishing.

Near midday, those who had gone into the forest returned. They had armfuls of leafy branches. All of the fishermen came together then and began stripping the leaves from the branches. Cabeza de Vaca watched with curiosity. They crushed the leaves with their hands and threw them into the basket. When the basket was full, they carried it out into the *ciwon*, shouting, "*Nal kau kau*," meaning shallow water. They scattered the leaves over the pond and churned the water to stir the leaves into it's surface. Then they withdrew and waited. Hardly an hour went by before the first fish floated to the top. He was breathing, but he moved very slowly. The fishermen snatched up the poles, splashed out into the water, and clubbed the fish. Some drug in the leaves had stupefied the fish. They brought the fish to shore and threw it into the basket. Then other fish floated up. They were not large, and there were only six of them by the time the day ended.

The fishermen were not happy with their catch or with Cabeza de Vaca. They kicked him again and motioned that it was time to go back. Cabeza de Vaca picked up the load of pole clubs and the basket of fish and started to leave. Suddenly, the fishermen were all over him. They knocked the poles from his arms and grabbed them up. They cocked back as if to crack his skull. He did not know what he'd done wrong but something had provoked them. They pushed him hard and shook their fists at him. They shouted names which Cabeza de Vaca was glad he did not understand. Then they snatched the basket away from him and dumped the fish out onto the bank. They pointed at the poles. It was time to try again.

Cabeza de Vaca picked up the poles and headed back through the flatwoods. He would never understand these dark little people. Half starved, they fish all day, then leave their catch to rot in the sun.

En route back to the river camp, the Indians found bird eggs from nests placed on the ground in the palmetto thicket, a large paper wasp comb bulging with pupae, and several locusts from a field. That, along with the rotten wood, ant eggs, and weed seeds crushed and thrown into a pot of water was what Cabeza de Vaca and the Indians would eat for supper.

That night, while he and Itch Vine were in their *añ*, he asked her why they had left the fish on the bank and not brought them to the camp.

"They will return in a few days when the *nats* have come."

"*Nats?*" he questioned. Cabeza de Vaca thought for a minute. "Maggots? You mean they are leaving the fish until they fills up with maggots?"

"They like the *nats*. They are tasty."

"But the fish will rot."

"It is a good taste, this rot."

Suddenly the hide flew back. A woman breezed in. A chunky little Chorruco with scars all over his body followed her. He smiled. His yellow teeth had gaps wide enough for fingers.

He spoke in his native tongue. "*Wi itu wankinto. Kulca. Icak cok cektsauke hite-u.*" Cabeza de Vaca looked at Itch Vine.

"He says he is the leader of the camp. His name is Kulca. It means grandson. He says he is the greatest thief ever."

Kulca pushed the woman at Cabeza de Vaca then slapped his cupped hand to his groin.

"*Kams*," he said in a husky voice. "*Tam.*"

"What is going on here?" Cabeza de Vaca said.

"He wants you to ride his woman," Itch Vine said. "And he wants to ride me."

"I'll do no such thing."

"It is our way. Do not argue with him."

The Chorruco stomped around the hut. He threw up his hands, snatched at Itch Vine, and shouted, "*Wi makhe-u, wi nikiil,*" meaning I swap wife. But Cabeza de Vaca shook his head. He pulled Itch Vine back. Then Kulca pulled out a small, skin pouch. He opened it and offered it to Cabeza de Vaca. "*Caje, caje,*" he said.

"He offers you his smoking leaves along with his wife."

"No," Cabeza de Vaca said. He shoved the Chorruco's hand away and pushed the woman toward the opening in the hut.

The Chorruco stared at him a moment then turned and stomped out spouting words over his shoulder. The woman followed him.

"Did you hear what he said?" Itch Vine said.

"I heard but I did not understand. Something about tomorrow."

"He said this is their last night at the camp. Tomorrow, we head up the river. The animals have returned to the forest. He just wanted his wife to make you happy."

"If I were any happier, I'd be insane."

A chill had come to the air. Cabeza de Vaca had bitter sweet thoughts about winter. There would be meat to smoke and eat, perhaps enough to carry them until spring, but the cold would pin them down. No one would venture far from the village. Most would stay inside by a fire. There would not be enough firewood to go around, and there would be fistfights and death. Others would die from the cold. Then there would be mourning and extra mouths to feed. It would be a lonely time, a time of waiting. Cabeza de Vaca had no time to wait. He needed to devise a plan that would get Oviedo and Alaniz off the island.

Slowly, the dugouts, loaded down with mats and poles, moved upriver. Most of the Chorrucos followed on foot on the bank. At sunhigh of the third day, they arrived at the village. It was a busy village. Others from distant camps had already arrived. Women fanned fires and chopped limbs. Young mothers carried babies in cradle boards looped around their foreheads with rawhide straps. The babies' heads were strapped to the boards to keep them from moving or to flatten their heads, Cabeza de Vaca still did not know which.

Several Chorrucos circled Cabeza de Vaca. Most had never seen him, but they had heard of him. They wanted to touch his beard. *"Katna-u,"* they shouted, meaning mouth fur. They jumped up to feel his blonde hair. They jostled and bumped him. It was annoying, but Cabeza de Vaca was careful not to anger them. The Chorrucos were small, but he knew they could kill a man in a moment if their laughter left them.

The village pulsed with a primeval rhythm. Twenty or so huts lay beneath towering pines like giant, fallen cones. Busy bodies moved in and out of the huts. A chorus of wails echoed through the trees. The smoke of several fires rose and drifted up the river corridor. Cabeza de Vaca noted that the Chorrucos were a little more advanced than the Capoques out on the Isle of Misfortune, but still he saw no gardens. What he wouldn't give for a handful of leaves from his wife's salad garden back in Jerez.

Cabeza de Vaca and Itch Vine were taken to a large hut that sat on a rise. Inside, he saw twelve of the hairy dark skins he had seen back at the camp. The skins were sleeping pallets scattered around a smoldering fire that occupied the center of the hut. He had never seen such a skin in all of Europe. He wanted to see this animal, this *cokon*. He wanted to taste its meat. Cabeza de Vaca spent the afternoon chopping firewood that had been brought from the forest. By nightfall, he was tired. "*Ue mon hehe*," he told Itch Vine. "My whole body is aching." He headed off to his hut. The large dance fire behind him was torched and a drum began to sound, its voice bouncing off the tall trunks in the forest. It seems the Indians always had a reason to dance, whether they had food or not.

During the week that followed Cabeza de Vaca tried to stay busy around the village. Staying busy kept them from beating him. He chopped firewood, mended huts, wove mats. His European skills made his mats superior to those made by the Chorrucos. It wasn't long before they were coming to him to exchange their old mats for new ones. They spoke to him in signs which he could easily understand. They still called him Pepok Pela, the shaman, but he had not been required to perform any shamanistic duties. Not a day went by that Cabeza de Vaca did not think of his countrymen and plan some route of escape. The thought never left him that there still might be survivors somewhere in the country. When he asked the Indians, they said no, they had not heard of any strangers in the land. He often found himself staring to the west. He wondered if that was the way to the prairie, to the *cokons*. If he and Oviedo and Alaniz escaped in that direction, perhaps they would at least have food. But that direction would not take them to Pánuco. They would, at some point, have to swing south and head for Mexico City in New Spain.

His opportunity came one morning at sunrise. He heard a crashing sound outside the opening of the hut he shared with Itch Vine and a dozen other people. When he rolled out to see what the

121

noise was, he found a pile of rabbit traps wrapped in one of the large, black skins. The Indian who had just dropped the bundle was called Canaike, which meant 'Has Ducks.' But Cabeza de Vaca never saw any ducks.

Canaike signed, 'We leave for the hunt, now. You bring.'

"*Yal*," he said and pointed at the traps.

The hunt party followed a trail west and north that wound through the pines. The twelve hunters looked more like warriors on a raid than they did hunters. They carried long spears with flint points, bows and quivers over their shoulders. Their large heads bobbed on their stout bodies. Their hair was wiry and thick, and their faces were painted blood red.

Soon, the pines gave way to great oaks and hickories. Then they came to the plain. Cabeza de Vaca's heart fluttered. The party passed quietly along the edge of the plain setting the rabbit traps at intervals along the way. All the while, they stayed within the canopy of the forest and stared out across the plain to the clumps of tall bluestem, looking for any movement. At one point Cabeza de Vaca asked them if the *cokons* lived out there. They said yes, but so did the Caddos. Cabeza de Vaca needed to know more. Was it good meat? Were the *cokons* easy to find? Easy to kill? The plain looked like much better land to travel than the marsh where there was no food, many inlets and rivers to impede travel, and mosquitoes in the night air as thick as soup. But before he could ask, Canaike, in deep concentration with his spear held before him, walked right into the side of a tree. The sharp flint point fell against his face and he bled profusely. The Indians immediately turned to Cabeza de Vaca. "*Peni, peni*," they said, meaning heal. They expected him to stop the bleeding.

Cabeza de Vaca had seen many cuts at the bloody battle of Ravenna, and he knew that direct pressure was likely to stop the bleeding. He saw no harm in helping Canaike. But for his own satisfaction, he closed his eyes, uttered a short prayer, and made the sign of the cross over his chest. As soon as he did this, a deer appeared out on the plain. The Indians froze. No one moved a finger. To move even one eye would be to give away their presence to the deer. Cabeza de Vaca could feel the tension in the air. And he could see the blood pouring steadily out of Canaike's forehead, but he dared not move. The deer had come around a cluster of big bluestem and apparently sensed them. He too froze. For the longest time nothing moved except the blood running down Canaike's face onto his chest and legs. Finally, the deer turned his back to the hunters and eased off into the grass clumps, his head held high, glancing left and right.

Cabeza de Vaca slapped his hand on the cut and pressed hard. Canaike flinched. The hunters dropped to the forest floor. They were very quiet, but Cabeza de Vaca could tell they were ecstatic. They had not had red meat in months. They signed back and forth. 'Pepok Pela the shaman, with his magical prayer and finger movements, has brought us a deer.' By the time they were ready to move toward the deer, the bleeding had stopped. Cabeza de Vaca removed his hand. The Indians smiled and pointed and signed again. 'Pepok Pela has magic in his hands. He has stopped the bleeding.'

Cabeza de Vaca knew he had made a mistake. He knew what had just happened was sure to fester and come to a head.

The hunters' attention turned fully to the deer, now. They moved quietly, along the edge of the woods. The wind blew off the plain into the woods so they knew the deer would not smell them. But they had to stay out of sight until they could get close enough to shoot their arrows. They moved like alligators, slowly and low to the ground, closer and closer to where the deer had stopped to eat grass. They slipped out of the woods and slithered across the plain floor. Cabeza de Vaca remained in the woods, waiting. The hunters were almost close enough, now. Just a little more. They stopped, eased up on their hands and knees, readied their bows, pulled the string tight.

Suddenly, six arrows flew out from behind a clump of grass beyond them. Two missed the deer, four struck him. The deer jerked. He turned and bolted. Six Indians leaped out of the grass. They wore breechclouts, soft leather shoes, and their hair was shaved except for a cockscomb down the middle that was greased and combed straight up. The Indians yelped and chased after the wounded deer.

The Chorruco hunters dropped back to the prairie floor. Cabeza de Vaca heard them whisper a single word.

"Caddos."

The Chorrucos were as mad as stomped ants. The Caddos had never seen them. The Caddos had killed their deer, the one Pepok Pela's magic had brought for them. Carefully, they followed the Caddos to their camp and peeked from the underbrush. The Caddos strung the deer on a limb, and two of the hunters cut away the skin with flint stones. The Chorrucos waited until all six of the hunters could be seen, then let loose a dozen arrows. The arrows swished through the air. Most missed their mark. Two hit the deer, two grazed the hunters, and one pierced a skinner's back. The Caddos yelped and screamed and ran off into the forest. All except the skinner. The arrow had apparently pierced his lung. He fell to the ground gasping for breath, his chest sucking air.

The Chorrucos leaped out and yelled. They raced around the camp, stomped the forest floor, and slapped their tattooed bellies with their open hands.

When they were sure the Caddos were gone, they turned their attention to the wounded skinner. They circled him, pointed at him, called him names. *"Tsan,"* they said, meaning thief. And *"Otse,"* meaning snake. Canaike, laying all the blame for his stupidity on the dying man, picked up one of the flint stones. He grabbed the skinner's leg and sliced off a piece of thigh meat. Cabeza de Vaca cringed. The skinner refused to cry out. He just stared in horror. Canaike handed the meat to one of the Chorrucos. Then he cut more meat from the skinners legs and arms. The Chorrucos placed the meat on sticks and roasted it while the skinner watched. The skinner's body was a mass of blood. Cabeza de Vaca felt sick to his stomach. He stared in disbelief while the Chorrucos stood and ate the skinner's flesh right in front of him. The skinner's face showed hysteria, now. Not that he was about to die or that his flesh was being eaten in front of him, but that when he died, he would not enter the sky above or the shades below. He would forever be suspended in nowhere.

Then the Chorrucos danced. They made wild faces and exaggerated gyrations. They danced and gnawed at the grisly flesh like ravenous lions until they had consumed all that they had roasted. Then they turned back to the skinner. His eyes were closed, now,but his chest continued to suck air. Canaike grabbed the skinners cockscomb hair. He cut a slice through his scalp and around the head. Then he yanked. The sound of tearing flesh drove Cabeza de Vaca into the darkness. He vomited. In all of his years of service to the crown and all the fighting and killing he had seen, he had never seen anything as nauseating as what he had just witnessed.

When all the excitement settled down and the skinner lay dead, the Chorrucos made a travois. They tied the half-skinned deer to the travois, jabbed six arrows into the body of the dead skinner, then dragged the deer off into the woods. Cabeza de Vaca was left standing beside the dead man. During his months of living with the Indians, that was the first time they did not pile the heaviest load upon his shoulders. He knew why. Now, he was the shaman.

In was late morning when the hunt party returned. The villagers saw the deer. They ran and circled it. The hunters shouted, *"I cak yako!,"* meaning, I eat a man. They told how Pepok Pela's magic had brought the deer. And how the Caddos had stole it and how they chased the Caddos away.

They showed the scalp, which they carried on a stick. The villagers circled Cabeza de Vaca and shouted. The hunters gestured toward Cabeza de Vaca, then Canaike, and said, *"Ok huya peneat,"* meaning, 'He cured him.' The Chorrucos pushed Cabeza de Vaca and shouted louder. Tonight, there would be a celebration. Tonight, they would drink the black drink.

The afternoon was filled with activity. Itch Vine remained in the hut. She told Cabeza de Vaca to go help the men. She would come and join him later. The big cooking pot was dumped and cleaned. New logs were brought to the fire. Men went into the forest and returned with armfuls of leaves and small twigs from the vomit holly. They put the leaves and stems in the pot and balanced the pot on stones over the fire. When the leaves were parched, they crushed them with poles and filled the pot with water, then covered the pot to prevent contamination from the women. Cabeza de Vaca noticed that the women were not allowed to help at their own cook fire. In fact, the women kept very quiet. They moved slowly and carefully and stayed away from the fire. The liquid began to boil. It spilled out under the cover and rolled down the side of the pot and sizzled in the coals below.

Throughout the afternoon, the deer roasted over hot coals, and the black drink boiled violently. When the sun set, a chill came to the air. The men painted their faces red. The drum and rattle sounded. The reed whistles shrieked, and the dance began. This time, only the men danced. The women remained off to the side, their hair pulled over their eyes, their heads held low. When the pot was uncovered, the liquid was black. The women turned away their heads. From then on the women did not move.

"Amlu! Amlu!" which meant, 'Let us drink'. A big gourd dipper with holes in the bottom was brought. The pot tenders sifted out the leaves and twigs. Then they stirred the liquid vigorously with the poles. A yellow froth appeared on the surface and the men shouted, *"Amlu! Amlu!"* One by one the men came to the pot with their *kapo amenen*, their drinking cup. They took out a big scoop, stepped back, and drank down the hot liquid. Swallow after swallow, they gulped the juice until their stomachs looked like they would burst. It was at this moment that Itch Vine made her mistake. There was a brief gap in the chattering of the Chorruco men. The black skin flap rustled on Itch Vine's hut. All heads turned to the hut. Out stepped Itch Vine.

"Wan!" The men pointed. Itch Vine was walking while the men were drinking their sacred drink. She had profaned their drink. If they did not get the black drink out of their bodies, every one of them would get sick and die. The women remained frozen but their eyes grew as wide as oysters. They stared at Itch Vine. The men punched and pushed their stomachs. They leaned over and spewed the frothy liquid out onto the ground. Then they tumbled the pot onto the sand and spilled the black drink onto the ground. The girl had contaminated their drink. The girl must be punished.

Cabeza de Vaca did not know what to make of this, but he knew something dreadful was about to happen. The men ran and grabbed Itch Vine. They threw her to the ground. They kicked her. Cabeza de Vaca ran to stop them but three men grabbed him and held him down.

"It is not bad," Itch Vine yelled. "They do not kick hard. Soon, they will stop."

Cabeza de Vaca saw that their bare feet and fists were pounding her but he was helpless. Eventually, they let Itch Vine up. They pushed her back into the hut. The men busied themselves with boiling another pot of brew from scratch. Cabeza de Vaca went to the hut.

Itch Vine was bruised in several places on her thighs and ribs. Cabeza de Vaca massaged her wounds to spread the pain. The kicking did not seem to bother her. The women were used to it. As the night wore on, the dancing, drinking, and drums continued. One of the women brought Cabeza de Vaca and Itch Vine some food and water. "*Lans al*," she said, meaning deer meat, and "*Na am*," 'You drink.' Cabeza de Vaca lay on one of the big black skins. Itch vine sat near him. They ate and talked.

"It was gruesome watching them eat that man," Cabeza de Vaca said. "There are deer and antelope and rabbit out on the plain. They don't need to eat men."

"They do it to gain his courage."

"Aren't they courageous enough?"

"All of the people in the land do it."

"We call those people *cannibals*. It is a name from the big islands far across the sea where the Carib People live."

"Our people eat only a small piece. It is a ritual. They are not *cannibals*. I have heard there is a land far to the south where they chop up the whole body and eat it with red sauce for food."

"Those people do not exist anymore. My people, the Spaniards, conquered them. A man named Cortés led them."

"Will this Cortés come here and conquer us."

"No. You do not have to worry about that. He is looking for gold, precious stones."

127

"Will you ever go back to them?"

Cabeza de Vaca thought for a minute. Not a day passed that he did not try to figure a way to get back to his people. "Tell me about the *cokon*," he said. "Can you eat them?"

"*Cokon* is very tasty."

"Where do they live?"

"Up on the great plain, toward the Red River, *Ta-i kuds*." She pointed north. They live in big herds and they eat the grass."

"Are they easy to kill?"

"Very easy. Our hunters wear a robe of their skin, and they sneak up on them. They jump out and chase them into a ditch they have dug. Then they throw their spears into them and wait for them to die. Very easy."

"Then why don't they go kill them? Why do they stay here and eat grasshoppers?"

"The land belongs to the Caddos."

Suddenly, the flap of the hut flew back. Two women younger than Itch Vine came inside. They were plump, naked, and had tattoos on their breasts. "*Hoktewe to*," one them said. "*A kmale*."

Itch Vine interpreted. "They say they have been sent to live with us for the winter."

"Other men do not have three women," Cabeza de Vaca said.

"They say you have magic hands. You are the shaman. The shaman always has three wives."

"I am no shaman. I do not have magic hands. And I don't need three wives."

"It gets very cold in the winter. The girls have heat. They will keep you warm.

"I hadn't planned to spend the winter here."

"Where will you go?"

"*Ta-i kuds ticto*," he said. He pointed northwest. "To the Red River." The two girls lay down beside him.

"The Caddos will kill you."

"I will take them things, sea snails, shells from the mounds. They can make knives."

The two girls snuggled close to Cabeza de Vaca.

"It is very cold up on the plain in winter. You will freeze." Their skin lay against his. They felt warm, soft. He thought about the winter cold. He knew it could be bad. He looked at the girls. They smiled. He looked at Itch Vine. She smiled. Oviedo and Alaniz would never leave Misfortune in the winter. Perhaps he should stay with the Chorrucos this winter, go to the plain in the spring, return to Misfortune late next spring when travel was easier, when the oysters in the bay were sweet and firm, the blackberries dark and full.

9

Spring, 1531
Village of Caddo

Father Sun awoke and shot yellow spears through the cracks of the big temple. Himatol kicked at the dirt floor beneath his feet. Dust jumped up and coated his deerhide moccasins and leggings. He had spent the night in the temple on the tall mound so he would be closer to Kills-the-witch. He had paced the floor all night, but Kills-the-witch had not spoken to him. It had been two moons since he last spent the night in the temple alone, without his eight wives to warm him. He had not slept that night, either.

A reed bed held off the floor by forked sticks sat in one corner. A thick buffalo hide was stretched over its top. In another corner were baskets of corn, beans, nuts, two large pots full of water, and ashes to keep away the weevils. Across the front wall, there was a single opening covered with buffalo hide and a wooden bench holding two flat pots. On the far wall, there were two empty boxes and an altar made of reed mats. A basket of gourds sat beside the altar. Perhaps Kills-the-witch was angry with him because he had not placed an offering in the boxes.

The Perpetual Fire at the center of the temple popped. A spark shot across the floor and burned itself out. Himatol had cast an eagle wing on the fire during the night and had spoken to the spiritual helpers—the moon, the clouds, the lightning, the cyclones. But still he had not received an answer to the problems that plagued his village. For a moment, he thought of his ancestors, the ones who had built the temple mound so close to the heavens, the ones who had great religious centers and vast fields bumpering with corn and beans. In his lifetime, Himatol had not seen the making of a single temple mound, and most of the big fields were no longer producing crops. How much longer could they last as a people? What had angered Kills-the-witch? Himatol must go to the people, have them bring gifts. He needed an answer.

He put on his best frown and walked outside. Himatol was the *Xinesi*, the headman, and everyone feared the *Xinesi* when he frowned. And fear brought about obedience. Standing on the rim of the big mound, he could see the entire village: women dressed in skirts of woven nettle and mulberry fringed with pierced seeds, pounding corn in log mortars and winnowing the meal to make flatbread, others tanning deer hides with the deer brains. They should be tanning buffalo, but the buffalo had been scarce for many winters. Too many. At the edge of the plaza, older women dyed rugs and reed mats and fired beautiful pots. Beyond the plaza he saw the seed house where they stored nuts, acorns, plums, and maize seed, and the smoke racks with bird, rabbit, prairie chicken, and turkey. But there was no buffalo on the racks, and there was no smoke coming from the big smoke house. Beyond the smoke house, he saw the houses, tall curved poles covered with grass. Food was scarce in the village, but at least they had food, unlike their enemies to the south who searched the rivers and shoreline for scraps left by the animals. Far in the distance, he saw the garden. That's where the men would be, in the garden.

Himatol scuttled down the steps. The morning breeze chilled his bare, tattooed chest and shaved scalp. The long tail of hair that grew from the center of his scalp whipped over his back. He crossed the plaza without looking left or right, and bolted through the village. Smoke from the racks stung his eyes, engaged his appetite. But he would not stop even though he had a perfect right to stop and eat anywhere or anytime he desired, for he was the *Xinesi*.

When he arrived at the gardens, the men and boys were busy chopping the ground with hoes made from buffalo shoulders. They were preparing the soil for beans, maize, squash, sunflower.

They wore breechclouts and moccasins, and their long hair tails swished as they worked.

Himatol slapped his thigh. A young boy blew a reed whistle. The workers looked up. They stopped their work.

"All night I have spoken with the spiritual helpers from the great temple," Himatol yelled. He was lying. They told me that when Father Sun reaches the high point in the sky, we must have council. All warriors must come. Tell everyone. And bring the *caddi* and the *tammas*." The workers searched each other as if to ask: Why did they need the *caddi*? The *caddi* built houses. They did not need new houses. Their village was shrinking, not growing. "All the clans must be there," Himatol said, "the Beaver, the Otter, the Wolf, the Lion. Tell the shamans to speak to the ancestors and bring gifts." Again the workers searched as if to say: What could be so important as to speak to the ancestors? "I will speak to the two *coconicis*." The workers dropped their hoes and stared as if to say: No, not the 'Little Ones'. The last time you spoke to the *coconicis* it cost us our osage bows, our pot drums, and our deerskin shirts."

One among them replied, "We will be there great *Xinesi*."

At sunhigh, Himatol stood on the rim of the temple mound. His hair glistened with bear grease, and the grease was decorated with duck down. His face and upper body were painted red, and he wore a long buffalo robe, the insides painted with animal designs. The tail of the animal dragged behind him. On the plaza below, the older men, the women, and children began to dance. Every able man marched single file up the steep steps. Each wore a buffalo robe and carried one or more gifts: an arrow, a pot, a mat. The *caddi* and *tammas* were among them, the *tammas* carrying their switches. Before each man entered, he left his robe and moccasins outside. Once inside, each placed a gift in one of the wooden boxes.

When all of the warriors were seated, Himatol entered. He snatched the heavy flap over the entrance behind him, shutting out the world. He took a fire stick from the Perpetual Fire and lit a leaf of tobacco. He dropped it into one of the flat pots by the entrance. Into the other, he poured bear fat and lit it. He pulled a feathered pipe from his breechcloth and carried it to the altar. He sat it inside

133

one of the boxes, then he kicked dust over the fire. The Perpetual Fire was out. The room became shadowy, the warriors silent.

"The *coconicis* are among us," Himatol began. Then he addressed the two spirit boys. "Our granaries are near empty and our flour corn will not be planted for four moons. There are no bears for tallow and fat, and the buffalo herds are thin. Our soils no longer produce abundant crops. The rains do not come like they used to. The witches make our children sick. Oh, *coconicis*, inform Kills-the-witch of our needs. Tell him we need a bountiful harvest, strong backs, victory in battle, and many women to serve the men."

For a moment, Himatol was silent. Then he spoke softly in a childlike voice. "We have heard your wishes. We have informed Kills-the-witch. He has said you must throw the rattle."

The warriors began to grumble. This wasn't looking real good. They hated it when their Xinesi threw the rattle. Himatol slipped up to the basket beside the altar. He reached down and retrieved a gourd, one in which only he knew the seeds had been removed. He threw the gourd across the dirt floor. It did not rattle. It had no voice. A unison grunt came from the throng of men.

"Kills-the-witch is angry," Himatol said in the sweet voice of the *coconicis*. "He wants more gifts, more promises."

Reluctantly, each warrior went back to the wooden boxes and gave more of his possessions. Some went outside and brought in their moccasins and placed them in the boxes. They returned to their seats.

"We promise to reform our lives and work harder," Himatol said in his natural voice. Then in the soft voice of the *coconicis*, "Kills-the-witch has heard your pleas and he receives your gifts. But there is something that bothers him. He is angry. He says that before the cold came last season, Chorruco warriors killed and ate one of the Caddo people. He says the Chorruco are moving into Caddo land, hunting on Caddo land, taking Caddo buffalo. The soul of the killed man lingers where no man lives, and the Caddos have never avenged the hunter's death."

The warriors gave another audible grunt. Wars were usually fought in times when food was abundant and little work was required. This was the season to plant, not the season to fight.

"We have heard the wishes of Kills-the-witch," Himatol said loudly. "Our shamans must drink their magic and sleep for one full sun. Tonight, we will cook and eat three hunting dogs at the dance. Our war heroes, the *amayxoya*, must drink red root and fish broth. Tomorrow, we will burn the temple and build the mound higher. The women will bring baskets of soil from the low grounds. We will do better so Kills-the-witch will give us a good harvest, a good hunt, good health, good war, good women, women with strong backs. Send out the smoke signals. Call up the Nanatsoho, the Nasoni, the Natchitoches. Send the message of Kills-the-witch to them. Tell them the *caddi* will build a war house. The men will bring the poles. The women will bring the grasses. The *tammas* will bring their switches, and he who moves slowly will be switched across his shoulders. There will be dancing, prayers, feasts, offerings for eight full days. Scouts will be sent out. New recruits will come. When Moon Woman is hidden, we will move across the plain to the south and strike the Chorrucos in their sleep. We will take their entire scalps and hang them over our doors. Captives will be brought here, and the women will cut off their fingers, gouge out their eyes, hang them with their feet above the ground. And when they die, we will cook them and eat them—"

Suddenly, the buffalo hide flap flew back. Light flooded the temple. A boy stood in the opening. He panted.

"Pepok Pela is coming this way," the boy said.

Silence dropped over the council. Finally, Himatol spoke.

"The shaman who lives with the Chorruco?"

"Yes."

"The one who heals broken skin? The one whose magic words and magic hands make deer appear?"

"Yes."

The warriors buzzed among themselves. Himatol said, "What does he want with us?"

"He brings gifts," the boy replied. "He will be here in four more suns."

"Hmmm," Himatol moaned. "Perhaps he is a spy, perhaps not.. We will treat him with respect, see what he wants. We will give him two women to keep him happy. Maybe he can give us

135

some of his magic. But I caution you. Not a word of our attack plan must be uttered around him. We will proceed with our plan. We will tell him the new war house is a new store house. We will bring him to our fire and let him hear our stories. But we will not tell him that before the grasses on the plain begin to turn, the Chorrucos will be no more."

Cabeza de Vaca moved steadily north. Canaike had volunteered to guide him as far as the first village. From the river valley of tupelo, gum, and bald cypress, they entered a gently rolling uplands of pine, oak, and hickory and crossed a river Canaike called Caycao. Slanting westward, the forest. thinned and prairies of bluestem began to appear. Canaike spoke of bear and deer and *cokon*, but Cabeza de Vaca saw no animals.

In a few days, they came to Nacono, the first village. The Naconos wept when Pepok Pela entered their town. Cabeza de Vaca conversed in signs and traded shells for turquoise and cotton blankets. Canaike returned to Chorruco, and a Nacono guide agreed to take Cabeza de Vaca to the next village. They followed specific trails and moved continually north. They saw chestnuts, pecan, and walnut, but it was too early in the season for the nuts. They passed through Neches, then crossed another river to Hainai and Namidish, all people connected to the Caddos. The big trees were absent, now. Only bluestem and scruffy bushes and grasses grew on the plain. The grasses were dry and brown and appeared dead except for green tips from a recent shower. The grasses reminded Cabeza de Vaca of his own life, an empty, dead shell with just a tweak of freshness left. He clung to that freshness every morning. There always seemed to be enough to carry him to the next day.

After a week, Cabeza de Vaca and his guide came to the Red River Valley. The trail dropped down off the plain and wound through a forest of trees, whose tiny new leaves twinkled in the morning light. When they came to the principal town of the Caddos, Cabeza de Vaca saw that the Indians were far more advanced than the Chorrucos or the Karankawas. Substantial houses were lined up along the river, and he could see people working in areas of specialization. There were potters, gardeners, weavers, cooks, even house builders. He noticed a very large house being constructed on a bluff along the river. As he entered the town, children circled him, old men watched from low openings, and the women wept.

These were the darkest people Cabeza de Vaca had seen since crashing in the surf off of Misfortune. Their heads were flattened. Their faces and bodies were streaked with red and black dye. The men had hair that hung like horse's tails down their backs. They wore breechclouts and moccasins and had repulsive tattoos of animal designs all over their bodies. The women had tattoos at the corners of their eyes and circling their breasts. They wore feathers, bones, and pretty stones around their arms, wrists, knees. Their hair was simple, parted at the middle and gathered and tied with a knot at the neck with red-dyed rabbit skins. The overall image, when Cabeza de Vaca compared them with Europeans, ranged from uncomely to hideous.

Suddenly, there appeared before Cabeza de Vaca a very dark man wearing a *cokon* robe with the tail still attached. The man was surrounded by an entourage. He made signs and spoke. He said his name was Himatol, and he welcomed Pepok Pela to their village. He beckoned a small Indian from his entourage, whom Cabeza de Vaca learned spoke both the dialect of the Caddos and that of the Karankawas, a dialect Cabeza de Vaca could understand, especially when accompanied by signs. He would be Cabeza de Vaca's interpreter.

Cabeza de Vaca gave Himatol his gifts and was given in return a bundle of osage orange branches cut to bow length. Not knowing quite what to say at this point, Cabeza de Vaca complimented Himatol on the order in his town, the large size of his temple mound, and asked why the new building was being constructed.

A frown came over Himatol's face, and Cabeza de Vaca could swear a hush came over the villagers. Himatol did not answer him. Instead, he announced that tonight, there would be a big dance and everyone was expected to be there. With that, he turned and padded away.

*   *   *

A stiff breeze jolted up the river valley. Cabeza de Vaca had felt many cold nights in Jerez, but his legs and back were always covered. Tonight, he wore only the coyote breechcloth Alaniz had given him. He shivered. He rubbed his bare chest. The sound of a dozen reed flutes drifted by. He looked across the village. In the distance, a huge fire blazed.

Cabeza de Vaca found a spot on a log near the fire. His interpreter came and stood behind him. The villagers began to gather. Women passed out food: roasted acorns, turkey, mice and snake, bowls of beans and boiled corn, and bear tallow. Two of the women were especially noticeable. They were large, bulbous women with big stomachs and wide rings circling their melon-sized breasts. Their bodies were painted in colorful streaks from their waist to their shoulders. When the women finished handing out food, they sat on reed mats off to the side. The two elaborately designed women did not take their eyes off of Cabeza de Vaca.

Himatol came to the fire. He spoke in a loud voice so all could hear. The interpreter spoke softly to Cabeza de Vaca.

"The Caddo people are honored that Pepok Pela has come to our fire. We hope his magic will keep away the witches. We accept his presence as a sign that Kills-the-witch has heard our prayers and will bring the buffalo back to the prairie. To give honor to Kills-the-witch, I will now tell the tale of our beginning."

While Himatol gazed off into the tree line to make adjustments for a dramatic telling, the two colorful women came and sat on each side of Cabeza de Vaca.

"In the beginning," Himatol said with a roar, "there was one woman. The woman had two daughters. One was full with child, the other had never spread her knees before a man. One day, the two daughters went to the lake. A horrible witch came and ate the daughter full with child. The other daughter climbed a tree and dove into the lake in order to escape."

Cabeza de Vaca shivered again. Both of the women beside him moved close and pressed their thick legs against his, then pushed their breasts against his arms. He immediately felt their warmth, and the chill went away.

"The daughter ran to the mother and told her the dreadful story. They returned to the spot by the lake, and they found a drop of blood in an empty acorn shell. The mother covered the acorn shell with another acorn shell and took it back to the place where they lived. She put the acorn shell in a pot and covered it. During the night, they heard a gnawing sound coming from the pot. In the morning, they came and looked into the pot and they found a boy the size of their finger. They covered the pot again and during the next night they heard the same gnawing sound."

Cabeza de Vaca was feeling more contented than he had in months. There were friendly people, food, a warm fire, and the two women whose closeness had begun to arouse him.

"The next morning, they came to the pot, and standing beside the pot there was a full-sized man. The man took a stone from his grandmother and went looking for the horrible witch. When he found the horrible witch, he killed her with the stone. Then the three of them went off to the sky, where the man ruled over all the land with his spiritual helpers—the moon, the clouds, the lightning, and the cyclones."

Cabeza de Vaca's eyes were closed now. He was tired. The tension of months in the wilderness—the hunger, the cold, the fear of not knowing when one of the Indians was going to turn on him and club him to death all seemed to drift away into the fat that surrounded his body.

"And now I have good news," Himatol said. "Pepok Pela has brought the *cokon* back too our land. Today, before the Sun-god fell onto the plain, our hunters spotted a small herd of *cokon* beyond the ridge to the south. Tomorrow, we will send the hunters back and when they return, we will have reason to dance."

Cabeza de Vaca barely heard the words of Himatol. He fell into the arms of one of the big women and drifted off to sleep.

The morning after the fire, after Cabeza de Vaca had slept in a large hut with his head between a pair of large, fleshy breasts, he had convinced Himatol to let him join the hunters, that perhaps his presence would bring them more luck. Himatol had swallowed that line of reasoning and let him go along.

139

Cabeza de Vaca's eyes bulged with excitement. He crouched with the hunters behind a hillock. Before him, not more than a couple of stone-throws away, stood six of the beastliest animals he had ever seen. They had dark coats, small horns, shaggy manes. And the beasts wore beards. They reminded him of oxen, but their shoulders were humped and their heads hung low. They ate grass. He watched as the hunters donned their *cokon* robes and face masks and moved slowly toward the animals. When they got within throwing range, they leaped out of their skins and threw their spears at the animals. Two animals were struck in the ribcage and tumbled to the ground. The others escaped. The hunters leaped on the animal and pounded his head with large stone clubs until they split his skull.

The hunters searched for several days before they found the *cokons*. Cabeza de Vaca was amazed at how slow the animals moved, how easily they were killed, and how much meat one animal could supply. Soon, he must work his way back to Misfortune, convince Oviedo and Alaniz that they should travel north, then west, then work their way down to Mexico City without ever passing through the marsh country.

He helped the hunters build two travois to drag the big *cokon* back to the village. The trip was slow and took them six days.

The night of their arrival, there was a great celebration. The Indians were very happy that Pepok Pela had found the buffalo. They beat the drums and danced until sunup.

Cabeza de Vaca went to his hut early. His two women followed him. He had noticed that the new building on the bluff was almost complete. He pointed and made signs and asked the women why the big house was being built.

The women were happy that he talked to them. They signed, 'Big house is war house. Soon, Caddo attack and kill Chorrucos. Chorrucos come to prairie, take buffalo, eat Caddo hunter. Soon, all Chorrucos die.'

Cabeza de Vaca's heart leaped. He didn't let his face show it, but fear raced through his body. He needed to know more.

'When do they go to war?' he signed.

140

'Soon,' they signed.

'How many will go?'

'All.'

'All Caddo warriors?'

"Yes. Nanatsoho and Nachitohes, too," the woman said. She smiled.

Cabeza de Vaca's mind raced. The Caddos were planning an all-out surprise attack on the Chorrucos. They were allying several tribes and would raise an army large enough to extinguish the Chorrucos. All of his friends would be killed: Kulca, Canaike, even Itch Vine, all the people who had fed him and kept him by the fire all winter.

That night, Cabeza de Vaca lay with the two women, their naked fat warming his body. But late in the night, when he heard them snoring, he slipped away. He had to go south, immediately—alone this time. He must warn the Chorrucos before they were all killed.

The trip took him a little more than a week. He followed the established trails and passed through as many villages as he could. In each, he was given food and rest and a woman to warm him.

In the afternoon of the seventh day, Cabeza de Vaca came to the twenty huts on the rise along the river. Smoke lay like a silver cloud in the void beneath the canopy of tall pines. Canaike was the first to greet him.

"*Pen!*" he shouted, meaning 'Friend.' Soon, he was surrounded by thirty or forty of the small people with the plate ears and wide mouths and scarred faces. They shouted "Pepok Pela," and "*Katna-u.*" They reached to touch his beard. They wanted him to make them more mats. Beyond the people, he saw Itch Vine and the two women he'd been given for the winter. He went to Itch Vine and asked that she tell the principal men to meet him in the hut where he had once slept with twelve others on *cokon* hides.

She returned with the old man who had the bulging stomach and sagging face. He came with four others. They sat around the small fire at the center of the hut. They beckoned Cabeza de Vaca

141

to join them. The old man lit a pipe and passed it around, then waited for Cabeza de Vaca to speak.

With Itch Vine's help, Cabeza de Vaca told them of his journey to the Red River Valley and how he was treated and of the new house that was sure to be completed by now. Then he told them of the plans of the Caddos, how they were uniting to eliminate the Chorrucos. The Chorrucos were shocked to hear such news. At first they did not believe him, but they looked into his eyes and they knew he was telling the truth.

'Why would they do such a thing?' they signed.

"Because of that," Cabeza de Vaca said. He pointed through the opening in the hut to the pole placed near the community fire like a flag staff. On top of the pole hung the scalp of the Caddo skinner who had been slain and eaten.

The men rose to their feet. They shouted solutions back and forth: We will attack them first. Yes, we will kill and eat all of them. No, we will move. We will take our village downstream and live closer to the Karankawas. The Caddos will not attack us there for fear that the Karankawas and Coahuiltecans will join us and destroy them.

In the hubbub of confusion, Cabeza de Vaca knew the Chorrucos would work out a solution, and he knew that solution would be to relocate downriver, for the small Chorrucos would not dare take on the more advanced Caddos.

Cabeza de Vaca stayed three more days to help the Chorrucos assemble their belongings and begin their trek toward the marsh country. He felt greatly relieved knowing they would not be exterminated. Then he and Itch Vine took their dugout and poled down the river ahead of the Chorrucos.

Summer, 1531
Isle of Misfortune

"Oviedo, Alaniz. It is I, the Provost Marshal!" Cabeza de Vaca shouted when he reached the Capoque village in the scrub. In

142

the nine months he'd been gone, he had grown bushy and scruffy. He was afraid Oviedo and Alaniz wouldn't even recognize him.

Oviedo rushed across the village and hugged him. He showed signs of continued beatings.

"We were afraid we would never see you again, *señor*," Oviedo said.

"I have good news for you, *amigo*. To the north, there is meat. . . red meat. There is an animal as big as an ox and just as easy to kill. His flesh will provide more food than we can possibly eat."

"But *Señor*, Pánuco is not to the north. It is to the south. The Capoques have told me that to the north the land goes on forever. And the people who live there—"

"The marsh to the south is impossible to traverse, Lupe." Besides, there is no food along the coast. If we head north and kill one of the big animals, we'll have enough roasted meat to last a month. We can then turn inland, bypass the coast, then head south, be in Mexico City before winter."

Lupe de Oviedo hawed as he spoke. He was making excuses. Cabeza de Vaca could tell he didn't want to leave Misfortune. He was afraid of something.

For a week, Cabeza de Vaca begged Oviedo and Alaniz to leave with him, but they would not. There was food on Misfortune—meager as it was—and they had a roof over their heads. They would stay and wait for a ship from Cuba or Spain or somewhere. Why didn't the marshal go on ahead and tell their countrymen in Mexico that the two of them wait on the Isle of Misfortune?

Cabeza de Vaca bade farewell to his two countrymen, to Itch Vine and Tadpole, and to the others he had befriended. The *saylas* were glad to see him leave. He was just another mouth to feed. He moved down the coast and lived awhile with the Doguenes. In the fall, he traveled inland to the village of the Mendicas, and when the weather turned cold, he sought out the Chorrucos. The Chorrucos owed him a favor. They put him up for the winter.

143

When the blackberries were gone in the late spring of 1532, Cabeza de Vaca returned to Misfortune. He found Lupe de Oviedo, told him once more it was time for them to escape. If he wanted to go south through the marsh country, that would be all right. Cabeza de Vaca had made friends with some of the Karankawas along the coast. He guessed that Oviedo and Alaniz were afraid to go north, perhaps they had heard that people to the north ate human flesh.

"I am afraid we won't be going anywhere this year, Marshal," Oviedo said. "Alaniz has taken ill."

"Alaniz, sick?"

"*Si*. Would you like to see him?"

Oviedo took Cabeza de Vaca to a mat house at the edge of the village. Inside, Alaniz lay shivering against the wall.

"Don Heironymo," Cabeza de Vaca said. "You look awful."

Alaniz was too weak to speak. His eyes were dark and sunken, his face drawn. He looked like he had lost thirty pounds. Cabeza de Vaca squatted beside him. He did not like what he saw. He had seen it too many times among the ranks of his fellow countrymen who had died during the first winter on Misfortune.

"He needs food," he told Oviedo.

"He can't eat," Oviedo said. "When I bring him fish or oysters, he throws it back up. The Capoques have given him up for dead. They will not come here. They say you are no longer welcome here, either, *señor*. Your life is in great danger if you stay."

Cabeza de Vaca spoke awhile longer to Alaniz, then prayed for him. He and Oviedo went outside.

"I am going to leave, Oviedo."

"Tell them to send a ship, *señor*."

"I won't leave without you, Lupe. I will come back for you."

"Where will you go?"

"I shall travel south and reconnoiter the coast, collect goods for the inland people. I will come back for you next spring when the tide is up in the bay. That will give Alaniz time to recover his health. You must look after him, Oviedo. Next spring, when the

144

weather is good, we will leave this place forever. You and I and Alaniz."

Once again Cabeza de Vaca headed south. Wherever he went he had his freedom as an independent trader. The Indians rejoiced when he arrived. They fed him, gave him their women. He was not a slave, not obligated to anyone. For that, he was thankful. But the loneliness grew immense. He longed to carry on a conversation with someone who spoke Spanish. The winter cold, the storms, the nakedness, the hunger, the many nights he spent alone in the wilderness were nearly more than he could bear. But he had promised he would do all he could do to stay alive, to carry out the will of God our Lord—whatever that will was—and to return to Misfortune and help his two countrymen escape.

In the summer, he headed north, took trade goods to the outer villages that were connected to the Caddos, the Naconos and the Neches and the others. Then, early in the spring of 1533, he returned to Misfortune.

"Where is Don Heironymo?" he asked Oviedo.

"He is dead, *señor*. He died this past winter. It was too much for him—the cold, the sickness.

"Did you give him a Christian burial?"

"*Si*. In the woods." He pointed.

"God our Lord has granted us favor, Lupe. We must seize the opportunity and depart from this land.

"I won't go north."

"Then we will go south."

"*Si señor*, we will go south."

The two men waited for a new moon when there were no shadows in the scrub. With Tadpole's help, they slipped away. Tadpole poled them to the mainland, then returned to the island. They moved swiftly down the coast, stopping to rest only when necessary. At the end of the first day, they came to a wide river. They had already crossed several ravines with Oviedo clinging to Cabeza de Vaca's arm, complaining with each step. Their legs were caked with dried mud, and sweat fell off them like drops of blood.

Cabeza de Vaca saw the river as a chance to bathe, to receive refreshment. But Oviedo saw it as something else.

"What do you mean, you can't swim?" Cabeza de Vaca said. He was stunned. They had many rivers to cross before they reached the slave station at Pánuco. "If you can't swim, why did you choose to travel south through the marsh? We could have turned inland and had food and shallow rivers."

"I did not choose, *señor*. You did."

"But you were afraid of the flesh eaters who live up on the prairie."

"I never said that, *señor*. I did not want to leave Misfortune because I cannot swim. I have been deathly afraid of water all of my life."

"But you. . . never mind. We will spend the night here. In the morning, we will find a log. You can float across."

"I don't know, *señor*."

"It will be all right, Oviedo. I will hold onto the log with you."

Two days later, they came to another wide river, and there was a repeat performance, Oviedo growing more fearful, Cabeza de Vaca encouraging him.

Finally, they came to the village of the Doguenes, where Cabeza de Vaca had been before. The Doguenes accepted the two men, gave them some food to eat, and told them that in two days, some of them would be going south to harvest pecans on the bank of a river. The two traders could travel with them.

When the party of pecan harvesters reached a wide bay, much too wide to swim, they built fires to attract the attention of some Indians they had seen on the far side. When the Indians came across, they were a group Cabeza de Vaca had never met. They called themselves Quevenes, but they seemed friendly.

Upon reaching the south shore, Cabeza de Vaca asked the Quevenes, using signs, 'Have you seen any men like me in this land?'

To his surprise, they said yes. Two men like him, and a large black man lived with the Mariames in the forest.

Cabeza de Vaca's heart leaped. He looked at Oviedo. Oviedo looked surprised. Cabeza de Vaca clapped his hands and yelped like anxious dogs.

'Are there any others in the country,' Cabeza de Vaca signed.

'No, they are all dead. Some from the cold. Some from hunger. Some killed by the villagers for sport.'

'Are the three who live with the Mariames treated badly?' Cabeza de Vaca signed. Then the Quevenes took a change of heart.

'Here is how they are treated,' they signed. The one doing the signing slapped Cabeza de Vaca hard across his chest. Cabeza de Vaca flinched, fell back. Others attacked Oviedo. They punched the two of them with their fists, smacked them with sticks, kicked them, even made balls of mud and splattered their bodies. It was all the two Spaniards could do to hold up their arms against the beatings.

The Doguenes backed off. They told the women who had come to help with the nut picking to get into the dugouts and cross back to the other side of the bay.

"I'm going with them," Oviedo said.

"You're what?" Cabeza de Vaca said.

"I'm going back to Misfortune. This is crazy. They are going to kill us if we stay here."

The Indians had stopped for awhile. They were preoccupied with what was happening with their dugouts.

"Don't show so much fear, Oviedo. They won't beat you long if you show bravery."

"I'm not showing anything. I'm leaving."

"You can't leave, now. We have finally located some of our countrymen."

"You go find them, Marshal. And when the four of you get to Mexico, send a ship for me. You know where I'll be."

With that, Oviedo left.

Cabeza de Vaca continued on with the Indians to the River of Pecans. The trees were full and the nuts as large as those Cabeza de Vaca had seen in Galicia. For days they picked the trees and mashed the nuts into meal which they mixed with small grains.

147

Whenever Cabeza de Vaca asked them to take him to see the Spaniards, they said no. He concluded that they feared the Mariames. Finally, a Doguenes Indian told him if he would meet him secretly one night, he would take him to meet the Spaniards.

That was the offer Cabeza de Vaca had been waiting three years to hear.

10

Spring 1533
Cactus Prairie

During the months the three men had lived alone among the Mariames, Dorantes repeatedly urged Castillo and Estevanico to escape and continue on toward Pánuco. But because none of them could swim, Castillo and Estevanico simply refused; there were rivers and bays along the coast. They had seen too many of their countrymen drown, and they did not want to follow in their path. But what of starvation, cold, and torture, which was all they had if they stayed, Dorantes had asked. It's better than drowning, they said.

But now Cabeza de Vaca was back, the one the *nativos* called Pepok Pela, and he could swim. He could help them cross the rivers.

"We will escape as soon as possible," Cabeza de Vaca told them. "But, I entreat you, we must not follow the coast; we must turn inland then go north. The *nativos* are of a better sort, and there are hairy cows we can eat. Then we will turn west and head for the South Sea, the body of water seen by Balboa. It forms the western shore of New Spain. From there we can move south to Mexico City. I implore you in the name of God our Lord to abandon the idea of following the coast. We must set forth on a new path to the north and inland."

That sounded good to Dorantes. It solved the problem of crossing the rivers. He was tired of having to carry Estevanico squawking and complaining on his back, while he pulled himself through the waters on a cord tied by an Indian guide.

"Why go north at all?" Castillo said. "I have seen the west. I was there with the Yguages. There are swollen ridges with nut trees and oaks more majestic than those in Spain. Beyond the ridges, there is a vast prairie where an abundance of prickly cacti grow. The flattened stems sprout like rabbit's ears and carry big thorns. Each fall, the Yguazes and others along the coast and farther inland—the Guaycones, Atayos, Acubadoes, Maliacones—all go there to harvest the pears that grow on the cactus. The fruit looks like big figs. Red and very sweet, the size of a hen's egg."

"I have eaten the dried pears," Dorantes said. "The Mariames brought them back to our village."

"In six months, the *nativos* will go to the prairie," Castillo said. "We can beg to go with them, and there, join up with some of the *nativos* who live farther on. By going from village to village, we can slowly move west."

Cabeza de Vaca didn't want to wait. "Has anyone heard of any survivors of boat four?" He asked.

"No," the three replied.

"Then why wait six months? We can head inland, now."

"We must be patient, marshal. We need the *nativos* for food and guidance. Without them, we die."

Dorantes added, "He is right, marshal. But we must be careful that the Mariames do not learn of our plan, or they will kill us."

Months passed before the men could go to the cactus prairie. During that time, Castillo was sold to the Lanegados. Later, when the three tried to meet up with him on the prairie, two women got into a fist fight forcing the Mariames to take the three back to their village. Their plan had failed. They would have to wait another year.

In the fall of what Cabeza de Vaca reasoned must be 1534, he and his two companions returned to the prairie. They slipped away from the Mariames' camp and found Castillo still with the Lanegados.

"I have news of boat four," Castillo told them. "But you will not like it. The Lanegados say there is a clan along the coast to the south called the Camoles. Apparently Peñalosa and Téllez shipwrecked on their shore, and because the men were so emaciated and feeble and could not raise a hand in defense, the Camoles killed every one of them. The Lanegados showed me some of their crossbows and lances they received in trade from the Camoles. They say their *iapels*—their heads, still lie on the shore, and their skin is half eaten away. A horde of green flies buzz around them and thousands of fat maggots crawl through the eye sockets."

Cabeza de Vaca looked away from the men. He remembered that last night when he had seen Peñalosa and Téllez drift out to sea with a broken rudder. He had thought then that he might never see them again. But what if he had tried to catch them? could he have saved them from such a painful fate? He uttered a silent prayer, crossed himself, and turned back to the men. "The prickly pear harvest is over. Soon, the *nativos* will be returning to their village in the east We do not have guides to lead us west. We must recommend ourselves to God our Lord and proceed north to the land of the cows." This time they were all were ready.

Across the vast prairie, dozens of clans who had migrated in for the harvest had established camps. At twilight, thorny acacias stood like shadowy scarecrows against a bronze sky veil. After dark, little fires flickered on the plains like a starry sky. On the mesquite racks above the fires, lizards, rabbits, nuts, and split cactus stems roasted in the heat of the coals.

Without prickly pears, food was more scarce on the prairie than along the coast. Starvation in that open country was a reality Cabeza de Vaca was all too aware of. Deep down, he could not help but wonder if they too, like the sweet pears of the prairie, would soon be gone. They must move quickly on into the cow country.

They approached one of the camps. Cabeza de Vaca stopped his companions just short of hearing range. He could never tell if a clan was friendly and would share their food, or if they would chop them down as the Camoles had done to Peñalosa and Téllez.

Suddenly, the *nativos* rushed out of camp. Cabeza de Vaca froze. The Indians surrounded them. They yelled and jumped up and down. They seemed to know the Spaniards—Pepok Pela and the ones from the coast who knew magic. The Indians were the Chavavares, and yes, they would love to share their remaining pears with Pepok Pela and the healers. They would even put them up in the lodge of their medicine men. Apparently, the Chavavares had not heard that the healers had been menials for the past several years.

Once settled, four *nativos* came and made signs that their heads ached. They wanted the healers to stop the pain. Cabeza de Vaca balked. It had been so long since the woman on Misfortune had been healed, he had almost forgotten. But the Indians had not. They thought the Spaniards could heal anyone, anytime, anywhere.

Surprisingly, Castillo stepped up, his strong hypnotic eyes focused on the Indians. Cabeza de Vaca stopped him. "No, we mustn't tempt God our Lord." Castillo ignored him. He laid a hand upon each forehead, breathed on each man the way the shamans had done, and crossed them.

Immediately, the four Indians leaped back. They shouted. They felt great. They laughed and slapped each other across the back, then ran away, only to return with prickly pears and venison. The Spaniards were dumbfounded, but they had not tasted meat in a long time and were overjoyed at the charred chunks.

Cabeza de Vaca turned to Castillo. "Captain, I do not think—"

"It is only a game, Marshal. Relax."

Word of the healing spread like a prairie fire. In the morning, Indians from the Comos, the Atayos, the Coayos, and Arbadaoes came with leg pains, back pains, head pains, and stomach pains. Castillo shrugged his shoulders, crossed them all, commended them to God—just a game he kept saying—and every one of them shouted that they were healed of their pain and ran to bring more chunks of venison.

Cabeza de Vaca could not explain it. Was the omnipotent power of God our Lord being unleashed here in this waste land? He recalled how when there was no food, God our Lord had been pleased to afford them *nativos* to sustain them under great want. Perhaps the power had been with them all along, and he just had not noticed.

For three days and nights, the Chavavares danced and celebrated around their fire. They ate the thick pear leaves they had dried, and they sniffed the smoke of a burning herb that made them act like dogs with paralytic madness. Cabeza de Vaca watched Estevanico curiously. Watched him sniff the smoke and parade untold numbers of women into his hut. Then Estevanico collapsed from exhaustion. When he finally woke up, he came to Cabeza de Vaca with a strange story.

"The *nativos* told me that when they sniff the smoke, witches visit them. There is one they call Badthing who makes their hair stand on its end. Badthing cuts them on the *pat* and *dom*." He touched his arm and breast. "Then he reaches in—"

Cabeza de Vaca held up his hand. "I have met this Badthing," he said. "Go tell them Badthing is a demon, and that as long as we are here with them, he will not come."

With winter cold settling in and the prickly pears gone and the four of them naked as the day they were born, Cabeza de Vaca decided they had better stay with the Chavavares until spring. They journeyed east with them for five days to a camp by a river the Indians called Guanpaclec—River of Mud.

While Castillo continued to breathe upon the sick and lame in camps along the river valley, Cabeza de Vaca joined a hunt party for the fruit of a tree that tasted to him like bittervetch of Spain. Thinking the party would return before nightfall, he left his animal fur bed behind. But that part of the country had no trails, and he soon found himself lost and separated from the others.

Night fell, cold settled in, and he thought he would freeze. Suddenly, there appeared before him a burning tree. Like Moses in the wilderness. Surely, it was a sign. God had answered his prayer.

153

Our Lord *was* with them, and He was making his power available to them. What else could it be; there had been no lightning?

He lit a firebrand, and for five days Cabeza de Vaca walked naked in the wilderness, eating nothing, praising God, remembering the forty-day fast the Lord Jesus had spent in the wilderness. At night, he slept in a hole covered with prairie grass surrounded by four small fires he lit with his firebrand, while God our Lord held back the deadly northern wind common that time of year.

When he finally met up with the Chavavares and his three *compañeros*, he learned that they too had wandered about searching for food. They were famished. But, that very day they found a great many trees full of ripe fruits.

Yes. God our Lord was with them. Cabeza de Vaca knew it in his heart.

Alonso del Castillo never believed the healings were real. But what did it matter; the game got them food. But now, the whole countryside was talking about the miraculous healings. He began to wonder when the game would end. The *nativos* had such an unpredictable sense of humor, the game could end violently at any moment. He'd seen them break into laughter over nothing, then just as quickly take up a club and kill a man for no apparent reason. He must be careful. These *nativos* were creatures of whim and instinct, not thought. With their childlike imagination, they'd make something up, then believe it was real. What if they imagined one of them was a demon or a witch?

One day, while the four were at the camp of the Cultalchulchas, a *nativo* arrived from the Susola camp. Would the healer come and save one of their *saylas* who was near death?

Death? Castillo grew cautious. But he had no choice. They would surely kill him if he did not go.

All four men and several Cultalchulchas escorts went and found the man lying in a lodge. A reed mat covered him. Castillo knelt, removed the mat, then stopped cold.

The *sayla* was dead.

He had no pulse. His body was cold, stiff. His eyes were rolled back. Did they expect Castillo to raise a man from the grave who had been dead a day or more? The game had just been elevated to a much higher level, and Castillo didn't like the stakes. He leaped up, backed away. For the first time he felt real fear. Sure, the Lord Jesus had raised the dead, but Castillo was not the Lord Jesus. Besides, Castillo's past had been clouded with a few, shall we say, uncommendable activities. Would not the Almighty God consider him a bit presumptuous if he continued this game and attempted to bring the dead *sayla* back to life? Would He, perhaps, even consider docking Castillo a few points on the day of reckoning for such activity?

Cabeza de Vaca had watched in silence. Now, he stepped forward. He knelt by the *sayla*.

Dorantes stood behind him. "He is dead, Marshal," he said.

"Like a fish on the sand," Estevanico said.

"Better back away, Marshal," Castillo said.

Cabeza de Vaca touched the man in several spots. "God our Lord is with us," he said. "It does not make sense that He, having once empowered us with His Holy Spirit, would forsake us in this time of great need." He leaned forward, breathed on the man repeatedly, prayed earnestly, crossed the man, asked God to put life back into his body, recited *Pater Nosters, Ave Marias*, rose, and without a word, departed.

Castillo placed the mat back on the dead man and followed him outside. What had the marshal done?

Expecting a miracle, the Susolas gave Pepok Pela two baskets of dried prickly pears. He gave the food to the Cultalchulchas, then the four returned to their quarters in a nearby lodge.

That night the Cultalchulchas stayed at the lodge of the dead man. Just before dawn they ran into the lodge where the Spaniards lay.

He was alive.

The *sayla* had come back to life and was eating and talking and walking around.

Cabeza de Vaca sat in quiet contemplation.

Dorantes and Estevanico jumped up in astonishment.

Castillo was shocked. What kind of miracle was this? There was only one kind that could raise the dead, the kind that came from God Almighty Himself. Had Castillo's touches actually caused hundreds to be healed also? What had become of the game? And what would this bring—this raising a man from the dead?

Castillo backed into the shadows.

11

Villages of the Tableland

The sayla really was alive. No one could explain it. No one tried.

The four men remained with the Chavavares through the winter. Every day, bands of *nativos* from the surrounding countryside came to be touched by Pepok Pela. When the crowd became too large, Cabeza de Vaca asked his companions to assist with praying and laying on hands. Dorantes did so dutifully. Estevanico was ecstatic to see that when he laid his big hands on someone and made the sign of the cross—he wasn't even sure what that meant—the *nativos* leaped up, proclaimed good feelings, and brought him food and trinkets. He attached the trinkets to his toes, his hair, around his waist, and danced around the fire every night.

Castillo refused to assist. He had stopped touching the *nativos* all together. It was not a game any more.

When spring arrived, it was time to depart. The Chavavares wept and begged the four shamans not to leave. As long as Pepok Pela was in their camp, Badthing could not harm them. No one could harm them. They would never be sick again.

But Pepok Pela had to leave.

The country was aflame with wildflowers, blooming acacias, yellow prickly pear flowers, and mesquite blossoms that dangled like hairy caterpillars.

The four men headed north. They spent three days with the Maliacones, a clan they had previously healed, but one that had to be healed again, just to be sure. Then they continued on to the village of the Arbadaos.

"My body feels like a swine at a pig roast," Castillo said. He dropped the tall bundle of sticks and firewood from off of his shoulders. He was exhausted. Two skinny dogs tied to a roof pole nearby barked at the noise. Dorantes sat in the dirt passing arrow shafts through a hole in a stone, shaving away the knots to make the wood straight. "My skin peels twice a year like a snake. Look at me. I am pierced in a hundred places, blistered to the bone. Look at these sores." He leaned down to show Dorantes the raw spots where the cord had cut deep into his shoulder. Blood trickled from a dozen scratches on his arms and legs. "The chaparral thickets are so dense out there, you get in, chop up a bundle, then you can't carry it out without getting pricked a thousand times."

God was punishing him. That had to be it. For not assisting with the healing ceremonies. But he wanted no part in that Holy Ghost stuff. Why couldn't things be simple like they used to be back at Salamanca: a peaceful stroll along the Tormes, a stretch on a shady bank, one of Desiderius Erasmus's humanistic dialogues in his hands, an historical treatise by Diego Hurtado de Mendosa lying beside him?

"Why don't you stay here and make combs or weave mats like Estevanico," Dorantes said. "They'd let you do that." Estevanico was sitting nearby on Cabeza de Vaca's deer skin. He leaned against a tree, eyes closed, fingers slowly weaving reeds and grass. "The Arbadaos are so busy searching for food, they haven't time to make these things. They'll trade you food for them."

Castillo looked aside. Arbadaos. Poorest creatures on earth. Sickly, emaciated, swollen from hunger. The only decent job they'd ever let him do was rub animal skins with wildcat brains, if you could call that decent. And food? The only food they had were green prickly pears, that puckered your cheeks worse than a Valencia lemon. And the only meat Castillo had were the parings he saved when scraping animal skins. Then if he tried to boil the parings, one of the *nativos* came by and grabbed them up. He didn't trust them. They were too impulsive, had no concept of appreciation. They had madman strength with animal intelligence, a dangerous combination. Besides, they believed in ghosts, and every civil-minded person knew that ghosts did not really exist, holy or otherwise.

"I'd rather be in the thickets," he told Dorantes. Then he turned away.

Why were they with the Arbadaos in the first place? They should be heading north to the land of the cows. They needed meat. Cabeza de Vaca, the great white healer, had made another wrong decision. Perhaps Cabeza de Vaca should not even be their leader. Anyone who believed the policies of Carlos Primero were better than those of King Fernando couldn't be all that bright.

The dogs barked again.

Castillo thought for a moment. He walked over to Estevanico. "Give me that skin."

Estevanico opened his eyes, hunkered forward. Castillo snatched up the skin.

"What are you going to do with that?" Dorantes asked.

Castillo ignored him. If he was going to survive in this acarpous land, he must make his own decisions from now on, not cater to some pocket-sized marshal who never even went to college.

He took the skin to the *nativo* who owned the dogs, made a trade, brought the dogs to Estevanico.

"Here. Butcher these. We're going to eat real meat, then we're leaving." Castillo was persistent

The three healers succumbed to Castillo's complaints and departed—Cabeza de Vaca, a little angry for having lost his sleeping mat, Estevanico, pleased to have meat in his stomach, even if it was dog, Dorantes, looking over his shoulder to see if they were being followed.

They were, and it made Dorantes nervous.

Dorantes and his companions plowed north, making stops at camps and villages along the way. At each village, the *nativos* asked to be blessed and in turn gave gifts of arrows. Dorantes gave the arrows to the crowd that had begun to follow them. That should keep them friendly. Then they continued on, the procession growing larger at each village departure.

The cortege spent several days passing through a high forest of hickory and oak, where their only food was prickly pear cactus stems baked in an earth oven all night. It was bitter, but it kept the four men alive.

They emerged from the woods onto a mesquite savanna and came to a village of fifty lodges. The stomachs of the Indians were swollen and heavy from eating pungent mesquite meal sweetened with soil from the earth pits in which they pounded the dried pods. They begged the healers to touch them.

But before the healers could do anything, the Indians who had followed demanded that the mesquite eaters first give gifts to the healers. Then the followers snatched away their bows and arrows. After the mesquite eaters were blessed and claimed complete recovery for all that ailed them, the followers took the bows and arrows and returned to their village.

A band from the new village now joined them: hunters, women with their children, old people hobbling along in their wake. The guides led them along a northern trail that rose to a tableland of open high hills and gentle slopes.

After walking a league or more, Dorantes spied something in the trail. A horde of Indians had rushed out of their village and were slapping their thighs with a loud smack. Those in front shook two gourd rattles with perforations to give the rattles a voice. Other Indians surrounded them. They touched their beards and said, *guagate*—beard. Dorantes hated crowds. He felt nervous. The Indians spoke and made signs that they had been waiting for Pepok Pela. The bearded healers were famous in their country.

"Where did you get those?" Estevanico said and signed. He pointed to the gourds.

"*Apel*," they said. They pointed to the sky. They signed, 'They come from heaven by way of the water.' "*Nathan*," they said and pointed north, upriver. 'Very sacred, used only for medicine dance. No one allowed to touch except shamans. We give to you because you make big medicine at our village. You are great shaman.'

The Indians gave the two gourds to Cabeza de Vaca and Castillo. Castillo quickly handed his to Dorantes.

Suddenly, the Indians picked up the four men and carried them to their village, a hundred circular, mat-covered huts on the bank of a small river. They were happy that Pepok Pela and the healers had come. The healers were gods. Now, no one in their village would ever die.

Dorantes felt pressed by the throng of *nativos*. What had they gotten themselves into? He became skeptical. Perhaps Castillo was right. They were not gods. Suppose one of the *nativos* died? Suppose one of them remained sick after being touched? What then? He didn't trust the *nativos*. He'd seen them change their minds faster than Estevanico could get lost. They were, in fact, the most inconsistent people in the world. You never knew what they were thinking, and their promises were about as reliable as a rotten boot cord.

What Dorantes wanted more than anything was to be away from there, away from the crowds. Be in Mexico—New Spain. If he ever got to New Spain he was going to get him the fattest, richest widow he could find and move up into the mountains so far no one would ever be able to find him. He was tired of serving his country.

The Indians danced and celebrated all night. In the morning herds of *nativos* came to be touched by the healers. But again, the followers jumped in. They yelled that the visitors must first give their possessions. The followers grabbed arrows, bows, beads, and shoes from those who had come to be healed. And as the three men touched them and made the sign of the cross, Dorantes saw the followers ransacking the village lodges, taking everything the Indians owned.

"This could be trouble, Marshal," he whispered.

But Cabeza de Vaca was in spiritual concentration. He seemed not to hear him. He touched one after another who came up to him, then prayed softly for each one. The *nativos* leaped into the air, their pain miraculously gone. Finally, Cabeza de Vaca said, "I

161

don't like what I see either, Captain. But there is nothing we can do about it until we gain more authority. The only concession is that those who are stripped of their possessions are reimbursed at the next village."

When they departed that village, they were accompanied by an abundance of women, the *nesh·hawnan*—the burdened ones—who carried water, gathered firewood, and cooked the food brought by the hunters and gatherers. At no time were the four men ever alone without the *nesh·hawnan*.

Dorantes felt like a prisoner. He stumbled along in the midst of the horde. Then he began to see mountains to the west. Two days passed and the mountains were still there. But where was Estevanico. He had not seen him since the mountains appeared. Finally, with Cabeza de Vaca busy with his ministry, Estevanico came to him, his body scratched like he'd been in a cat fight. Dorantes decided not to ask him what happened. He'd seen him with a pack of Indian women almost every night, except for the past few nights when he was not seen at all.

"The *nativos* want us to go into those hills to visit their kin," Estevanico told him.

"You tell them Castillo says no. We go north." Castillo had gotten mighty autocratic with his demands. Dorantes didn't know what had gotten into him. The lanky captain wasn't even speaking to Cabeza de Vaca anymore.

"They say they are enemies of the River People who live to the north. They want to go west to the hills."

"Tell them soon we will turn and follow the sun." Dorantes noticed that Estevanico was acting more Indian than Spanish or Moorish or African or whatever it was he used to be. In fact, Estevanico seemed to be almost enjoying himself.

"But they say—"

"It doesn't matter what they say. Castillo is in charge now, and he says north is where the cows are and where they grow plants, like those gourds you have dangling around your waist like bull *huevos*."

Estevanico looked at the gourds, gave them a jiggle then shut up.

The Indians begged and pleaded but to no avail. The four men continued north. Eventually, the Indians abandoned the healers and turned back. They would not go to the village of their enemy. For a brief period, the four were alone. They continued on to the banks of a beautiful river where there was a village of twenty lodges. The River People were in tears, wailing, hanging their heads. When Estevanico asked them why they were sad, they told him they had heard that those who follow Pepok Pela will rob them of their meager possessions.

'No, no,' Dorantes signed. 'We are alone. Do not have fear.' He didn't want to get the *nativos* riled up, mad at him for bringing robbers to their village. Then he looked over his shoulder. He hoped they were still alone.

The River People looked around too. No one had followed them. They became happy. They took the healers to a large *cooch*, a mat house on the river bank, and gave them food and water and let them rest.

At dawn, it happened. Just as the River People had gathered to be touched by the healers, the attack came. The Thigh Slappers, who Dorantes thought had previously turned back, ran into the village shouting and signing.

'Gifts must be offered first or you anger the Children of the Sun.' They ran from *cooch* to *cooch* plundering, grabbing up bows, arrows, strings of beads, ochre, little bags of mica the *nativos* had collected from the rocks. Everything they could get their hands on. 'Must treat Children of the Sun with great respect and never anger them. They have the power to take your life.'

Dorantes shook his head. *"Vamos de mal en peor,"* he uttered—they had gone from bad to worse.

'After they bless you, you must take Children of the Sun to where there are many people, must take everything the people have and give to Pepok Pela to be blessed. That is the custom.'

An old shaman, looking afraid for his life, brought a large copper rattle and handed it to Dorantes. Dorantes didn't want to insult the Indians; he took it. But he gave the rattle to Estevanico, who seemed to have become the depository for everything, most of which hung somewhere on his body. Then he watched as

Estevanico took the rattle to the river's edge and shook it gently. Dorantes had noticed that his old friend still had his bad days. It was that Apalachee girl, the one Estevanico had given the golden rattle to—Ka·konee. He was remembering her. He missed her. Dorantes was sorry for ever getting Estevanico mixed up in this mess. If he ever gets to New Spain, the first thing he is going to do is give Estevanico his freedom. But how long would Estevanico survive without Dorantes to keep him out of trouble?

In three days, after the Children of the Sun had blessed the River People and given the gifts to the Thigh Slappers, they departed. Dorantes looked behind them. More than half of the River People had joined the procession.

They followed the river the first day, then turned west into a valley between the mountains. They plodded across deep canyons, sloping hills, through thickets of sumac, cottonwood, cedar, soothing their burning feet in little streams that raced beneath granite cliffs. Then they turned northwest and crossed the mountain. As word went out of their great healing powers, traveling bands of Tonkawas joined them, and their procession grew larger every day.

One afternoon at sunset, they came to another river. Their guides went ahead to find a village and announce the customs and terms required of people visited by the Children of the Sun.

Cabeza de Vaca did not like the customs and terms; the stealing was getting out of hand. Besides, the gift of God's love should never be sold—not at any price. The Lord Jesus had already paid the price with his blood on the tree. But Cabeza de Vaca did not want to voice objections to Castillo. The young captain had grown cold to him, and Cabeza de Vaca knew why. He was struggling with his faith. Cabeza de Vaca had seen the lost look in his eyes when the three of them were laying on hands in the name of God our Lord. Eyes that were normally strong enough to make men bleed had turned sad and empty. Cabeza de Vaca had stayed away from Castillo during this last leg of their journey, letting him make decisions for the group, giving him time to wrestle with his spiritual and emotional conflict. But he knew if they were to ever get out of this adverse land alive, they would have to work together as a team. Somehow, he must mend their torn relationship, help Castillo with his spiritual struggle.

In the morning, they brought an Indian who had been shot through the back with an arrow many moons earlier. The arrow was still in him. The Indian was in much pain. Would Pepok Pela bless him and make the pain go away?

Cabeza de Vaca touched the man. He felt the point. It had pierced the cartilage and was laying next to his heart.

"I don't think we should pray over that one, Marsh," Estevanico said. "Better get out your knife and go to work."

"We can't be cutting into these *nativos*," Dorantes objected. "What if he dies?"

Cabeza de Vaca looked at the swollen skin. His thoughts drifted back twenty-five years to when he was a young man and had joined the army of King Fernando. He was sent to fight the French in north central Italy, in Bologna, Ferrara, and Revenna, where twenty thousand men had died. Fernando had waited much too long before pulling the Spaniards out. Hundreds had fallen at Cabeza de Vaca's feet with head injuries, crushed arms, spear-torn sides. How many times had he stooped to plug a gushing wound, sew torn skin with a needle and thread? Was this *nativo* any different? Why shouldn't he remove the arrow point, help the man as he had helped so many others? Perhaps Estevanico was right. He should take up a knife, do the same here as he had done so many times in Revenna, then commend the man to the hands of God our Lord.

He looked to the heavens and prayed silently. But out of the corner of his eye, he saw Castillo back away into the shadows. He took up a flint knife, the sharpest he could find, then placed a stick in the wounded man's mouth. The man spit it out. *Nativos* didn't seem to feel pain like ordinary men. But were these heathens ordinary men? It was said that since they knew not God our Lord, they were little more than animals. Yet Cabeza de Vaca had seen a look of compassion in their eyes that he'd never seen in any animal. These were men all right, but men who had never met with the power of the Holy Spirit. He glanced toward the shadows where Castillo stood. The young captain had also not met that power.

Cabeza de Vaca spent the better part of the morning cutting through the *nativo's* chest, slowly picking out the flint point. Then, he sewed him back up with a deerbone needle. Dorantes' face had grimaced a hundred times, but the *nativo* never flinched once. He just stared into the leaves overhead.

The villagers who had watched him asked for the arrow point, then raced off shouting a new proclamation: The Children of the Sun are more than great shamans. They are gods who go inside your body, fix it, then put it back together. You must give them everything you own. If you hide anything, they will know it, and they will cause you to die instantly, just by thinking about it. The Sun, the giver of life and everlasting mystery, tells them everything.

Estevanico had never been a god before. He liked the idea, him touching people, muttering things like, "This one's all yours, Allah. He's too gone for me to do much with," then making the cross sign like Dorantes had showed him, sometimes saying the other thing: "Hell, Mary. Full of grass. The Lord is with you." Then the sick man jumping up, letting out a shout, going and bringing Estevanico some rabbit stew, or a new bow, lending Estevanico his wife for a few nights and her being so anxious to please, him being a fertility god and all. This God business wasn't bad at all. Of course it had its downside, him having to touch so many people every morning before he could even pee, staying up half the night blessing food when he could be in his lodge wham-bamming his princesses. And the walking? He was going to have to get him one of those thrones, sit up on a couple of poles, a princess on each side of him, couple more on the ground fanning him with them big palm leaves. He wondered where he could get palm leaves out on the prairie.

By the time the Children of the Sun had journeyed west by north, re-crossed the river and entered a great plain that turned out to be thirty leagues wide, over three thousand Indians had joined the procession. For leagues behind the Spaniards, they followed in family groups and clan platoons, leaving behind their arguments, their border-battle grudges, their gathering-ground claim disputes to accept new responsibilities: dig worms, collect spiders, club

166

hares that leaped by the hundreds across the plain, snare quail, shoot deer in the nearby hills, collect and carry water and portable mat houses, bring it all to the Children of the Sun to be blessed—every day. No one would dare eat a thing until everything had been blessed by the gods, even if it took half the night—every night.

Estevanico pranced at the head of the pack. He was always in constant conversation with the multitude of women that circled him, served him food—no worms, *gracias*, just boiled rabbit, *gracias*—and serviced him all night in one of his four big lodges.

He had even come to respect the *nativo* men. He admired them in a wild sort of way. They were hardy, free, could look you right in the eye and tell you the biggest lie in the world without a smack of a clue that you were being duped. He liked that. Besides, they had high repute for boogers, witches, and *fantasmas*, just like the low people in Azamor, where Estevanico had lived as a child.

Estevanico wore a long string of eagle feathers that spilled from his great mass of hair—which Dorantes kept telling him looked like a pack rat's nest—to the ground, colorful beads around his arms and ankles, mica chips glued to his cheeks, the two gourds and copper rattle tied around his waist. The women had painted his face and belly with white dye. He felt like one of the *nativos* himself—the chief *nativo*, actually.

The procession continued across an arid, sandy wasteland where there was no game. Many Indians turned back to avoid starvation. Cabeza de Vaca gave a huge load of gifts to the principal men to distribute to those departing, and blessed them before they left.

Learning that the great plain continued north forever and that the cows had not come this far south for three seasons, the team turned south. They forded a chest-deep river, then crossed a shrub savanna of tall, dry grasses. They came to a mountainous region of slanted plateaus and lofty peaks covered with juniper and oak and open ranges of yucca, greasewood, and sagebrush. During the day they dragged through torrid passes of gray-white sand flanked by wine-red mesas. At night they slept in their portable houses beneath craggy cliffs where coyotes howled and mountain lions cried.

One afternoon, coming off the mountain, Estevanico decided to tell Dorantes a secret he'd been keeping.

"You never kept secrets from me before."

"It's not really a secret. It's just this thing."

"This thing?"

"I was talking to my princesses. . . my servants. . . one night while I was resting, waitin' for my breech snake to wake up—"

"One day your breech snake is going to fall off your body from depleted exertion."

"Andrés, you know I don't do none of that *deviated insertion* stuff."

"Go on with your story."

"Like I was saying, I was telling them how one day when I become a mortal, I'm going to be a conquistador and have a great adventure, conquer golden cities and all. They said I needed to have a vision quest first. I said what's that, and they said I had to go into the woods alone and I would find out."

"Is that when you disappeared for three days?"

"I was on a vision quest, Andrés."

"Did you receive a vision?"

"Well, sort of. I was in these woods in the mountains and it got real dark, so I looked for a place to sleep. I thought some animal might eat me if I slept on the ground. I looked up and saw this limb with a fork and I said to myself, now that would be a good place for Estevanico to sleep. So I climbed up the tree But when I got out on the limb, there was already someone in the fork—a bobcat. He hissed and snarled and leaped on me, slapped me like he was making chopped liver. Then the limb broke and we hit the ground. I took off running, the bobcat right on my tail. My foot went into one of them suck-holes in the ground and I went to tumbling. I rolled off the side of this cliff-like thing, bumped my head against a rock, and fell down into a ravine so thick with briars that it felt like an ocean of glass. I couldn't see how I was going to get out, and I couldn't see how any bobcat was going to get in. My head felt like a herd of horses'd been dancing on it, so I just curled up and went to sleep. That's when it happened."

"That's when what happened?"

"There was this old owl over my head, and she made this funny sound, like she was talking to me. Then I saw a vision. Me and three hundred copper-skinned princesses, they naked as a skinned snake except for little bells on their toes. Me with my big shiny moron hat on my head, solid gold rod in my hand, and this really great adventure about to be dumped on my lot."

"Then what?"

"That's it. Sun came up and I didn't see anything else. So I got up and started figuring a way to get out of the briars."

"Did you tell your princesses?"

"I told them, all except the part about the suck hole and me falling and all. Didn't seem right that a god should fall in a bunch of briars. I told them I had to fight a bobcat."

The mountain trail turned and broadened. The precession continued on. Then. . .

"Would you look at that," Dorantes said.

Below them was a river flanked by multistory adobe houses set in cliffs. Fields of pumpkin, beans, and calabash lay beside the houses.

The procession had dwindled down to a few hundred, and these started to grumble and complain. They were in the land of an enemy. The river, they told the four men, was the Grand River, and it ran forever in both directions. The people were the Jumanos.

"These are the first permanent houses we've seen since we left Apalachee," Cabeza de Vaca said. "And these people actually plant."

The Indians refused to go a step farther. The Jumanos would kill them if they went down into the river valley.

"Give them the rest of the gifts," Cabeza de Vaca told Dorantes. "Tell them to keep the faith, and we'll come back to see them some day."

Estevanico said goodbye to all his princesses. He gave each a hug and a little feel to get him through whatever it was his three companions were going to drag him through.

The Indians wailed and cried, took the gifts, and turned east. The four men and a few guides who agreed to go with them headed down into the valley.

The town looked deserted of men. They were met by women. The women did not speak but led the four into a large house whose walls, to Estevanico, looked like a hairy animal, long strands of straw hanging from clay.

As their eyes adjusted to the cool darkness, they saw the village men kneeling four and five deep, their heads hung low, long hair pulled over their faces.

"Allah get gone," Estevanico said. "So this is where everybody's hiding. They know who we are, too. See, they piled all their stuff out in the middle of the floor. I'll do the honors." He strutted up to the pile.

Estevanico made some noises, shook his rattle, rattled his gourds, moved a few things around, said, "Bless all this stuff," then clapped his hands to get the Indians attention. Slowly, each sat up. Estevanico moved through the crowd. He touched every man. This god business was easy, best job he'd ever had. And look at all the stuff he was getting.

The Jumanos gave them beans, squash, and corn. Castillo looked at the food. Finally, something civil.

Castillo and Estevanico watched as a woman pulled hot rocks from the fire and dropped them into a calabash of water. The water boiled. She added vegetables, then held up a skinned and gutted animal and said "*kawa*"—rat. She threw the rat into the boiling water and said "*ko*" and made chewing motions with her mouth. She smiled and showed a mouthful of rotted teeth, then she spit into the soup.

"Ask her where she gets the maize," Castillo said. "I do not see any in the fields."

Estevanico signed and spoke to the woman. Castillo shook his head. Estevanico always seemed to know every language even before he got to a village. It was as if he were one of them.

"*Aki*," the woman said. She pointed and spoke further.

"She says it comes from upriver where there are richer towns with lots of maize and hides, cotton things and a fruit called *chacan*. She says they haven't had any rain here for a long time and can no longer grow maize. She says why don't the Children of the Sun make it rain?"

A voice came from behind them. "Tell the woman Alonzo del Castillo, the great healer of the Capoques, will be happy to pray for rain."

Castillo jerked his head around. It was Cabeza de Vaca. What was he saying? The marshal was surrounded by the principal men of the town.

"After all. Castillo was the first Child of the Sun, the first to bring God into our presence."

Estevanico did as Cabeza de Vaca told him. The Indians yelped and ran off to prepare for the ceremony.

That night, there was a feast and a celebration. Castillo didn't like the predicament Cabeza de Vaca had placed him in. He struggled with the request but eventually decided that if a Moor could pray and lay on hands while copulating with half the women in the country and not get struck down by lightning, why shouldn't he at least go through the motions?

He came to the fire and stood in the circle of Jumanos. He paused quietly. He thought about Gutenberg's Bible, tried to remember a rain story. Then it happened again, a passage uttered by the prophet Samuel, about Elijah, flashed in his mind. Castillo raised his hands and said, "Now, therefore, stand and see this great thing which the Lord God Almighty will do before your eyes."

The words sounded strongly presumptuous to Castillo, but he uttered them just as he had memorized them. Then he knelt as Elijah had done on Mount Carmel. He placed his head between his knees and waited.

But it did not rain.

He rose and walked out of the circle. What else could he do? He had played their little game, once again but the game was over. Now what?

171

As he passed Cabeza de Vaca, he heard the marshal say, "It did not rain right away for Elijah, either. You must tarry as he did. Tarry and keep the faith, Captain."

That night Castillo was restless. He tossed on his fur skin. Had he mocked God? You can fake healing from sickness, but how can you fake rain? Then, how can you fake rising from the dead? That man *was* dead. Now he's alive. That shocking moment would not leave him.

Just before dawn, it rained.

By the time Castillo joined the others back at the circle, it was pouring. The Jumanos danced in the mud, leaped at the thunder, shouted *ka, ka*—hear, hear.

Cabeza de Vaca smiled. "Your faith has given them rain, Captain. Now, they can plant their fields."

Castillo just shook his head. How could this be?

The four stayed with the Jumanos a week. Then they went upriver. They lived off of the deer tallow and powdered straw that was given to them by the Indians of the adobe towns through which they passed.

After seventeen days of travel, Castillo stopped.

"The villages we meet are not getting any more civil. We must make a decision. We can turn north where the Jumanos say are rich cities with multistory houses. Or we can turn west and follow the sun across the barren desert where the Jumanos say not even a bird flies.

No one spoke. Apparently they were waiting for Castillo to make the decision as he had for the past several weeks.

Finally, Castillo turned and stared at Cabeza de Vaca. "I leave the decision to the Provost Marshal. He is the one in charge of this expedition."

Cabeza de Vaca returned the stare, then looked north across the rising green terrain, then west across the barren desert. He spoke resolutely.

"West. We will follow the sun across the desert to the South Sea, then turn south, the way to New Spain. After all, we are the Children of the Sun."

MEXICO

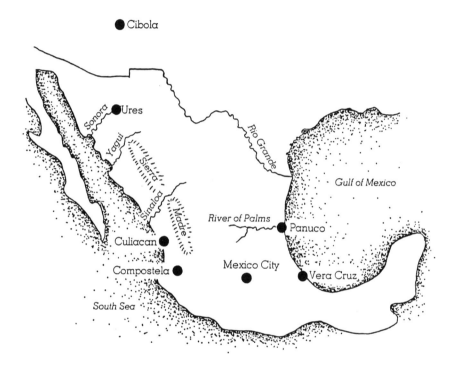

So we went on our way and traversed the whole country to the South Sea, and our resolution was not shaken by the fear of great starvation, which the Indians said we should suffer. . .

—The Account of Cabeza de Vaca

12

Christmas, 1535
Compostela, Mexico

Nuño Beltram de Guzmán was incensed. He stood at his second
floor balcony looking down on the festivities in the street below. He
was a large man with broad shoulders, his athletic frame covered by
a *sayo*—a jerkin whose bulging top hid his padded doublet. His
head sat in a slashed-band collar that puffed up under his square
jaw.

The skirt of the *sayo* was full and hung to his knees in
multicolored folds of triangular gores. On his legs and feet, he wore
purple knit hose held snug by a wide ribbon with tassels tied above
the shin and a pair of buskins made of special order sheepskin. He
chewed on the end of a Havana cigar. He spat. The murky brown
sputum landed half in the street, half on the first and only
wrought-iron rail in Compostela. He turned to face the squat
captain standing in the archway behind him.

"*Madre de Dios!* Where do you think the brown-asses went
off to, *capitán?*" he said.

"I do not know, *señor*. But I tell you the villages are empty.
They left their crops, everything. Vanished, just like that." The man
snapped his fingers.

Guzmán stared at the fat little captain. If he pushed him
over, he swore he'd be taller lying sideways. The captain was Diego
de Alcaráz. He wore a *carmeñola* skull cap on top of his perfectly
round head, with a slit in the front held together with agleted

175

rawhide that lay against his forehead making his eyes appear crossed. His rotund body was clothed in doublet and hose laced at the hem. Bridging the gap between the upper sections of the hose was an enormous cod piece held stiff by some unknown object. The whole effect made Alcaráz look like a giant engorged tick with a huge erection that wavered when he walked.

"Then you must sail farther up the coast, captain. And you must do it tonight."

"But *señor* Governor, what good would it do? The Indians are not there. Besides, the celebration of our Lord has begun and the men are tired. They need rest, refreshment, a few nights with the *putas.*"

"*Que lástima*—what a pity," Guzmán replied.

The fat little captain still called him Governor. Even though his title had been stripped from him two years ago, Guzmán still wielded power. However, time was running out for him. The new viceroy had arrived in Mexico City, and there were sure to be investigations about his slave hunting. And his archenemy Hernán Cortés had returned. This time, he claimed to have discovered a long peninsula jutting down into the South Sea from the land of Cíbola.

The Seven Cities of Cíbola. The thought pinched Guzman's mind.

Had that been when his troubles began, leaving the country unattended to chase after a myth? He turned back to the wrought iron rail. He wiped the sputum with his hand, dragged his hand over his *sayo.* He remembered when he was the supreme power in New Spain. . . only nine years ago.

He had been appointed governor of Pánuco—that had cost him his *cojones*—and head of the *Audiencia*, a position that gave him absolute authority. His first job: ship Hernán Cortés back to Spain to answer questions about the chaotic situation in New Spain and charges of pilfering revenues from the crown. That was the year the new expedition had left San Lúcar for La Florida. What was that commander's name? Narváez? What a minceball. He guessed those poor *diablos* had all perished. At least that is what Narváez' seamen had said when his ships arrived in New Spain after

176

sailing the coast for nearly a year trying to find him and his 300 *soldados*.

That was also the year his Indian slave Tejo told him that when he was a little boy, he had accompanied his trader father far to the north and had seen seven large cities as big as Mexico City and that the streets were filled with gold and silver.

Gusman had immediately assembled an army of thousands, including Spanish soldiers, Aztecs, and Tlascaltecs, and set out in search of the Seven Cities of Cíbola. He built a chapel at Tonalá and founded the towns of Santiago de Compostela and San Miguel Culiacán, but he never found the Seven Cities.

When he returned to Mexico City, he learned that Cortés had returned from Toledo with a new title: *Marqués del Valle de Oaxaca*, and that Cortés was mad as a kicked dog that Guzmán had confiscated some of his properties and accused him of killing his first wife Catalina. And close in Cortés' shadow came a new *Audiencia*, who ousted Guzmán and delivered a royal decree forbidding slavery.

The search for the Seven Cities of Cíbola had cost him plenty.

Guzmán got around the decree by issuing a directive stating that any Indian considered hostile or a threat to the colony could be taken into slavery. This allowed him and his *amigo íntimos* to continue slave hunting. He sold thousands of Indians to the mine operators and *encomenderos* of the Indies, until the king, responding to pressure from the new *Audiencia* and high officers of the church, stripped him of his governorship.

He turned back to Alcaráz. "There is a rumor in the street that a *licentiado*, Diego Perez de la Torre, has been appointed *Juez de residencia* to conduct a rigid investigation of my affairs with respect to slave hunting. He is due to arrive in March. This may be our last raid; it must be a big one. Big enough to afford us a *finca grande* somewhere in Cuba or near Santo Domingo where we can raise tobacco or cane." He thought he saw Alcaráz flinch. He did see him reach down and squeeze the contents of his elongated codpiece. "I hope that is not my Christmas present, *capitan*. I was given one just like it two years ago."

"Oh no, *señor*. It is only a rolled parchment."

"Then you will assemble the men and sail at first light?" He knew Alcaráz would. The captain was in too deep. Besides, he hadn't an *amigo* in the world. All of Guzmán's partners and attendants had deserted when the new *Audiencia* arrived—all except Alcaráz."

"*Sí, señor*." At first light."

"And *capitan*, I suggest you not stop at Culiacán. The vice-governor is there. It is best that he not know of our little business. Sail on to the Sinaloa, then take the horses north beyond the Yagui."

"But *señor*, the Yagui is flooded this time of year."

Guzmán ignored him. "Find those brown-asses, *capitan*. Flush them out of hiding. This mission must not fail, or we are *carne picado*—chopped meat, if you know what I mean."

The river was flooded. The four survivors could not cross.

There wasn't any way Estevanico was going to perch up on Dorantes' shoulders across that muddy sluice. He lay at their camp on a cotton blanket given to him by the Indians at Ures, his body much leaner than it was when he'd left Spain eight years ago, but hard and taut. He watched the horde of Indian followers standing by the river, facing the rising sun, catching the sunlight with their hands, rubbing it over their bodies. Maybe he'd get some of his copper princesses to rub some of them rays all over him. No, too early to play hide the sausage. He'd better rub himself. He rose, went and stood with the Indians, raised his hands, and rubbed sunlight on his body. His mind drifted back to the events of the past several weeks.

With the Jumanos as guides, they had left the grand river and traveled a hundred leagues across a land so barren they had had to eat powdered straw to survive. And you could forget about eating dogs. Those hairy little round-heads on the desert were so small they had less meat than a canary. The four continued across rusty mesas with big yellow cones sticking up and wide valleys of sage and cactus. Their mouths were drawn alum-tight, and buzzards circled around over their heads.

Then they came to a mountain, whose distant snow-capped peaks reminded Estevanico of the snow-fingers on the high sierra. How he had wished he was in Granada, sitting on the old caliph's knee, listening to tales of high adventure —General Tariq attacking King Roderic in Andalucia, Boabdil spilling the guts of the Abencerrages all over the fountains at the Alhambra. He wondered if he would ever find the great adventure the old caliph had told him about. He wondered if maybe Allah, instead of smiling upon him, had thrown up on him.

From the mountain, they dropped down into a river valley. The Jumanos and the Powdered-straw People went ahead to the village of Ures to announce the customs associated with a visit from the Children of the Sun before collecting their gifts and returning home.

At Ures, Estevanico had seen more permanent houses, cotton shawls, gardens of pumpkin, beans, maize. The women there painted their faces like the Moors of Barbary, and the men got drunk off the juice of a great thistle they called *pitahayam*—of which Estevanico consumed heartily and made a two-day dancing spectacle of himself. He had seen mesquite bread and sun-dried melons and preserves made of saguaro cactus, great, long-haired sheep sporting huge horns high up on the crags, and poison-tipped arrows that would rot the flesh right off your body. He had also seen soap made of yucca root and beads made of coral from the South Sea, which the Indians said was a two-day journey, but that the way was sparse and barren and had only a few villages.

At Ures, the four survivors had blessed the Indians and eaten a mountain of deer hearts before leaving with an entourage of attendants and a new harem for Estevanico. Cabeza de Vaca said they should not travel west to the coast but south, between the mountain and the sea, the way to the Christians, to New Spain. Now, after several days travel, they were stopped by the flooded Yagui River.

Estevanico glanced at the Indians around him. He wondered why the women wore dresses that hung from their neck to the ground, while the men were all naked, except for the trinkets they stuck on their bodies. Estevanico had collected lots of trinkets

179

himself. He especially liked the five emerald arrow points the Ures Indians had given to Andrés. He strung them around his neck with some turquoise beads. The Indians said all that stuff had come from the north, where there was lots of gold and silver and seven big cities with houses stacked on top of other houses. Secretly, Estevanico had wanted to go north when they had turned south to cross the desert. The desire still churned within him—go north to the land of the seven cities, be a conquistador, conquer riches and beautiful princesses, fulfill the promise the old caliph had given him. More than anything else, he wanted to do something so great he would never be forgotten. But the good marsh had insisted they turn south. Estevanico had not argued. Who would listen to a Moor slave turned fertility god, anyway?

Estevanico stretched, yawned, his eyes searching left and right. Maybe he'd see a new bauble he could trade a blessing for.

That's when he saw it.

It was hanging around the neck of an Indian not twenty feet away. The shock of it caused Estevanico to freeze. He couldn't even speak. "Andrés," he finally breathed without moving his lips, his eyes still locked on the ornament. His feet slowly backed away. He turned and ran at full stride. "Andrés!" Louder now. "Andrés!" Until he ran headfirst into Castillo.

"Whoa, Estevanico. You still have time. The day has just begun."

"Time for what?"

"Whatever you're running for."

"Come with me." He pulled Castillo by his arm. "You got to see this."

He raced back to the river. He stopped. He pulled Castillo behind him.

"See? There." He whispered. He pointed with his nose to what hung around an Indian's neck. He didn't want to cause any waves at a sunrise worship service. It wasn't like he didn't have no respect for the sun. After all, it *was* his father, him being a Child of the Sun and all.

"Dios mío!" Castillo said. "That's a buckle from a sword belt, and it has a horseshoe nail tied to it. Spaniards must be in the area. Run, bring the provost marshal."

When Cabeza de Vaca and Dorantes arrived, the marshal voiced caution. He knew the Indians as well as the others. "We can't ask him where he got it outright, he'll lie or make something up, thinking he has in some way insulted us or broken a custom and drawn our attention. To maintain our authority over the Indians, we must continue to carry ourselves with utmost gravity, speaking only rarely."

"But how can we ask him without breaking our code of quiet?" Dorantes said.

All heads turned to Estevanico. There was one of the four who had no code of quiet. Had no codes at all, for that matter.

"No hay problema," Estevanico said.

He went and stood by the Indian, caught a few sunrays, rubbed them on his chest and arms, then with perfect nonchalance signed, 'Where did you get your neck piece?'

'It came from the sky.'

Now they were getting somewhere. A sky god had dropped it in his lap when he was out on the trail. Estevanico tried again.

'Who brought it from the sky?'

'Men with beards, like those.' The Indian pointed to the three Spaniards. 'They come to river, ride big animals. They bring spears, shiny knives. They kill two of us.'

Estevanico's three companions moved closer. Their eyes were wide with excitement. They had seen what the Indian signed. When the Indian finished, the four men knew that Spaniards had been in the area but had left in big boats by the sea. They needed to hasten their journey; perhaps the Spaniards were still somewhere in the country. They were excited. It had been too long, too far, too many years without seeing a fellow countryman. They wanted to talk to a Christian.

Finding a wide, deep area upstream where the waters ran slow, they and the Indians crossed the river on logs and continued south through dense valleys and over rolling hills on the west shoulder of the mountain. They moved with much haste, now, staying in villages only long enough to ascertain that Spaniards were indeed in the country. Every day joy and anticipation grew. Then they began to see abandoned villages, burned crops and houses. The farther south they went, the fewer people they saw. Spaniards had been there, all right. The Indians were fleeing; most had already gone. Those who remained had no food. They ate bark and roots. They were near starvation. The four travelers again went through a time of great hunger. The Indians had nothing to give them. Why had this happened? Estevanico asked the marshall. The land is so rich and beautiful. Why burn it?

"Slave hunters," Cabeza de Vaca said.

The Indians told them the bearded ones raped the women, took them and the children and half the men, then burned their houses. Those who escaped had gathered at a secret place high in the mountains where the ascent was difficult. If the Children of the Sun would only come to the high place, all would be well again.

They went.

Cabeza de Vaca looked rankled. He muttered to Estevanico, "For civilized people to drive simple, peace-loving families from their homes, enslaving and killing them, is barbaric and certainly against the wishes and orders of His Imperial Majesty."

Estevanico nodded. Even though it wasn't *his* majesty, he wasn't about to prompt the marsh to a speech when he was on his high horse.

The mountain Indians welcomed them with open arms and gifts of shawls and backloads of maize, which the marshal gave to Estevanico to distribute among the starving Indians who had brought them.

Then he beckoned Estevanico to his side to be sure he was communicating well. He signed to the Indians, 'I will track down the bearded men and make them stop. Peace will return to your land. Soon you can return to your villages and replant your gardens.'

The Indians believed him. Runners were sent to those in the forests and low hills to come out of hiding. In two days the travelers were off the mountain with a procession of hundreds. The Indians said they would be safe as long as they were with the Children of the Sun.

They continued south. They saw hitching posts and camps where the slave hunters had been. They met Indian scouts, who said they had spied the Spaniards three days on. Everyone was tired. They needed to rest, make camp. But Cabeza de Vaca said he could not rest his fluttering heart. He took eleven Indians and Estevanico and continued on, even though Estevanico's heart wasn't fluttering at all.

In three days, they came upon them—hairy-faced, metal-clad, spur-jingling Spaniards on horseback at the far end of a trail.

"*Caballeros!*" the marshal yelled. Now, Estevanico's heart fluttered. The horsemen turned. The Indians cowered. Estevanico curled his fists behind his body. He and the good marsh hardly looked like civilized people: barefooted, in loincloths made of some weird hairy cow that lived up on the great plain, which they never found, the marsh as brown as the Indians, Estevanico with so much dye and decorations hanging on him he looked like one of those trees that Martin Luther fellow decorated every Christmas up in Alsace. Those *loco* Spaniards might just decide to hog-tie them real quick like, make another double slave out of Estevanico.

"*Caballeros! Gracias a Dios!* We have finally found you," Cabeza de Vaca shouted.

The horseman rode up to them. They circled them. They appeared totally confused at what they were looking at: a white-haired, bearded Indian speaking Castilian Spanish, a plumed and spangled *negro*, naked Indians clinging to them like they were ninny pups.

The provost marshal was in tears.

Captain Diego de Alcaráz was suspicious. Instead of slaves, his horsemen had brought to his river camp two of the strangest looking creatures he'd ever seen. He listened as the white-haired one explained.

"We offer thanks to God our Lord for having chosen to bring us out of captivity even so melancholy and wretched."

"Who'd you say you was with?" Alcaráz said. He shifted his big body from one cheek to the other on a camp stool that was hardly large enough to contain one of his cheeks.

"Pánfilo de Narváez. The governor of La Florida."

"Never heard of him. And there ain't no governor of La Florida." Only governor around here's Nuño Guzmán and they done kicked him out of office."

"It doesn't matter. Narváez died at sea."

"Oh, it was a ship you was on?"

"No, I tell you we have been on foot—eight years now."

Alcaráz studied him. He must be demented. The *loco hijo de puta* must've deserted the army eight years ago, took a slave with him, then got lost somewhere. And the *negro* ain't even talking, just looking. Must be a *mudo*, lost his tongue, thinks he's some kind of captain-general, all them medallions hanging on him. Alcaráz had better play it safe, act like he believed them till he got them back to Compostela, then arrest them, maybe even get a reward.

He noticed how the Indians were staying close to the two *lunáticos*, treating them like they was some kind of chief or something. Maybe the *lunáticos* could help him flush the Indians out of hiding.

"Say, *señor*," Alcaráz began. "We're kind of in a plight here, completely undone and all, y'know, *señor*. We're supposed to take some Indians back to the city, help build a new church, and seems like they took off, hiding out somewhere. To make matters worse, *ir de mal en peor*—we run out of rations. Maybe you might can help us a little."

"How is that, captain?"

Jesus, the man is dense. Alvaráz leaned forward. He spoke slowly. "We need Indians, *señor*. Indians and food."

The man seemed to understand this time. He rose. He dispatched fifty Indians and the *negro* to guide three of his horsemen into the wilderness.

Now, we're gettin' somewhere.

184

*   *   *

During the next five days, the white-haired man indulged himself in thanksgiving meditation. He spoke little to Alcaráz or his men. Then about midday, Alcaráz looked up and was caught in absolute surprise, utter *asombro*.

His horsemen had returned. They were followed by the *negro* and two other long-haired Spaniards in buffalo loincloths, and they, by a great gang of Indians carrying big pots of corn. Sweet Jesus. That was going to make one hell of a haul. He and Guzmán could buy the biggest *finca* in the Havana hills from the rewards they'd get from these *esclavos*.

Alcaráz' hungry men took the corn from the Indians and roasted it. Alcaráz musn't waste any time lettin' them Indians know he was in charge and that they were on their way to Compostela else, they'd soon feel the lead of an *arquebusier* in their belly. He signaled for his *sargento* to have the rest of the men circle the Indians and begin tethering them in chains.

"Hold it right there, *señor*." It was the white-haired one. "Those are free and peace-loving people, who have been farming these fertile lands since the dawn of time. They pose no threat to the Spanish colonies and have taken no belligerent measures other than to protect their homes."

Who the hell was this guy? Looking like some freak-o *mestizo*. Telling Alcaráz what he won't going to do. Alcaráz was the one with the lead balls, in more places than one. Those *lunáticos* didn't have *excremento*.

"I am Alvar Núñez Cabeza de Vaca, *alquacil mayor* and acting governor of La Florida, representative of Your Cesarean Catholic Majesty. And you, *señor*, are a *ladrón*, a common criminal. I insist, as these Spaniards are my witness, that you render a certified statement of the date—time, year, and day—when I met you, and also the condition in which I come. Further, I command you to stand fast or you and your men will soon find six hundred angry Indians sitting on your heads. You can't load those guns fast enough to stop them, Captain.

Que merda. This *hombre* meant business. He didn't sound demented now. Not with that big talk. If Alcaráz didn't know

185

better, he'd say his voice sounded almost regal. But his appearance. And the Indians watching him like they was just waitin' for the word. Maybe Alcaráz had better slack off a bit. Wait and see how things develop. Maybe try a different approach.

"Order your men to lay aside their weapons, Captain," the sheriff said. "These people come in peace."

Alcaráz thought for a minute. He was right. He couldn't shoot all them Indians if they all attacked at once. But he sure as Hell could shoot the high sheriff and that *negro* and them other two. Then the Indians would scatter, he'd run them down, shoot a couple to show he meant business, take the rest back to Compostella, coffled belly to butt all the way, strung out like a string of fish across two mountain ranges. Wouldn't Gusman drop a big one down in them fancy sheepskin boots of his when he saw all them Indians?

"*Pronto* Captain."

Alcaráz nodded to the *sargento* to obey the order.

The sheriff then turned to the Indians. He shouted to them while the *negro* signed an interpretation.

"Return to your villages. Replant your fields. There will be no more raping or killing or taking slaves. These men will return to their homes and never bother you again. You have my word on it." The Indians fell to their knees. They hid their faces with their hair.

Dios mio! Those Indians thought the sheriff was a god. He'd better fix that real quick like. Alcaráz stepped up. He called for his own interpreter and yelled to the Indians.

"This man's an impostor. He's not a god or a medicine man or whatever it is you think he is. He's just a mere Spaniard who got lost. He's got no supernatural powers and no legal authority here. You are stupid if you obey him. On the other hand, I am a most gracious servant of God." He raised his open hands to the sky. "It is God's will that you obey me and follow me to a land where there are great fields of maize and beans, where you will be given a house and food and never have to hunt again. Don't listen to this man. He's but a sick Spanish soldier made of flesh and blood. I have full authority in this land."

Alcaráz pulled the rolled parchment from his erect cod piece. The cloth flopped loosely back against his leg. He unrolled the parchment. It was the directive Guzman had issued five years earlier giving him permission to take as slaves all Indians he considered a threat to the colony. And he certainly considered naked savage who didn't worship the Lord God Almighty a threat.

The Indians looked at the sheriff, then at Alcaráz. One of them signed a reply. Alcaráz' interpreter backed away. He would not interpret what the Indian signed.

"What?" Alcaráz looked at him. He looked back at the Indians, back to the *negro*. "What did that Indian say?"

The *negro* stepped up.

"He said the Children of the Sun come from where the sun rises; you come from where the sun goes down. They heal the sick; you kill the well. They come naked and barefooted; you come in shiny clothes. They walk as we do; you ride big animals and carry fire sticks that destroy. They give gifts to the people; you burn our villages, steal our people. It is best that you get your moon ass on up the road"

Two days passed before Alcaráz figured it out. Now, he knew how he'd get rid of them naked-as-a-frog *lunáticos*. Then he'd be free to make the biggest grab of his life. Won't them Indians be surprised when they find out their gods just disappeared off the face of the earth. He snapped his fingers. He smiled. All he had to do was cooperate with them a little longer.

13

Culiacán, Mexico

"*Señores,* are you sure this is the way?" Dorantes yelled up to the three horsemen who rode in front of them. They had traveled through a dense forest without food or water for several days. Seven of the contingent of Indians accompanying them had died from lack of water. The others were weak, and the four travelers near total exhaustion.

"*Sí,*" the lead man said over his shoulder. The two beside him said nothing.

"He is lying," Estevanico whispered. He studied the backs of their heads. "We are going in circles. First the sun is over here, then it's over there."

"Marshal." Dorantes beckoned Cabeza de Vaca to his side. "Are you sure these men are honest?"

"Alcaráz seemed sincere when we left his camp. He told me that I was indeed right in my accusations and that he was only following the orders of Nuño Guzmán. He showed me the parchment of Guzmán's directive then offered his humble apologies. He said the *alcalde* Zebreros was a righteous man and would lead us to San Miguel Culiacán, their northernmost outpost. With all the Indians gone back to their villages, it seemed the best plan."

"We can't go much farther without water, *Señor* Zebreros," Dorantes yelled up to the horseman. "Are you sure you carry no water?"

"*Si,*" came the reply. The man kept riding.

Estevanico didn't like the three horsemen. He'd seen them drink from hidden containers. "He's lying again."

"Then we must stop awhile," Dorantes yelled. "These Indians were not the healthiest when we left camp. I fear we may lose more if we do not rest."

The horses stopped. The four travelers and the Indians fell by the way to catch their breath.

"We will search for water," Zebreros said. The horsemen nudged their horses. They started moving off into the forest.

"*Señor,* shouldn't you leave one of the horses in case you get lost?" Dorantes asked.

The horses kept moving.

"We will need a horse to find our way, *señor.*"

The horses and riders disappeared into the bush.

Estevanico and his three companions stared blankly after them until the last rustle and clank vanished from their ears.

"They won't come back," Estevanico said. His mouth was as dry as dirt.

"I can't believe I let them trick me," Cabeza de Vaca said. He look humiliated.

"They tricked us all, Marshal," Dorantes added.

The men sat quietly for a long time. Estevanico started figuring. After all the *mierda* they'd waded through, and after all the beatings by the *nativos* on the coast, they'd still managed to survive. Now, so close to real Spaniards, were they going to cock up their toes and expire right here in these dark woods? But water was such a thin thread of existence. Without it, they couldn't last more than a few days, and they'd already used up those days, even an extra one. He needed to get out of there, find a mud hole or something. There were no sweetwater sinks on the mountain slope. No flowing rivers or freshwater creeks like there were in the low flatlands east of the cactus prairie where he'd lived as a double slave for so long. And there'd be only salt water in the direction of the South Sea. He'd learned how deadly that could be when it was drunk.

He glanced around at the Indians. They were sick. They stared blankly into space. His companions were resting with their eyes closed, maybe holding back tears. Maybe even quietly dying, themselves. But Estevanico wasn't dying. He was stewing. Every moment he sat, another tendon or muscle jerked in readiness for the moment his mind would give the command. He was mad at what the horsemen had done to them. He knew his lean, hard body was trimmed tight and nowhere near ready to drop off the hook. There was something different about him, something special. That's what the old caliph had said. He was black, not white or copper. He was big, not small or medium-size like the others. He was a Moor, not a Spaniard or an Indian. Even out on the trail when he'd seen the Spaniards and the Indians get the leaping heebies—some dying from it—he'd felt a measure of strength and confidence still lying dormant within him. He'd been unlucky, all right, just like the rest of them. But he knew a secret, a magic trick the great Cristóbal Colón had told him long time ago on that dark wharf in Palos, and he heard those words echoing deep within him right then. "You can make luck change, little one." Estevanico knew it was time to do just that, to call upon that extra measure of strength lying dormant inside him. To make luck change.

He rose to his feet. He was surprised at his own quickness. His companions opened their eyes. They reached to steady him, apparently thinking he had gone mad.

"I'm going for water. I will be back before nightfall. Do not move from this spot."

He headed off into the bush in the direction the horsemen had gone. He left the Spaniards and the Indians gawking. He would not go uphill, there was no water at the top of a mountain. He would not go downhill, that would take him to the salty sea. He would go across the mountain, always in a gentle downhill direction. A stream, if there was one, would be at the meeting of two hills. If not, he wasn't sure what he'd do. As he hiked, he blazed the trail. He broke young saplings, left them bent in the direction of his companions. He made marks in the ground with his foot, arrows pointing back.

191

He began to see woody vines with star-like leaves hanging from the trees. He recognized them as ones the Indian medicine men used to cure stomach ailments. He knew the plant was full of water, and water ran downwards. He found two good-sized rocks and smashed one of the vines. He lay on the ground and held the bruised vine over his open mouth. The drip, drip, drip, of the slightly bitter juice falling under its own weight from such a great height wasn't the sweetest drink he'd ever had, but it partially quenched his burning throat and gave him stamina to move on, winding down into the dark woods.

"Get those horses saddled up!" Alcaráz was excited. It was time to move out. Zebreros would be in Culiacán, now, counting his gold coins. The four *lunáticos* and the sick Indians would be lying in the woods somewhere waiting to die—if they won't dead already—and hundreds of Indians would be planting beans and corn back at their village, waiting to be coffled.

A page brought a stool and sat it by Alcaráz' horse. He helped the captain onto the stool, then up over the saddle onto the horse. The horse gave a snort at the weight dumped upon him. The two aglets bounced against Alcaráz' round forehead. He adjusted his codpiece—now re-stuffed with the rolled parchment—to point straight up, then kicked his horse.

"When we get to the first village, I want you to fan out and surround them," he ordered. "I don't want a single one of them to escape. First thing I want to see is three dead Indians laying on the ground. Show them we mean business. Then we slowly move in, chain them, then move on to the next village. And keep that little *pene* in your breech hose. We don't have time for no bone dancin' this trip.

Melchior Díaz, captain and vice-governor of the province, sat in a straight-backed oak chair in his headquarters at Anhacán, adjacent to Culiacán. He listened to Zebreros' story.

Díaz was a plain man with simple features. He had not been born a gentleman. But because he was honest and merciful, he had won his position out of merit. His doublet and trunk hose were overlaid with a pale blue *sayo*, whose skirt struck him mid-thigh. He might easily be mistaken for a common soldier if not for the raven black bonnet he wore on his head. The bonnet carried the sword-cross of Santiago, trademark of a master *bonetero* from Toledo. Because Toldeo wool was shorn from only live sheep and the reverse sides of Toledo bonnets dyed red, a sign of good health, Toledan *boneteros* boasted the finest bonnets in all the world. Díaz' bonnet was adorned with a tall, white ostrich plume.

"That is incredible," he replied. "From the Narváez expedition, you say? I remember when they left Spain. I thought they had all perished."

"*Señor*, I am afraid if we do not hurry, the last four survivors will be gone also."

"Tell me, *alcalde*, how did they come to be in this predicament?"

Zebreros looked down. He spoke softly. "Alcaráz ordered me to abandon them in the barren land. I didn't want to do it, *señor*. But he threatened me with certain, ah, information he has about me. Embarrassing information, *señor*."

"You mean he paid you handsomely?"

Zebreros leaped to his feet. He slammed the small bag of coins into the wall across the room. "It is devil-money, *señor!*" he said. "I beg your forgiveness. Alcaráz and Guzmán are the last of *los bandidos*. I will never again ride with them on a slave hunt. If you will only forgive me for this action."

Díaz had suspected that Guzmán was somewhere behind this escapade. It had been difficult to comply with the law and be vice-governor to a man like Guzmán. Díaz hated slavery, not only because it was illegal, but for humane reasons. And he hated the directive Guzmán had issued that gave a free hand to his captains to hunt slaves. His own predecessor at Culiacán, Diego Fernándo de Proano, had been tried and found guilty for branding and selling Indian slaves. Díaz would never participate in such inhuman activities.

He also knew that it was just a matter of time before Guzmán would fall, for the *juez de residencia* had finally arrived in Mexico City and was at that very moment discussing the activities of Nuño Guzmán with the new viceroy. And if Díaz could convince the Narváez expedition officers—provided they were still alive—to apprise the viceroy of Guzmán's actions against them, the ex-governor would finally be tried and banished.

"Can you take me to them, right now?" Díaz said.

"*Sí, señor.* They are not more than three leagues from here."

When Díaz and his entourage arrived at the Sinaloa River at a known Indian camp, he was surprised to find the three Spanish officers and the *negro* there, fed and resting. He leaped from his horse. He hugged the men and wept with them.

"We thought you were all long dead, *señores,*" he said. "The ten women who came with your ships said a Gypsy seer predicted that all on the expedition would die a horrible death. Then when you did not arrive for years. . .

"If it hadn't been for Estevanico here, we *would* be dead," Cabeza de Vaca replied. "He found these *nativos,* then led them to us."

The *negro* said, "I am supremely at your service, *señor* vice-governor." He bowed low and long until Captain Dorantes nudged him.

"Actually, I am legally governor until another is appointed, but Guzmán refuses to step down."

The men settled down by the river's edge and shared stories. Then Díaz asked, "I know you are anxious to move on to Mexico City, *señor,* but I would be most appreciative if you would remain with me in Culiacán long enough to see that the Indians are indeed settled back into their villages and that the slave hunting has ceased."

"It would be our pleasure, *señor,*" Cabeza de Vaca said.

"And one other thing, *señor.* A viceroy has been appointed to Mexico City, a shrewd and sagacious young man named Don Antonio de Mendosa. He has the power to arrest Nuño de Guzmán and put an end to the merciless activities of Alcaráz. If you would perhaps tell him what you have seen in the wilderness. This Guzmán is an *hombre malvado,* wicked and evil to his core. Once he hanged several Indians for not sweeping the street in front of him when he came to their village. He is brutal and arrogant. A *caballero* named Francisco Vásquez de Coronado arrived in Mexico City with Mendosa, and it is believed that he will replace Guzmán once Guzmán has been deposed. But so far, no one has been able to make him sit down and shut up. *Ay de mí*, what a brute. If you would be of assistance—"

"Is there a notary in Culiacán who can give me a certified *testimonio* of Guzmán's directive authorizing his captains to take slaves they consider a threat to new Spain?"

"*Sí*, that can be arranged."

"Then I will help you oust this *engañador*."

In Anhacán, Cabeza de Vaca and his three companions devised a plan. Estevanico and two of the Indians—ones who had been with them and knew of their healing powers—were sent to tell the hundreds of Indians in the area to meet them at Culiacán for a great council. Estevanico took the magic gourds with him to show his authority.

A week passed and no one had come. Suddenly—

"It's them!" Dorantes pointed. Estevanico, the two Indian guides, and three other Indians came across the town plaza. No one else was with them. The headmen presented gifts of turquoise, feathers, and beads to Cabeza de Vaca.

"Marshal," Estevanico began. "These are headmen from three villages. They wish me to tell you that they have heard the stories and know the power of the Children of the Sun, but they do not trust the Spaniards. At this very moment, Alcaráz and his men are rounding up their people, locking them in chains. Several have been killed in the raids. These three are taking a big chance in coming here alone, but they need to know the truth. They want to hear it from the *señor* vice-governor here."

Díaz stomped in circles. "I can't believe he continues after all this."

Cabeza de Vaca found anger rising in him also, but he decided to let the vice-governor take charge; he would act more as an advisor or assistant.

"Tell them to go tell Alcaráz that the four men he tried to kill are alive here in Culiacán and are on their way to Mexico City to testify against Guzmán. Tell him to halt all activities, release the people he has captured, and return to Culiacán immediately. Then tell the Indians that the Children of the Sun do not lie. If they will come to our council fires, the Children of the Sun will tell them how they can live in their villages without any Spaniard ever bothering them again."

Estevanico signed the message and the headmen left. Within a matter of days, Indians began pouring into Culiacán. Small fires burned all around the town. Díaz sent gifts to the camps. Then when the time was right, the headmen and leaders came to the central fire. Cabeza de Vaca nodded for Díaz to speak first.

"I swear before the great God in the sky that neither I nor anyone from this town will ever invade your villages again. None of you will be enslaved. This man you call Pepok Pela is an honest man, a man who has traveled about your country for many winters telling people about the great God in the sky. If you listen to him now, believe in him and do as he says, you will have peace in your land." Díaz stepped aside. Estevanico remained to continue signing, for he had always been the best at it.

Cabeza de Vaca had waited a long time for this opportunity. Before, while he was considered to be a god and regarded so highly, he never felt like he had control of things. He believed his mastership was tenuous and that he, like the others, had to obey those customs and terms or they would topple from grace. Now, he had the authority of the Spanish guns behind him. And the hundreds of Indians who had gathered were far less belligerent and more family oriented than the previous ones. These Indians were simple farmers, who treated their wives with respect. They would listen and obey what he had to say, for the sake of their families. He began.

"It is true that the Spaniards have enslaved you, but only because you are not Christians. Your fathers have taught you to worship a man in the sky you call *Aguar*. You pray to him for health and for water for your fields. You believe *Aguar* created the world and everything in it. This being is the same as the one we call

Dios. If you will call him by the name *Dios* and build a church in each village and place a cross at the entrance, and whenever a Spaniard comes, greet him with a cross instead of a bow, the Christians will look upon you as brethren and treat you well. They will be your friends and not harm you. If you do not do this, they will overrun your land, if not these before you, then those who will surely follow."

The Indians bowed to Cabeza de Vaca and said they believed him and would do as he said. Cabeza de Vaca lowered his head and uttered a prayer. "May God in His infinite mercy grant that in this day of Your Majesty and under His power and sway, these people will become, willingly and sincerely, subjects of the true Lord who created and redeemed them." Then he looked up to Díaz and his three companions. "Now, on to Mexico City and this Nuño de Guzmán matter."

14

Mexico City

It was a clear morning in May when the four travelers rode out of Culiacán accompanied by twenty mounted soldiers, six Christian civilians, and several hundred Indians. Alcaráz had returned, and in a most apologetic manner reported that the Indians had gone back to their villages and were building churches, planting gardens, and showed no fear of him. Díaz had sent a message by post and pouch to Mexico City that four of the Narváez expedition survivors were on their way.

Castillo again took the lead. He felt redeemed of any misgivings or wrongful thoughts he may have had in the last months—years even. He still didn't know if the rain at the Jumano village was coincidental or God ordained, and he wasn't asking. He quietly accepted it as a message from God Almighty that Alonzo del Castillo was on the right path. Not only had he been spared while hundreds had died—some a frightful death—but he had all his wits about him and his confidence had returned.

But something was wrong with Cabeza de Vaca. Castillo could sense it. The marshal appeared weary, forlorn. Something was dragging him down. He never spoke of Jerez or his family during his eight-year journey, but now he had begun to speak of home. Could it be that he was taking responsibility for their recent brush with death, indeed, the entire eight-year brush with starvation? Castillo must make an effort to show the marshal the support and respect he well deserved, show him that he was not to blame for anything except getting them out of the wilderness alive.

After more than a hundred leagues of travel, the party arrived at the two-story *residencia* of Nuño de Guzmán in *Compostela*. The street outside was littered with dung from chickens and pigs who foraged the city for scraps of food. Castillo stared at the animals. How long had it been since he'd seen such creatures? And wouldn't they make a wonderful staple food supply for the starving *nativos* he'd lived with along the coast? But his thoughts were quickly replaced by anger as he and his *compañeros* faced the broad-shouldered man in sheepskin boots who came through the arched doorway. This was the man responsible for them almost dying, not Cabeza de Vaca.

"*Bienvenidos, ciudadanos,*" the man said, his arms held wide as though he were hugging them all. "Come into my home; I have prepared a place for you. Your attendants will be taken care of."

Castillo held his tongue. He and his companions went inside where four *catres* were pushed against the wall, fluffy pillows and cotton blankets folded at the foot of each. Cabeza de Vaca appeared to be in deep thought, so Castillo introduced himself and the others. "And you are Nuño de Guzmán?"

"*Sí, señor.* And these are your beds. I have ordered clothes to be brought to replace your, uhh—" He stared at their nearly naked bodies. "*Está a su disposición*—my home is your home."

The man was fawning. Castillo wasn't going to get sucked into any sugar cane hospitality from this animal. He could hold back no longer. "*Señor,* you are responsible for the death of seven of our companions."

"Why, Captain. Surely you would not hold me responsible for the actions of an insubordinate officer operating illegally in the far reaches of my jurisdiction." Guzmán had apparently heard of their recent mishap.

"You *have* no jurisdiction, *señor* Guzmán. We are on our way to Mexico with a *testimonio* of your directive authorizing your captains to capture and sell Indians as slaves." He showed Guzmán the parchment.

200

Guzmán was visibly embarrassed, at a loss for words.

"I am sure the new viceroy and Cortés will be very interested in what we have to say," Castillo said.

At the mention of Cortés, Guzmán jerked his head around. He looked squint-eyed at Castillo. "Hernán Cortés is a whoreson. Did you know he took in a fourteen-year-old Indian girl as a mistress when he—"

"Now, just a minute, *señor*," Dorantes interrupted. "Cortés used the Indian girls given to him as a means to introduce Christianity to the heathens—a great improvement over the corruption imposed by the colonists of Columbus's day. The girl you speak of, Malinche of Tobasco, was one of the first to convert to Christianity. She even took a Christian name. You cannot elevate yourself by attempting to reduce those around you." Dorantes spoke out in defense of Estevanico's hero. It would be inappropriate for a slave to reprimand an ex-governor.

Guzmán looked into the stern faces of all four men. He obviously could not compete with men who had him dead to rights. "Your clothes will arrive soon," he said. "Dinner will be brought an hour after sundown." Then he stormed out.

After dinner, the four men tried to sleep on the cots, but the mattresses were too soft, the cotton blankets smelled of sweat, and the pillows crimped their necks.

Estevanico was the first to slip to the floor and stretch out on his cow-skin rug. Soon, the others followed.

At the first light they were up, trying to pull clothes over tough, callused skin that had not felt clothes in years. The snug-fitting hoses scratched their legs, the doublets and jerkins bound their arms, the boots pinched their feet. But they knew they could not ride into Mexico City half-naked.

The rest of the morning was spent trimming beards, shortening hair, getting used to the clothes. By noon, they were on the road again.

Guzmán had not returned, even to bid them farewell.

Along the road to Mexico City, another hundred leagues or more, Spanish families—*peninsulares, criollos*, mulattos, mestizos, quadroons—who had heard of the miraculous survival of the explorers lined the road. Thousands met them and cheered. Many joined the entourage.

When they came within sight of Mexico City, Cabeza de Vaca asked the *sargento*, "What is today's date?

"It is Sunday, July 24, 1536, *señor*."

The four men raised their chins and made their way triumphantly toward the capital. They followed the long causeway from the east that passed over islands dotting Lake Texcoco, which surrounded the city. The causeway would lead them directly to the sacred precinct where the Aztecs once sought to please their gods with burnt offerings of hearts ripped from men's chests. It was now a great Christian center. They passed numerous *chinampas*—island gardens, dikes, aqueducts, and canals built by the Aztecs to transport their tributary goods.

They crossed broad plazas, now spacious market places flanked by razed adobe houses and temples sitting upon tall, limestone-stepped pyramids. Nothing in Spain, Portugal, or Morocco could match the magnificence of the city that just a few years ago was Tenochtitlán, the Aztec capital. But, thanks to Hernán Cortés, the city now belonged to Spain. Crowds waved flags and cheered as the heroes paraded along the wide street. Bells from the *campanario* of the first church in New Spain, built upon the site of the main Aztec temple, tolled across the city. It was the eve of the vespers of Santiago, the day Spanish colonies celebrated Spain's patron saint, James the Apostle. Tomorrow there would be celebrations all over the city, a bull fight, dancing. But today, it was as if the celebration had already begun. St. James had delivered the four shipwrecked men just as he had delivered Spain.

Emissaries of the Viceroy and the *Marqués del Valle* came out to greet them, welcome them home, take them to the housing quarters at the viceroy's palace, a scaled-down copy of the king's residence in Spain. The emissaries said the viceroy and the marquis would greet them formally tomorrow after vespers. There would be a *fiesta grande*. Tonight, they were to rest from their long journey. Tomorrow, they would attend the *corrida de toros*. Then the celebration. *Mañana. Buenas noches.*

Inside the palace quarters, Indian servants dressed in clean white linens and wearing crosses around their necks moved leisurely back and forth bringing clothes, figs, oranges, watermelons, roast lamb, and bread made from wheat—foods the four men had not tasted for a long time.

That night they were again restless. They were not used to such extravagance and comfort. One by one they removed their night shirts, slipped to the floor, and slept in the manner to which they were accustomed.

The following night was warm and thick. The frogs along the lake's edge croaked incessantly. The four men had been guests of honor at the bullfight, then spent the afternoon resting. Now, they were dressed and ready for the *fiesta grande*. They left their quarters and followed a walk to the main entrance of the palace. Their boots clunked noisily on the cobbles. Their clothes pinched at every bend of the body. Cabeza de Vaca had insisted that Estevanico be treated as an equal to the three officers, for without his magical fingers they would not even be there.

Cabeza de Vaca felt nervous. It had been a long time since he had attended a formal affair. And, as Spain had led the world in fashion, there would be sights, even customs, he'd soon see that would be totally unfamiliar to him. Plus, he had something on his mind.

Two *vigilantes* stood at the wrought iron gate, their halberds leaning against their shoulders reflecting the yellow of the gate lanterns.

Inside the *sala de espectáculos*—the great room—the big chandeliers had been lowered by their ropes and pulleys to just above the guests' heads. Thick candles along the edges guttered and spit wax to the painted canvas that stretched over the oak floor below. The room buzzed excitedly with conversation that was muffled by the folds of tall satin curtains.

Cabeza de Vaca stopped inside the double doors. He gawked at the gala scene before them. The younger women wore elaborate damask farthingales that flowed from their tiny waists like cathedral bells and veed in the front to reveal colorful petticoats. Their small breasts were accented by low-waisted, tight-fitting bodices with stiff, lace collars, puffed pickadil shoulders, and sleeves with wide cuffs and silk undersleeves.

The older women wore loose overgowns open down the front to show off their satin gowns, knotted sashes, and linen collars held aloft by wire frames. The old-fashioned gable hoods Cabeza de Vaca remembered were not to be seen. They had been replaced by flat-topped hoods that exposed the fronts of the *señoras'* center-parted hair.

The men were likewise in the latest fashion: daggers with long silk tassels strapped around knee-length jerkins, colorful capes with flattened collars that spilled to their shoulders, and velveteen-lined gloves held in their hands. Some of the men still wore their generously dimensioned gowns, which gave them an almost square silhouette.

A flamenco guitar strummed in a nearby corner. Suddenly, the guitar stopped. Eyes lifted, heads turned, and conversations ceased. For a moment no one moved. Everyone stared. Cabeza de Vaca looked at his companions. They were attired in poor fitting, unmatched clothing and boots of a less fashionable period. A regal-appearing man with high, dark bangs stepped out of the crowd, his long ermine-collared gown of rich brown brocade lined with silver cloth and slit from the floor to his knee, flowing majestically as he moved.

"*Saludos!*" he bellowed. He held up a *caliz* of wine. "*Los naufragios*—the shipwrecked men—have returned with stories of strange worlds."

"*Saludas!*" the crowd responded. *Los naufragios!*"

The man came forward. He was followed by two *hidalgos* and a courtly lady.

"I am Antonio de Mendosa, viceroy to New Spain."

Cabeza de Vaca introduced himself and his companions. The guitar picked up where it had left off and the buzz resumed, but this time with eyes cut toward the strange-looking men whose faces were scarred and brown from years of exposure.

Mendosa hugged each man then turned to introduce those behind him. "Francisco Vásquez de Coronado from Salamanca. Coronado arrived with me in Vera Cruz only months ago."

Coronado was less regally dressed than the others. He wore *calzas bragas*, old style breech-hose with holes at the thighs where his pale yellow hose were laced, the upper edge of the breeches covered by a matching yellow jerkin. He was barely in his twenties but appeared bright-eyed and ambitious.

"*Bienvenidos, señores.* I know your trials have been many."

"*Señor*," Castillo said. "Have I not been told that the first printing press to New Spain arrived on your ship?"

"*Si, señor*, but credit for its importation goes to the viceroy, not I. Soon, Mexico City will be mass producing its own books."

Castillo turned to the viceroy. "*Gracias, señor*, for bringing the stateliness of Spain to the colony. Will you be printing any Bibles?"

Mendosa smiled proudly. "I am sure we will, Captain."

"I long to hold a Bible in my hands once again." He turned back to the youngster. "*Señor* Coronado, we must speak of Salamanca."

Mendosa continued, "*Verdad.* And may I introduce *Señora* Cortés, daughter of the Count of Alguilar."

The lady stepped back and curtsied. The men bowed. Cabeza de Vaca noticed something familiar in her motion. She was the most elegant lady at the celebration. Her head was covered with a minute cap banded in gold, held down by a roundlet enriched with pearls and rose-colored stones to which was attached a braid-casing that spilled to the small of her back. Around her neck and shoulders and half-way down her breasts, she wore a *gorguera*—a partlet with delicate rows of embroidery and drawnwork so sheer you could see the milk white of her breasts. Her dress was a figured, crimson velvet *brial* with snug-fitting Gothic sleeves and a full skirt slit down the front to show the crimped forepart to which was attached tiny, velvet bows. Never had Cabeza de Vaca seen such courtly fashions. Her eyes were close set, and her nose was pointed, Her moves were those of Cabeza de Vaca's wife, whom he had left in Jerez de la Frontera so very long ago. He missed his wife immensely at that moment.

"And her husband," Mendosa continued, "the *Marqués del Valle*, conquistador of New Spain, Captain-General and owner of the entire valley of Oaxaca and the town of Cuernavaca—Hernán Cortés."

Cabeza de Vaca saw Estevanico's eyes brighten up. He and the two captains bowed to Cortés. The conquistador was slender but strongly built with broad shoulders. His fair complexion made him appear less vigorous than he was known to be. His black hair was wavy and cut square below his ears. He appeared more military than most of the men. His slightly bowed legs were covered by bulging upperstocks with gold braids lying over a puffed satin lining. A tight band just above the knee held rose-colored netherstocks. His elegant doublet matched the upperstocks. And around his waist hung a magnificent, filigree-handled sword and a large, gold medallion.

Cortés bowed back. "So what has become of my old friend, *señores?*"

Cabeza de Vaca knew Cortés was being facetious; He and Narváez had been bitter enemies, not friends. He did not like the conquistador's tone. "The governor is dead, *Señor* Cortés. Swept to sea on a leaky, horsehide boat in a midnight storm, after starving for six weeks. If he was lucky, he drowned. It not, he drifted until thirst and dehydration slowly choked the life out of him."

"I am sorry for asking, Marshal. I meant no harm."

"I've waited a long time to meet the great Hernán Cortés," Estevanico said. He stepped forward and bowed low. He waited for Dorantes to bump him.

"Not so great, anymore." Cortés said. "The year your men set sail for La Florida, I was called back to Spain. And I am sure this had nothing to do with Narváez' abrupt departure after such a long delay," he said parenthetically. He seemed to be sparring with Cabeza de Vaca, perhaps because the marshal was second in command under Narváez. "They stripped me of my governorship of New Spain, and when I returned with my new wife," he nodded to the elegant lady beside him, "Nuño Guzmán had interfered with my rights. Since then, my activities have been checked, and I fear my popularity has waned."

"How soon they forget how you killed Moctezuma and got all of those riches," Estevanico said.

"Moctezuma was stoned by his own people. I did not kill him. And greater riches have since been found by Francisco Pizarro when he choked the god-king Atahualpa of the Inca Empire in Peru."

"I have not heard such a story." Dorantes said. "Where is Peru?"

"In the mountains on the main, south of Vasco Balboa's isthmus. Pizarro landed there four years ago, when you and your governor were lost in the wilderness."

"*Our* governor was already dead, *señor*," Cabeza de Vaca said. Cortés's voice had something sharp in it, too impulsive. Dorantes had apparently not noticed but Cabeza de Vaca had, and he didn't like it. "Captain, why don't you and the *marqués* go get some refreshment. Take Estevanico with you. I am sure he has many questions about the *great* conquest. And Captain Castillo, perhaps you and *señor* Coronado would like to join them and talk of Salamanca. I have business to discuss with the viceroy."

"Don't pay Cortés any mind, marshal," Mendosa said when everyone had left. "*Verdad.* He is bitter for not being named viceroy of New Spain. But the fact is, the sovereign does not trust him. Once, when he controlled all of New Spain, he was an absolute ruler and came close to establishing an independent kingdom. At least that is what is rumored. Spain wishes no one to ever have that much power again. But that is history. Come, tell me of your adventure in the wilderness to the north." He led the marshal into the room, where they were swallowed up by the buzz. Cabeza de Vaca gave him a brief account of their trials without any exaggerations.

"That is an amazing story, Marshal. You must put it in writing in the form of a brief report as soon as possible, while the facts are fresh. Perhaps it should even be a joint report with input from your companions."

Cabeza de Vaca's eyes brightened. "That is it!" he exclaimed.

"That is what, *señor?*"

"That is why God our Lord preserved me. He wants me to write an account of everything I saw and heard in the years we wandered through those remote lands. Not merely a statement of positions and distance, animals and vegetation, but of the diverse customs of the many barbarous people I saw. Yes. An account of much exactness. And though some things may sound novel and difficult to believe, they will be credited as strictly faithful." He glanced up into the emptiness beyond the chandeliers and thought to himself: *La Relacion—The Account of Cabeza de Vaca.*

He turned back to the viceroy. "You shall have your joint report señor, but when I return to Spain, I will write a full account of our wanderings. But first I have a matter of utmost gravity to discuss with you." Finally, he was going to speak of what had been bothering him. For weeks his thoughts had been heavy with one overpowering thought. He knew he should be happy that their long journey had come to an end, but until this concern was resolved, his mind would not rest.

He told Mendosa of the activities of Guzmán and Alcaráz and of his desire for the welfare of the Indians, to which Mendosa replied. "I share your sympathies precisely, Marshal. Your report will be passed on to the *Juez de residencia*, who is at this moment at the Castillo de San Juan de Ulua collecting information about Guzmán's slave shipments. Surely, it is but a matter of time before Guzmán is extricated and his captain punished. I assure you I am committed to enforcing laws that free the Indians from slavery, prohibit forced labor, and administer the death penalty to anyone caught branding slaves."

That was what Cabeza de Vaca had wanted to hear. A heavy load was lifted from him. No one knew the Indians more intimately than he, and he considered them as human and as deserving of freedom as any man on earth. It was to this end that he had decided, somewhere along the way, to return to Spain and devote all of his energies for years to come.

"Now, tell me, Marshal. What are your plans for the immediate future, bearing in mind that nothing in the Indies occurs immediately?"

"Return to Spain and establish my status as governor of La Florida, now that Narváez is dead. Then—"

"Too late, marshal. Early this year, King Charles appointed Hernándo de Soto from Barcarrota *adelantado* of La Florida."

"What?"

"It is true. Thinking you were all dead, the Sovereign took this measure. Spain still seeks the riches of La Florida. De Soto was a conquistador with Pizarro when he conquered the Incas. He returned to Spain a very rich man. With his military experience and wherewithal to finance a full-scale expedition, he was the most appropriate candidate for the job. At this very moment, he is organizing an expedition twice the size of yours to sail to La Florida early next year. In two or three years, he will reach the northern provinces of New Spain." Then Mendoso took on a serious stare. "Marshal, I have a matter I must discuss with you."

Gently, he touched Cabeza de Vaca's elbow. He guided him to a corner where there were no listeners.

"Pizarro and Hernándo de Soto followed rumors that there were riches high in the mountains of Peru. They chased those rumors and returned to Spain very, very rich. There are rumors here, too Marshal. Rumors that there exists in the northern provinces, seven cities of gold."

"The Seven Cities of Cíbola," Cabeza de Vaca said.

"*Sí*. You have heard of them?"

"I have."

"Well?"

"*Señor* Mendosa. I did not see any wealth in all the land of La Florida, only extreme poverty and emptiness."

"But everyone is saying—"

"I saw a few iron cinders, some galena with which the Indians painted their bodies, a few pouches of mica, some chunks of turquoise, and five stones that appeared to be emerald. I only heard stories that there were villages to the north that had multistory houses, but we had already seen these in the river valley of the Jumanos. They were mere adobe dwellings set in the cliffs. But I cannot emphasize enough that the Indians spoke to us only by signs, these being interpreted mostly by Estevanico—who himself is prone to exaggerate—and that lies and truth are on equal planes to

209

the Indians. Any stories that we may have heard of riches to the north are likely to be spurious."

"Then you did hear rumors?"

The viceroy was not going to let up. There was gold in his eyes, and there was nothing Cabeza de Vaca was going to say that would tarnish it.

"*Señor* Mendosa, you are an indefectible host. But I fear if I do not mingle with your guests, I shall not be re-invited."

"We shall speak further of this matter, marshal."

With that, Cabeza de Vaca walked away. He wanted to talk to others about the growth of the colonies, and about Spain. Had anyone been to Jerez recently? Did anyone know Hernándo de Soto? But first, he wanted a handful of grapes. How long had it been since he had eaten grapes? Why didn't the Indians cultivate them? He'd seen them growing wild in the forest. Birds and raccoons ate the fruit before it was even ripe.

A long mahogany table sat against one wall. It held bowls of fruits, cheeses, and breads from Spain and the Indies. At one end of the table a huddle of men and women had gathered. He could hear their oohs and aahs and a voice coming out of the middle of the huddle. It was Estevanico's.

". . .and the whole countryside is full of silver mines and gold mines. If I'da had a cart, I would have brought you all a cartload. The Indians are so simple they haven't even invented the wheel yet. They don't know what riches they're sitting on. They just squat in their gold mansions, which are stacked one on top of the other up to the sky, and sweep pearls and jewels as big as your fist out the front door. I myself once had a necklace of five emeralds that had diamonds and sapphires stuck all along the edges, but I traded it to one of Alcaráz' soldiers for a piece of bread."

Cabeza de Vaca felt the blood of his face drop. This was exactly what he had hoped not to hear. He knew that to Estevanico this was only a game. A game that was so much a part of Estevanico's personality he had to play it or he wouldn't be Estevanico. But the exaggerated stories—lies actually, for Estevanico was more Indian than Spaniard—would lead to false hopes and possibly expeditions into the north country that could bring harm to the Indians.

Then he caught sight of a young man on the edge of the huddle whose appearance made his heart skip a beat. The man was listening intently, clinging to every word that spilled from Estevanico's mouth. The man's eyes were wide. They were filled with adventure and dreams backed by a full measure of youthful lust and unfettered desire.

The man was Francisco Vásquez de Coronado.

15

Cíbola

Háwikuh bolted up. He sat still as a lizard. Sweat dripped from his hot, barrel chest and fell to the fur mat where he'd been sleeping. In the pre-dawn darkness, he listened to his heart bump. He tried to focus on the shadowy objects around him. The voice of the oracle had been so clear, it was as if he were right there in Háwikuh's room. But he knew he wasn't. He knew the voice had come from inside, from a vision. Every night during the past moon the oracle had visited him in his sleep—prompting him, warning him. And this day, Háwikuh of the Bitchi;kwe—the Dogwood Clan—and head of the *Kiva* of Eldest Brothers, must announce the most dangerous decision he'd ever had to announce since being appointed High Chief by the priests of the seven Zuñi villages of Cíbola.

For a moment he considered lying back down on the soft mat. He touched the fur. The mat had been a gift from his woman when they were joined. He had watched her make it from sunup to sundown one day, rolling rabbit furs around yucca cords, tying them together with hemp until she had a wide, flat pallet. He loved the mat. He'd slept on it every night since they were joined.

A soft light drifted through the wall opening, now. Háwikuh could see his woman Wupatki lying on her mat, her long naked body pressed against the coolness of the adobe wall. She had been named Wupatki because she stood like a "tall house." But Háwikuh loved his tall, big-boned woman. As a youngster, he had asked the ruler's permission to join with her. When he wove a blanket and placed it at Wupatki's feet, she covered her nakedness with it. At that moment they were joined, and she was never again seen unclothed, except when she slept at Háwikuh's' side in the darkness of their clay home.

Wupatki had borne Háwikuh two sons, Inihti and Kiasiwa, who grew tall themselves and joined with women of the Turkey and Macaw Clan and moved to their village. She also borne him a little girl. The girl lay curled on her side, wrapped in a feather robe on a mat of willow branches, facing west beneath the dirt floor of their square room, as if she were sleeping. Háwikuh had placed a deer hoof rattle beside her before returning the dirt to her grave.

Wupatki had cared for them all. How many days had Háwikuh sat in the doorway playing his juniper flute, watching her take up a hand stone and crush dry maize on her lava rock, then crush it finer on her sandstone, and finer still on her flat granite? And how many days had he watched her coil clay into cooking pots, pitchers, bowls, and water storage jars, coating them with a thin wash of fine clay, hardening them in the fire, then dipping her yucca brushes into plant dyes and crushed minerals and painting beautiful designs of birds and animals on the sides?

He looked along the far wall and saw Wupatki's three *metates* tilted slightly downward to three willow baskets. Farther along the wall, he saw a basket of hand stones, food bowls, water jars sealed for times of drought, a stone mortar and pestle, and a storage basket of beads. Heavy juniper rafters filled with willow brush and topped with a thick mixture of stone, clay, and straw sheltered his family from the night air. Cotton blankets and an empty baby cradle with a layer of gray dust hung from the rafters.

Háwikuh knew he would not sleep any more this day, knew he must leave the adobe house right away; he had something of great importance to do. Besides, houses were for women. *Kivas* were for men.

He rose to his feet. He was not a tall man, a full head shorter than Wupatki. But he had thick arms, and his head was flat across the back and wide at the ears. As an infant, his head had been tied to a hard cradle board until it flattened out in the fashion of the chiefly clan.

His hair was long and wound in two bobs at the sides of his head and one at the rear, held in place with deer bone pins. He fastened colorful woodpecker feathers over his left ear and a walnut shell inlaid with turquoise just above his forehead.

Háwikuh slipped his feet into a pair of finely-woven yucca fiber sandals. From the bead basket, he retrieved a large, four-strand necklace with hundreds of small turquoise beads mined out of the deep pits to the northeast. He slid the beads over his head, then tied a cotton breechcloth with cedar bark fringe around his waist.

Now, there was one additional thing he must do this day. In a corner, hidden under a bear skin for protection, he pulled out two small clay pots and a little bag made from the skin of the great mountain sheep. He felt the bulge of the stone-carved bear fetish inside the bag and the grainy mixture that covered it. Then he tied the drawstring to his breechcloth. He would need the strength of the bear when he spoke to the tribal elders. He dipped his finger into the walnut oil of one pot, then the crushed red clay of the other and painted stripes on his cheeks and forehead. He returned the bowls and grabbed a bundle of prayer sticks decorated with tiny, bluebird feathers. Then he headed out the door.

The morning breeze felt cool on his moist skin. It brought the scent of sagebrush from off the plain. Háwikuh crossed the rooftop terrace and climbed the ladder down to the ground, stopping long enough to make water in the corner of his ground floor storage room. The liquid quickly disappeared into the earth, leaving a puddle of yellow bubbles to burst into the face of the flies.

Already, the morning haze had grown as white as the heart of a bean. He must hurry if he was to beat the Sun Father to the mesa.

He headed off through the village. He passed the earth ovens where the women baked their flat-bread. He walked east along the narrow corridors beyond the ceremonial *kiva*, where soon he would meet with the tribal elders. He passed more storage rooms and living rooms and the village dump.

Háwikuh's joints popped. He was not so young any more. His legs were stiff, his teeth rotting from years of eating sweet maize, and ground short from the grit from Wupatki's sandstone *metate*.

Near the edge of the village he climbed up three ladders, crossed three terraces, and ascended a final ladder that took him to a high platform on top of a stone tower. His leg muscles ached and his breath was short, but his eyes raced across the wide plain to the distant mesa set against the morning sky. If only his legs could race as fast as his eyes.

But he had out-raced the Sun Father. His fiery glow had not yet peered over the mesa where the Ancient Ones had once built their stone houses among the copper-colored cliffs and crags of sandstone and shale.

The stone tower had been originally constructed as a watchtower to guard over the fields of maize, beans, and squash. But these days it was more often used by the village priest, who shouted reminders to the villagers below—things that were necessary for them to live a long, peaceful life: no drunkenness, no human sacrificing, no unnatural coupling, keep the ceremonies, do the dances, maintain harmony, keep the balance.

He turned and looked across the village: little cubicles of adobe brick rooms stacked one, two, three high, rising like stepping stones to the sky. And a hundred piñonwood ladders, their poles extending far above the terrace walls like dry reeds at the edge of the lake. The people were coming out on their rooftop terraces now, climbing down the ladders, the farmers going to the fields, the rabbit hunters to the plain, the weavers to their tall looms in the underground *kivas*, the women stirring juniper logs in the big ovens, donning head rolls, balancing pots of maize meal on the head rolls.

Today the plaza was empty, except for a young girl combing her brother's hair with a bundle of straw and Nanahe the Hopi trader pulling the strap of his back bundle across his forehead, preparing to make his return trip to the northwest.

But tomorrow, the plaza would be filled with farmers from the other six villages of Cíbola. The smoke signals had already called them to come to the ceremony for planting instructions, for it was the time of the *Ik'ohbu Yachunne*, the Turning Moon. The Sun

216

Father had traveled north as far as he would go. Tomorrow, Sun Father would begin his long journey back to his home to rest. If the farmers did not plant their third and last maize crop soon, it would be eaten by the Frost Spirit.

Tomorrow, the sound of the flutes and drums would echo up the long corridors. Palowahtiwa would release his eagles and turkeys from their wicker coops and pluck their feathers for the ceremony. The priests would dance the Antelope-Snake Dance while the people watched from their rooftops, their legs hanging over the walls, feet resting on the juniper poles that pushed out of the upper walls. Then the people would climb down and form two lines and dance the Basket Dance to give thanks for the earth's harvest. Háwikuh loved his village and all its ceremony. He only hoped there was enough ripe maize from their first crop to feed all the visitors.

Suddenly, the adobe walls burst out of the morning haze in a brilliant gold hue. Streaks of yellow gilded the village wall and painted the corridors the color of ripe maize. It was as if the village had turned into gold. Háwikuh turned. Sun Father had jumped from behind the great stone mesa that sat on the distant earth like a sleeping giant.

The entire plain, with its narrow canyons, piñon-juniper forest, and sagebrush valleys, was blanketed in gold, even the fine meadow and natural springs in the south, which gave drink to bobcats, deer, and elk. And to the north, too, where fields of maize, squash, and beans grew.

Háwikuh squinted through the deep furrows of his face. The breeze brushed the patches of grama grass that circled a jagged peak rising off the plain. The shadow of the great mesa lined up *exactly* with the jagged peak, just as he knew it would, for it was the time of the Turning Moon. But this year's ceremony would be marred with fear. For Háwikuh must tell the elders the message of the oracle and his dangerous decision.

He carefully laid the prayer sticks in a row on the tower wall and released the drawstring of the goatskin sack. He removed the bear fetish, held it in his closed fist, then raised his arms high. He uttered a low chant and dumped the remaining contents over the wall: a mixture of turquoise flakes, crushed shell from the Sea of Falling Sun, and maize meal.

The breeze caught the offering and scattered it across the plain below. If Háwikuh had not made this offering on this special day at this exact time, he would have displeased the gods, the balance would have been offset, and there would not be enough rain to grow the crops.

Now, all that remained was to meet with the tribal elders tomorrow in the ceremonial *kiva*, tell them of his decision—the *only* decision as far as Háwikuh could determine.

He turned back to the village. He looked down at the empty plaza and wondered if his people would be forced to retreat to the mesa top like they did in the days of his grandfathers.

A dust devil rose out of the red soil and danced a solitary dance across the plaza floor before falling back to its earth home.

Not a good sign.

Next morning, Háwikuh was up at dawn again. He placed the stone bear in a medicine bundle and took the bundle down the ladder. Already, the farmers were pouring into the village. There was excitement everywhere as separated families reunited and food was swapped for stories.

Wupatki happily greeted her sons and their women and her grandchildren, but Háwikuh remained out of sight. He had more important things he had to do. He had a secret meeting with his special unit of Bow Priests. At midday, he met the farmers at the plaza. He reminded them of the message of the Turning Moon: plant as soon as possible. He gave them instructions on how and where to plant—as if they didn't know already—because it was part of the ceremony of thanksgiving, and he must keep the ceremonies to please the gods. Maintain the balance.

By mid-afternoon, it was time.

He walked up the long corridor to the ceremonial *kiva*, a round room four man-lengths across with a cribbed roof of poles, brush, and clay. The room stood only a half a man-length above the earth, but the floor was sunken a full man-length deep into the earth. Háwikuh glanced at the houses circling the *kiva*, the women busily rushing in and out. Houses were for women; *kivas* were for men.

He stepped through the round roof-hole and climbed down the ladder to the cool chamber below. There was a stone-lined fireplace with an adjoining ash pit in the center and low on the opposite wall, a ventilator hole. In the floor was a *sipapu*, a small hole to allow the Ancient Ones to enter from the Underworld. In the wall opposite the ventilator hole was a *kachina* niche lined with small stones and holding several carved *kachinas* representing the ancestral spirits who lived in the mountains to the west, disciplinarians of the people.

Today, there was no weaver at the tall loom, no one spinning cotton or knapping flint, no one swinging the stone hoes, picks, hammers, axes, and drills that stood in the corner. A roll of hemp rabbit netting lay beside the tools.

The elders were all here: Acus from the mesa top two days beyond the mountains, Totonteac from the hot lake, Mats'a:kya, all of them. Háwikuh glanced at each one of them. They sat on painted buffalo hides in a circle around the empty fire pit. They wore thick beads of olivella and abalone, turquoise and polished seeds. He hated to have to tell them what the oracle had told him.

When Háwikuh's foot touched the cool floor, the elders' voices stopped. Háwikuh slipped to the head of the circle. He removed a clay cloud-blower from the medicine bundle. He filled it with tobacco and seasoning leaves. He lit it and blew a cloud to the four corners. The pipe had a clay frog attached near the bowl that would surely bring rain to the new crop. Then he removed a quartz crystal, a bone whistle, the clay bear, a small bag of maize seeds, and a wooden flute. He placed the objects on a colorful blanket in front of him and blew a chant on the flute, then gave his attention to the elders.

"Wise brothers, our people have been since the gray mist covered the earth. We have suffered many disasters, but we have always survived. In the days of the Ancient Ones, Cloud-swallower the giant ate the cloud breath of our sacred gods and the souls of the dead from where the rain comes. Snows in the north and rains in the south ceased. Mists on the mountains were drunk up. Waters

219

in the valleys dried up. Then Grandmother Spider destroyed Cloud-swallower. But fearing the waters would not remain in the valleys, the Ancient Ones took their planting sticks and moved from their pit houses on the plain to the cliffs and mesas. They built stone houses and *kivas* high on the ledges in the great stone walls, where the Basketmakers of the gray mist had once lived. They planted their crops on the flood plain below. But then the angry rain gods made great gullies that stole the flood-plain waters."

Háwikuh rolled the black turquoise ring on his middle finger. He did not want to be saying these things. "Hunger took the land and bitter wars between brothers divided the people. It forced them to return in small colonies to the plain and to the grand river far to the south and to the stone forest in the west. They left their cliff homes to the rabbits and ravens. Then the A·pa·chee came, the 'Enemy People.' They raided the fields, so our people came back together. They united as the Seven Villages of Cíbola to better protect the land."

"Hold, wise chief," the elder Halone said. "Thus it was in the days of the Ancient Ones, but why do you speak of our legends of disaster when times are so good? When there is balance and rain and plenty of maize? When the Zuñi of Cíbola are considered the richest of all the people from the Sea of Falling Sun to the Great Plain?"

"Wise brother, I will tell you. Many winters ago, when I was a small boy, an oracle lived in the village, one who was blind and crippled, but the wisest in all the land. The oracle spoke of a day when a new race of people would come up from the Land of Everlasting Summer, a people with white faces and shiny bonnets. They would break down our wall and burn our storerooms and trample our people."

"Why, here, brother chief," said Atishoa from the village of Kyaki:ma. "I do not see such a people in our land."

"Such a people have already overthrown the Aztecs in the Land of Everlasting Summer," Háwikuh said. "With coats of iron and bonnets of metal and short canes that spit fire and make thunder, they rode giant, biting animals into Tenochtitlan and overthrew the houses. They have built a new town on the ruins of Moctezuma and moved into his great temples."

This news stirred the elders. They had sat quietly through Háwikuh's tales. Now, their heads swung left and right, uttering phrases of disbelief.

"The oracle has returned." Háwikuh dropped his head. He stared at the objects in front of him. "Every night during the Turning Moon, he has visited me in a vision. He warns me that the time for the fulfilling of his prophecy is near. The people with the bonnets of metal will be at our gate before the next ladder rung rots."

"If that happens, the intruders will disrupt our cycle of ceremonies," Halone said. "There will be drought and famine and war. The spirit beings will abandon our breathways, and we will have an unhealthy life road."

"We must carve many *Ahayudas*," Atishoa said. "We must place the War Gods in the sunlight to eat themselves up and decay to the earth. All we ask for is rain, peace, and long life, not war."

Háwikuh listened carefully as the elders gave their solutions, waiting for one that might be better than his.

Finally, one said, "We must fast and scrub with yucca seeds to remove the spiritual stains." It was Halone. "Plant our prayer sticks, then retreat to Dowa Yalanne where the red dust blows."

The elders grunted in shock. Dowa Yalanne meant they were in very serious trouble. No one of their generation had ever had to retreat to the mesa top village on Maize Mountain. But their grandfathers had, to escape the A·pa·chee.

"The old village is still there, just a day's journey from here. There are hundreds of rooms, *kivas*, plazas, huge storerooms, a catchbasin for rain. There are only three narrow trails to the top. These can be guarded by a child."

"Our fields are not ripe," Totonteac said. "We would run out of stored grain by the end of the Turning Moon. We have no time to plant new fields. Our people would starve."

Acus jumped to his feet. He wore four cords of beads strung with bone tubes. They clacked when he moved. "Then we must climb to our terraces, remove the ladders, and throw sling-stones and shoot arrows until all the intruders are dead." Acus was more hardened than the other elders. Living atop a mesa, he and his warriors had a habit of throwing off the high ridges anyone they did not like. He was feared by many in his own town, and his warriors obeyed him religiously. He had the best warriors of Cíbola. "We must scalp them and hang the scalps on the outer wall for all to see who would cause harm to our villages. "

"Many women and children would die," Halone said. "Is that what we want?"

No one answered. The elders sat silently for awhile. They too stared at the power objects on the blanket. No one had a solution. Then one by one, the elders looked to their high chief, Háwikuh. Finally, he spoke.

"I have searched among the Bow Priests in all seven villages, and assembled the finest bowmen in the land." Háwikuh did not like his plan any better than the other plans. It was dangerous. It could bring war to all the land of Cíbola.

"Most of them are from the village of Acus, but every one of them has killed and scalped and shoots as true as the path of a falling stone. I will station them outside the village wall. When the white-faces send their scouts, we will demonstrate how accurate our bowmen are by shooting into a post. The white-faces will take the message to their leaders, who will be amazed at our strength and accuracy, and they will return to the Land of Everlasting Summer."

"How many have you assembled, brother chief?" Acus said.

"To please the spirits of the four corners of the earth, I have assembled double four. Forty-four."

"How many is that, wise brother?" Totonteac asked.

Háwikuh emptied the bag of maize seeds. He laid forty-four of them in a row across the blanket. The elders leaned forward and studied them. Halone pushed an occasional seed off to the side. He pointed a long-nailed finger at the seeds and said, "That's one father and his son, and his son a young farmer. That's a lot."

"The Bow Priests are stationed outside the village wall at this moment. Come, they will demonstrate their worth."

The elders climbed out of the *kiva* through the smoke hole and followed Háwikuh across the village. The Sun Father had traveled to a low spot in the western sky now, and the village had again turned gold. Outside the wall, the Bow Priests were in a huddle, talking. They were all dressed alike: deerhide breechcloths and wrist guards, a string of abalone with a large turquoise stone at the bottom, and a single owl feather in their hair—the sign of death. When the elders approached them, they stopped talking. Two stone throws beyond them there was a large boulder. Near the boulder, a piñon pole about the size of a man had been sunk into the ground. Háwikuh walked to the pole. He put his back to it and began pacing back toward the gate, counting. *"Topinte, kwilli, hai, awite. . . ."*

He counted to forty-four before stopping. He was very close to the gate, now. He beckoned the Bow Priests to come. He formed them into two ranks, one behind the other, facing the pole, their backs to the village wall. "Arrows pulled," he shouted. The Bow Priests nocked their arrows and pulled the cords tight. The second rank aimed their arrows between the shoulders of the first rank. "Acus, I give you the honor. Most of the Bow Priests are your warriors. They will shoot on your third count."

Acus stepped up, a slight smile appearing at the corner of his mouth. He looked as though he approved of this procedure. He raised his arm and shouted. *"Topinte, Kwilli, Hai!"*

Forty-four arrows twanged free of the bow cords all at once. They sliced through the yellow haze of the late afternoon and struck the piñon pole all at the same time, each arrow striking a spot in the upper half of the pole, the height of a man's chest.

Acus yelped.

An owl flew out from somewhere behind the boulder.

Not a good sign.

16

The Wilderness

"I'm getting married."

Estevanico rolled over on his fur pallet next to the cot at the palace quarters. He squinted up at Dorantes, who stood over him. "What?" He rubbed his head, his *huevos*, his eyes. "I thought we were going back into the wilderness."

Months had passed. Cabeza de Vaca had returned to Spain to begin his account. Castillo had married. Dorantes had moved into the city. Estevanico remained at the palace housing quarters where he received free food and clothes. The two friends still spent many days together roaming the ruins of the fallen city of Tenochtitlan, just as they had roamed the ruins at Córdoba when they were younger.

"Things change, *amigote*." Dorantes had a gleam in his eyes that Estevanico had not seen in a long time. "Remember the lady Mendosa introduced me to, María de la Torre? She is rich, old friend, has extensive properties and receives many rents from Asala and Jalazinto. She has asked me to come and live with her in the country."

Estevanico's heart dropped to his belly. That was just what Andrés had always wanted. But Estevanico couldn't live in an expensive home in the country where there were no *señoritas* to dance with, no gamblers he could beat at their own game. And what of his long friendship with Andrés? And what of the expedition?

Actually, Estevanico didn't want to live in the country or the city. He couldn't get used to the clothes. He only wore them when he went out prowling. And he still couldn't sleep in a bed. It was too soft. He didn't like the rich foods. Too much cane sugar. The meats were too fatty. He wanted to return to the wilderness where he belonged, people respecting him, bowing down to him when he walked by, him touching them with his big hands, blessing them with his quick-fingers, them being most appreciative of his services, offering him princesses and stuff, him moving on to the next village and the next and the next till finally he came to his lot, the great cities of gold—Cíbola—children sweeping pearls aside so Estevanico could pass, buxom princesses hanging emeralds and diamonds around his neck, rubbing all up on him, roads paved in silver, houses made of gold, gleaming so much Estevanico'd have to squint as he strutted along, everybody cheering 'cause the Child of the Sun had finally come to bless them, take away their pain, fix it so they'd never die. Estevanico knew the Seven Cities were there. He'd heard the Indians speak of the gold houses.

"Mendosa has changed his mind about sending us to reconnoiter the wilderness for him." Dorantes said. "Coronado is planning an expedition to search for the Seven Cities of Cíbola. It appears Mendosa has taken that young upstart under his wing, made him a member of the city council, elevated him to gentleman status, and now plans to support him fully in his search for the Seven Cities."

Estevanico's heart dropped farther, down to his *huevos*. He gave his *huevos* another scratch. Now, what would he do? How could a great adventure fall to his lot if he couldn't get to his lot?

"It is time for you to be a free man, *amigote*."

"Free?" His heart fell all the way to his knees. This was the worst possible news Estevanico could hear this day.

"You have earned it, my friend."

He was already free with Dorantes. He never had to worry about food or a place to sleep. Dorantes always provided that.

"You have been a faithful friend and servant all my life. As long as I can remember you have been at my side. It is the least I can do to give you your freedom."

Now he'd have to get a job. Get up before the sun does. Work. He'd never had a real job. He didn't want a real job.

"Doña María has a house full of servants, already. You'd only be in the way. Besides, you wouldn't like it out in the country—too quiet."

Where was Estevanico going to sleep? Viceroy'd eventually boot him out. He didn't like the sound of this. How could Dorantes even think of such a thing? Estevanico remained silent through the void that followed Dorantes' announcement.

"Or," Dorantes finally said—very slowly. "Mendosa has asked me if you'd be interested in joining a small expedition into the wilderness to pave the way for Coronado, pacify the Indians and explain to them that the Spaniards will not be coming to enslave them."

Estevanico's heart began to rise.

"You would accompany a Franciscan priest named Marcos de Niza, a cosmographer who accompanied Pizarro in Peru. Two others will join you—*Fray* Antonio de Santa María and a lay brother named Daniel."

His heart was back in place, now. Thumping mightily. "When do we leave?" Estevanico was ready to leave this morning—right now.

"Not so fast. Mendosa says you will be the guide and translator for the expedition. But at all times you will be under the command of Fray Marcos, and you must obey him in all and everything."

"No problem, Andrés. That's easy. I can obey. Tell them I am ready any time." Estevanico was wide awake now, sitting tall.

Dorantes stared at him, apparently in doubt of Estevanico's ability to obey anyone. "I knew you would want to go. First, I have a gift for you. Wait here."

Dorantes went outside, then returned with a shiny new morion helmet with a broad, crescent-shaped brim sweeping up to points at the front and rear. A crest rose from the crown like an ax blade. A tall, fluffy, red plume was attached to the back.

Estevanico leaped to his feet. "Andrés!" He was speechless.

"And look." Dorantes handed him one of the medicine gourds he had saved from their journey. He had decorated it with feathers. "Remember the story you told me of your vision quest when the old owl sat on the limb and sang your vision to you? Well, I decorated your medicine gourd with owl feathers. See?" This is the great adventure you always spoke of, Estevanico. Show the gourd to the Indians and they will know you come in peace."

It wasn't more than a week before the expedition was underway, the four men, two greyhounds, and a few Indians to carry their supplies until they reached the free Indians beyond the Sinaloa. Estevanico wore his loin cloth, at the moment covered by a loose-fitting *quezote* that hung from his neck to his ankles and allowed him free movement. But at the first available opportunity he would ditch the coarse Moorish jerkin and continue in the more comfortable Indian attire, whether the *frail* liked it or not.

The small party passed through Compostela and Culiacán. The people came out to cheer them along the way. At the Sinaloa River, they camped with the Opatas, the people who had saved Estevanico and his companions from dying of thirst months earlier. Estevanico gave away his *quezote*. He donned his morion, dressed his toes with bells, his waist with feathers, and hung beads of turrets, cones, and prickly murex the Indians had gotten from the sea around his neck, arms, knees. He shook the medicine gourd in his hand and walked from Indian to Indian touching each one, "Hell Mary, full of grass, the Lord is with you." Blessing them, "Hell Mary, full of grass, the Lord is with you." Taking away their pain, "Hell Mary, full of grass, the Lord is with you."

That night the Indians danced. The *fraile* complained of Estevanico's abuse of the sacraments and liturgical procedure, but Estevanico did not care. He danced naked and drank the strong concoctions and sniffed the sacred herbs into the late night hours. There was no Allah out in the wilderness to criticize him, no Jehovah to tell him what he couldn't do. There was only the Child of the Sun, who obeyed no one. He alone had the power in the wilderness. He alone knew the way to Ures. From then on it would be Estevanico the conquistador who would be in charge.

228

Estevanico did not sleep at all that night. The magical herbs gave him superhuman strength. At daybreak, he was back on the trail, the two big greyhounds at his side, a harem of princesses around him, servants carrying his gifts—turquoise, hairy cow blankets, arrows.

On he marched, strutting ahead of the padres. From village to village, up the coast between the sea and the Sierra Madre mountains, his entourage growing larger every day. No longer was he a slave. No longer was he a Moor. He was Estevanico, the Black Conquistador, a god in the wilderness marching to his glory. He had need of nothing. But the Indians needed him. The padres needed him. He was important. The padres would be lost without him. He alone knew the language of the Indians. Just let the padres fall in somewhere at the rear of the ranks.

They camped at the Yagui River, where Estevanico had first seen the Spanish slave hunters. In the morning, *Fray* Marcos came and spoke to Estevanico. He knew he had no control over the Black Conquistador, so he told him he thought it best if Estevanico went on ahead, and he and his companions would follow a few days behind. That would give Estevanico all the freedom he'd need to do the things he thought he should do to pacify the Indians.

That sounded great to Estevanico. The padres were sort of dead weight anyway, always complaining about the way Estevanico handled things. What did they know about the ways of the wilderness? What did they know about blessing people, about being a Child of the Sun?

But if Estevanico would send a wooden cross back from time to time so the padres would know everything was all right, a little cross if he found a village, a big cross if he found a town as big as Mexico City, they would surely appreciate it.

Sure, that would be no problem, a little cross or a big cross.

Next day, Estevanico was in Ures, the village of deer hearts. There was a great reunion and many blessings and an all night celebration, Estevanico sleeping in the village ceremonial house with seven new princesses. Seven was a good night's worth of pleasure for him. One for each of the golden cities of his lot.

In the wee hours of the morning, he lay staring into the brush ceiling. He thought about how he'd made his luck change, how he was going to keep right on doing it. He was never going to be unlucky again.

At daybreak, he continued on out of Ures. His Indian guides knew where he wanted to go—north to the seven golden cities. After sixty leagues he came to a river. There, he built the largest cross a man could carry. He sent it back to *Fray* Marcos. That ought to get the padres excited.

He continued on up the river valley another fifty leagues to a trade trail the guides said led from the sea to Cíbola. He sent another cross back twice as big as the last one. So big he had two Indians carry it. That ought to teach the padre to lag. Estevanico felt omnipotent. Just up the trail, perhaps another seventy leagues, his glory awaited him. He could taste it in the air. He could smell it in the breeze.

The train of servants, guide, and princesses followed the trail northeast. They crossed mountains and deep canyons. They passed towering mesas covered with black rimrock and carved with primitive drawings: butterflies, a crooked arrow, spirals. The riverbeds were dry and glowed with soft white sand winding into groves of cottonwood. Great canyon walls rose in layers of white and yellow sandstone capped with volcanic rock. They crossed a sagebrush flat, then made their way down into a canyon where a cool thread of water weaved through a narrow pass.

They followed the river and crossed an old silt pan covered with a crusty layer. Beyond the silt pan was a scrubby juniper-piñon forest. And beyond that a wide plain.

The plain was nothing but sand and rock where tumbleweed rolled and mottled coyotes searched for jack-rabbits too old to run. Out on the plain the sky seemed much larger than the earth. It was a timeless land of jagged peaks, odd-shaped pinnacles, desert mirages of distant oases shimmering on a sea of sand. And around the rim of the plain, great buttes and sandstone mesas layered one against the other.

Estevanico squinted. Far across the plain, on the shoulder of a round hill, he saw a city rising out of the earth in giant stair steps—the first of the Seven Cities of Cíbola.

He made camp. He followed the procedure of Cabeza de Vaca, he called for three of his guides.

"Go to the city. Tell them the Child of the Sun has come to pay them a visit. Tell them they don't have to fear any more; I come from the Land of Everlasting Summer to take away their pain. Show them the medicine gourd." He rattled the gourd. He handed it to one of them. "Tell them it is a holy gourd, and in my hands it will perform magic. They will never have to know sorrow again."

The old priest was on the tower when he spied the three Indians advancing up the plain. "Travelers on the plain," he yelled down.

Háwikuh was at the plaza with the elders. He heard the warning. He went to the tower. "How many?"

"Three."

"Traders?"

"I don't think so. They carry only one object. They dress in the manner of the Opata Sono-li. They have no weapons."

"Open the gate and allow them entry," Háwikuh told those who had come with him.

Háwikuh met the three messengers. He heard their story but looked at the gourd suspiciously. "I have never heard of any Child of the Sun. Send him away. We are celebrating the *Ik'ohbu Yachunne*."

"What?" Estevanico exclaimed. "And you gave them my gourd?" The Indians nodded. "Never mind. They will understand when they see me. I have seen this happen before. The ones who are the most unfriendly always turn out to be the happiest. Bring my things. We're going into the city."

With the two big greyhounds at his side, his naked princesses circling him, his guides carrying his gifts behind him, Estevanico sashayed across the plain up to the closed gate. He was surprised to see the city was not made of gold and wasn't as big as

231

he thought it might be. But there were six other cities beyond this one. Surely this one was some kind of outpost town. Like Culiacán was to Mexico City. That was it, sort of like a gateway. He'd just go on in there, bless them up real good. Get him some fresh princesses, some more turquoise and stuff, then head on up the plain to his glory.

The gate opened just wide enough for three men carrying bows and animal skin shields to come out.

"What is it you want?" they asked.

Estevanico told them who he was and what he could do for them and the custom of the land when a village was visited by the Child of the Sun. He told them about the padres who were soon coming and how they would teach them a new way of worship, and how they would be a different people once Estevanico came into their village.

The warriors signed back. They would take this message to the elders. Meanwhile, he an his people could camp there by the big stone down in the *arroyo*.

The sober-faced elders sat on their buffalo skin mats around the silent fire inside the *kiva*. Háwikuh sat at the head. He puffed hard on the cloud-blower.

"Wise brothers," he began. "Just three days ago I told you of the warning of the oracle. And now, outside our wall, there is one who says he is from the Land of Everlasting Summer. For two days he has sought to enter our village, but we have not opened the gate. We have sent him blankets and turquoise, still he does not leave."

Acus interrupted. "He is a spy for the evil ones. He wears the silver bonnet, and he sends no gifts. We must not let him in."

"Hold, brother," Halone said. "He carries no weapon. He can do us no harm."

"He carries the feathers of death. Look at this." Acus held out the gourd decorated with owl feathers. "Many feathers, not one. Many will die, not one. We must never let him in." Acus rose to his feet. "He says this is a holy gourd and can make us live forever. It is nothing but a buffalo gourd. Look at these markings.

232

It is from a village along the Grand River." Acus threw the gourd against the *kiva* wall. It burst into splinters.

Háwikuh sat silently. He listened to the arguments. The man looked harmless enough from where he had watched him from the wall. Still, he wondered.

"Do you see how large he is," Acus said. Acus sat back in the circle. "He is from a race of giants." The elders grunted their concern. "He asks for our young women. What does he want with our women? He already has a hive of women. What vile thing is he doing with them? He must be coupling unnaturally. No man can couple with that many women naturally."

"But wise brother, he is black," Halone said. "The oracle said the new race would have white faces. Maybe he is who he says he is. He has no giant biting animals."

"No? What about the giant dogs he has with him. They are big enough to eat seven of the dogs of Chi·hua·hua for a single meal."

"But they are not big enough to ride. The oracle said—"

"I say we put all the women on the terraces, raise the ladders, then invite this Child of the Sun to the village dump and bury him."

"What say you, brother chief?" Totonteac said.

A thick cloud hung around Háwikuh's head. He lay his pipe aside. He just wasn't sure. The man *was* black. Why would white men send a black man to speak for them? The man said he wanted to change the Zuñi. Who needed change? He said he comes from the Sun Father, but Háwikuh had watched him swagger out of Hemlock Canyon, the Sun Father reflecting off his bonnet, the big red feather blowing in the wind.

"In the morning, we will proceed with our plan, wise brothers," he said. "We will accompany the Bow Priests to the gate, and they will demonstrate their strength and accuracy. This Child of the Sun will see how true we shoot into the pole. He will leave in amazement and report what he has seen to whoever he represents. Then we will turn to planting our fields."

The elders grunted. They rose. Acus said nothing. He remained seated. Háwikuh headed for the piñon ladder that would take them up to the village. The others fell in behind him. When Háwikuh put his weight on the first ladder rung, it broke in two, rotted from age.

Not a good sign.

Estevanico woke at dawn. He stretched and looked toward the city. In the next moment, a brilliant wash of sunlight exploded from behind the distant mesa and gold-coated the houses and the city wall. Suddenly, Estevanico was transported back to that long night at the Alhambra when the wind howled down a narrow passage and the sun kissed the tops of the thirteen towers before dropping behind the high sierra.

That was the night Granada fell, the night they shot the old caliph. He thought about the old caliph and the promise he had made to Estevanico: When the adventure falls to your lot, be ready. It will linger only a moment. Latch on to it, and you will find your glory.

Estevanico was ready—more ready than he'd ever been. He would pounce on the adventure with his whole big body, ride it all the way to his glory. He had come a long way, waited a long time for this day. He'd traveled all over Spain with Andrés, keeping him out of trouble. He'd crossed the Ocean Sea, survived the wrath of Huracán, been to the new cities of West India. And how many times had he faced death from Indian attacks, disease, been lost at sea in a leaky boat, brushed against starvation, thirst. Yet, he had made it. The old caliph had said he was special. He had paid the price, made all the sacrifices a man could be expected to make and then some, just like Cristóbal Colón said he should that night in Palos. After this day, the Black Conquistador would be remembered forever. All that was left to do was for Estevanico to reach out and take his glory.

Then the gate opened. It swung wide this time. Estevanico watched. He counted. Seven elders followed by forty-four bowmen all dressed alike. Now, they were getting somewhere. Now, he could talk directly to the headmen. Not to some message boy who couldn't keep his story straight. Soon, the headmen would see him clearly, realize who he was, bow down to him, give him all the stuff they had.

Estevanico stepped forward. He climbed upon the backs of two of his guides. He stepped to the top of the boulder, his big black body stark against the white haze, his morion helmet glowing as gold as the thick medallions of Tenochtitlán. He removed his loin cloth and sandals, tossed them to the ground. Now, they would see his supernatural magic. His powerful muscles bulged in the morning light. Feathers, bells, and trinkets dangled from head to toe. He spread his legs, raised his arms, held his big hands palm up as if supporting the immense sky. He was prepared to receive his glory.

"I am the Black Conquistador, Child of the Sun. Bring your young women, your cow hides, and your jewels and lay them before me and I will. . ."

When Háwikuh saw the stranger climb upon the boulder to speak, he stepped back from the others, leaving Acus to prepare the Bow Priests for the demonstration. The remaining elders moved off to the side.

Háwikuh stepped forward now, away from the line of the Bow Priests. He looked upon the stranger with curiosity and wonder. Never had he seen such a powerful specimen of a man. He hoped that those he would return to were not of the same size, or he might have trouble containing his women—both young and old—to the rooftop terraces.

The pole stood close to where the people of Sono-li huddled around the big rock. It glowed as if made of pure gold. The powerful black man continued to shout all the things he was going to do to the village. Háwikuh turned. The Bow Priests were lined up, now. He nodded to Acus.

"Arrows pulled!" Acus shouted. The elders shifted so they could all see the arrows fly. *"Topinte!"* Acus shouted. Háwikuh turned back. He focused on the spot in the top half of the pole. It was in perfect range for the black stranger to see.

But the black man hadn't even noticed the demonstration had begun. His big white eyes stared over top of their heads to somewhere beyond them.

235

Háwikuh looked back. All the village women were lined up on the terraces staring directly at the powerful body of the black man.

"*Kwilli!*" Acus shouted.

Háwikuh dropped his eyes down to the Bow Priests. He wanted to see the arrows release, all at exactly the same time, as if they were one. It was then that he noticed the Bow Priests seemed to be aiming high. They could never strike the pole with that aim. He could hear the black stranger behind him promising things his people had only dreamed of having: never die, never be sick, perfect peace, happiness, forever.

"*Hai!*" Acus shouted.

Then Háwikuh knew. He raised his arms. He took a quick breath to shout out to the Bow Priests to stop, that they were aiming too high.

But it was too late.

Forty-four arrows twanged free of the bow cords all at once, sliced through the yellow haze of the morning, and struck their target all at the same time—the upper half of the black intruder's powerful body.

The black man died instantly. He fell forward and tumbled into the arms of his awaiting princesses.

> *Then and thus, was killed by our ancients, right where the stone stands down by the arroyo of Kia-ki-me, one of the Black Mexicans from the Land of Everlasting Summer.*
>
> —Zuñi Indian legend

236

AUTHOR'S NOTE

ESTEVANICO died never knowing he had reached his goal. He was a major participant in the greatest adventure of the New World conquest, and is famous today as the discoverer of the American southwest and as the first black man to explore America.

In 1537, ANDRES DORANTES tendered the Joint Report—the earliest account of the expedition—to the *Audiencia* in Santo Domingo. He attempted one return to Spain, but the leaky ship was forced back to Mexico. Dorantes spent the rest of his life in affluence managing his wife's estate and serving under Mendosa as an officer in the conquest of Jalisco. He and Maríe de la Torre raised eleven children. Descendants of the Dorantes family still reside in Mexico City today.

ALONSO CASTILLO later sailed to Spain, but soon returned to Mexico where he was awarded half the income from the Indian village of Tehuacán. He and his wife produced eleven girls and lived a long, quiet life in Mexico City.

Of the men left behind—THEODORA and the NEGRO PORTER at Mobile, LUPE DE OVIEDO at Misfortune, NARVÁEZ, his pilot ANTON PEREZ, and his page CAMPO, ASTURIANO and FIGUEROA along the coast of Texas—nothing was ever heard.

JUAN ORTIZ, the youngster put aboard ship when Narváez began his march through Florida, returned to Cuba and subsequently joined a rescue party back to Tampa Bay sent by Narváez' wife Maria de la Valensuela. There, Ortiz was captured by Hirrihigua of Ucita, tortured, and held prisoner as the only white man in today's Florida for eleven years. When Hernando De Soto landed at Ucita in 1539, Ortiz was rescued. He joined the De Soto expedition throughout the American southeast and served as interpreter. He died at the Village of

Utiangue (Autiamque) in south-central Arkansas in the winter of 1541-42.

CABEZA DE VACA arrived back in Spain to his faithful wife in Jerez in 1537. The king was fascinated by his account of the expedition. De Soto, who had just been appointed *adelantado* of La Florida, offered Cabeza de Vaca a high position if he would join the expedition, but Cabeza de Vaca refused. In 1539, the king appointed him governor of the Province of Rio de la Plata, a faltering settlement in South America. He served from 1540-43 until his subordinates, tiring of his rectitude and attempts to stop the abuse to the natives, trumped up false charges against him. He was imprisoned for two years then returned to Spain where he died in 1557 friendless and lonely. His account, *La Relación*, was published in Spain in 1542. A second edition published in 1555 was called *Naufragios* (Shipwrecks). Cabeza de Vaca is remembered today for his written account of the expedition, for being the first to describe the plants and animals of the southern United States—buffalo, armadillo, gila monster, opossum—the first to describe the protohistoric cultures of the south and the pueblos of the southeast, and the first to carry the gospel to the sixteenth century inhabitants of today's United States.

HERNANDO DE SOTO, with his 600-man army arrived in Tampa Bay in 1539. Where Narváez had found only a few villages on his journey to Apalachee (Tallahassee), De Soto, traveling farther inland, found about two dozen, including Ocale and Apalachee, whose inhabitants repeatedly attacked the Spaniards. Near Aute, De Soto found mounds of charcoal (from the forge), trough mortars, and horse skulls that marked the camp of the Narváez company. De Soto died during his exploration of the southeast and was buried in the Mississippi River. Descendants of his escaped pigs still roam wild in the southeastern US.

FRAY MARCOS DE NIZA, having lost contact with Estevanico and claiming to have seen Cíbola from a distance (but probably got no farther than southern Arizona) returned to Mexico with tall tales that Cíbola was greater than the city of

Mexico and that he had learned that the cities beyond it stood ten stories high. Marcos provided nothing to the exploration of the southwest, but his exaggerations did inspire Mendosa and Coronado to spend a fortune on the subsequent Coronado Expedition.

In 1539, Mendosa appointed FRANCISCO VÁZQUEZ DE CORONADO Governor of New Galicia, Guzman's territory. In 1540, Coronado's expedition of three hundred soldiers and hundreds of Indians headed north. They found Háwikuh's town and initiated the first major battle between Europeans and Native Americans, forcing the Zuni to evacuate. Coronado sent parties west, who saw the Grand Canyon and the Colorado River, wintered his main army near Háwikuh, then headed east into the Great Plains of Texas where the Spaniards saw thousands of buffalo. They then turned north into Kansas but never found any wealth. In 1542, the year Cabeza de Vaca's *La Relación* was published, Coronado returned to Mexico, where soon after he was relieved of his governorship. He died in Mexico City in 1554. Coronado is remembered as the so-called conqueror of the legendary Seven Cities of Cíbola and as the first explorer of the American Southwest.

NUÑO DE GUZMAN was ousted in early 1537. Failing to get an appeal from jail in Mexico City, he was sent back to Spain where he remained in detention in Valladolid (Narváez' hometown) until his death in 1550.

MELCHIOR DÍAZ, the most experienced veteran on the frontier, was selected by Mendosa to guide Coronado over the best land route. He became a captain in Coronado's army. While leading a detachment west of the Colorado River (probably in the sand dunes near the base of the mountains of San Diego) Díaz hurled his spear from a running horse at a dog who had been chasing their sheep. The spear stuck in the ground, Díaz' horse overran it, and the spear punctured the captain's bladder. He died twenty days later.

DIEGO DE ALCAREZ served as lieutenant under Díaz. Casteñado (of Coronado's expedition) later wrote that Alcarez was a "man unfitted to have people under his command." Near the Arizona border, he was wounded by a poisoned arrow. His flesh became putrid, fell from his bones, and he died a painful death.

HERNAN CORTÉS returned to Spain in 1539. He received no honor and secured no assistance in recovering his property in Mexico. In 1541, he lost much of his remaining wealth in an unsuccessful expedition against Algiers. He retired to a small estate near Seville where he lived until his death in 1547.

In 1541, FRANCISCO PIZARRO was assassinated in what is today's Lima, Peru. His secretary Xeres wrote, "...his sword flew out of his hands, and then they slew him with a prick of a rapier through his throat."

Most of THE INDIANS met by Cabeza de Vaca and his companions in Florida and Texas are extinct today. The ZUNI of HÁWIKUH were forced into submission, and by 1680 their town was abandoned. Today, Háwikuh lays in ruins a few miles south of Zuni in western New Mexico.

EDITOR'S NOTE

An English translation of Cabeza de Vaca's account is available from Arte Público Press, Houston, Texas. It is an annotated translation by Martin A. Favata and José B. Fernández titled *The Account: Álvar Núñez Cabeza de Vaca's Relación.*